Contents

Acknowledgements

The manuscript for this book was almost finished when Graham Tate died suddenly. His insights, expertise and enthusiasm are all represented here as testimony to his high personal and professional standing in the international software engineering community. In later years, Graham became increasingly convinced of the need for rigorous modelling of the software development process as the key to producing high quality information systems effectively and efficiently. We wish to acknowledge Graham's significant influence on our ideas and the production of this book. We also wish to acknowledge the support and encouragement of Graham's wife, Dr June Verner, who is also a researcher and author in the field of software engineering.

A huge debt of gratitude goes to our own wives and families; to Patricia, Adrian, Nigel and Matthew Sallis and Sue MacDonell. Many thanks go also to our friends and colleagues in Computer and Information Science at the University of Otago. Finally, we thank Janet and Roger Green for their hospitality and Professor Bob Spence at Imperial College for library and computing facilities during Philip's sabbatical in London in 1993 when a good deal of the work for the book was carried out.

We also acknowledge the assistance of the reviewers whose constructive comments helped us in the development of this book:

Andrew Barnden	Monash University
Hamish Bentley	Queensland University of Technology
Vanessa Chang	Curtin University
Deidre Jinks	University of Technology, Sydney
Grace Loo	University of Auckland.

Philip Sallis
Stephen MacDonell

About the authors

Philip Sallis is Foundation Professor of Information Science at the University of Otago in New Zealand, a post he has held since 1987. Prior to this he held academic positions in Sydney and London. In 1979 he gained a PhD in Information Science from The City University, London. He has a BA in Computer Science and History from Victoria University in Wellington and a Dip Grad in Theology from the University of Otago. Philip is also an Anglican priest. From 1991 to 1993 he was President of the New Zealand Computer Society and is a Fellow of the NZCS.

Philip has published and presented conference papers in system development methods and software engineering topics. He also conducts research, and has published, in computational linguistics. He has held a number of positions on international research and conference committees, including SEARCC, IFIP and UNESCO. He has been a member of government task groups, particularly in the areas of IT in schools, and industry liaison. He has also acted as a consultant to various educational, government and commercial organisations.

Philip is married to Patricia and has three teenage sons, Adrian, Nigel and Matthew. He has a small farm in the rural parish of Middlemarch where he provides pastoral care and priestly ministry.

Stephen MacDonell is a Lecturer in the Department of Information Science at the University of Otago in Dunedin, New Zealand. He received a BCom (Hons) degree (First Class) in Information Systems in 1988 and an MCom (with Distinction) in Information Science in 1990, both from the University of Otago. In 1993 he received a PhD in Engineering from the University of Cambridge. This was followed by a year's postdoctoral work and the appointment to his current position.

Stephen has published in the areas of software development and software metrics. He also maintains research interests in software process management and modelling, and in automated development approaches applicable to the commercial systems domain. He is an Associate Member of the New Zealand Computer Society and the ACM.

Stephen is married, to Sue.

CHAPTER 1

An introduction to software processes

HOW TO READ THIS BOOK

This book can be used as a textbook for software engineering courses. It can also be read by practising software engineers, or indeed anyone who develops software, as a source book for professional updating. It comprises a set of topics reflecting contemporary thought and practice. These topics can be read individually and from that point of view the book offers a source for clarification and exposition of current software engineering practice and management. The exercises associated with each chapter are intended not only for content review but also for creative thinking about the issues addressed in each chapter.

Each chapter is focused on a central issue: software management for control and improvement. The principles, issues, paradigms and methods discussed in these chapters are, in a sense, the building blocks of software management. In contrast to many other software engineering texts the emphasis is on management of the software *process*. Thus it does not follow the more traditional path through an instance of 'the system development life cycle' (although issues associated with development tasks, activities and products are discussed). The thrust of the book is thus one of providing an approach to software process management for control and improvement.

THE CURRENT STATE OF SOFTWARE

Many software engineering books begin by shocking their readers with stories of system failure and software inadequacies. Rather than producing a litany of such woe, it suffices to say, that although productivity aids such as computer-aided software engineering (CASE) tools and fourth generation languages (4GLs) have accelerated the production of software, and in some cases improved product quality, there are still more than enough examples of systems not meeting users' requirements, not achieving acceptable reliability, costing more, and taking longer (Davis, 1993).

The realisation, particularly over the last decade, that successful systems depend to a large extent on user participation in design, and collaboration in development of software, has meant a general improvement in the relevance, usability, quality and performance of systems. The change in attitude of system developers from one where users were essentially excluded from the development process until the software had been written, to the contemporary user–development partnership, has been paralleled by the emergence of system development tools which are more integrated with computer-based software project management methods. Much of the impact of these tools has been due to other changes in technology such as concurrent processing and multi-user systems. These development environments, examined in detail in Chapter 9, actively facilitate collaborative work.

Some critics observe that application software is still far from perfect in conception, development and operation. While this is valid, there is no doubt that enormous improvements in quality and performance have occurred in recent years. We would suggest that, where these improvements are most obvious, participation in the development process by users and developers can be clearly observed (refer to Chapters 6 and 7 for further details on the issue of user participation in the software process).

The fact is that we now know how to produce better software. The reason that this is often not done is the result of poor management, caving in to outside pressure, cutting corners, and not ensuring that our knowledge is actually used in practice. This book is intended to help to remedy the situation.

WHY HIGH QUALITY SOFTWARE IS SO DIFFICULT TO PRODUCE AND TO MAINTAIN
1.3

It is interesting to note that the fourth generation of programming languages emerged primarily as a product from the computer industry, rather than from research laboratories. This was essentially due to the pressure on organisations to deal with the applications backlog problem. The disparity between the demand for new systems over the past decade compared with the much smaller increase in available qualified personnel, together with the impact of productivity improvements, is illustrated in Figure 1.1.

If this backlog of applications demand is not in itself enough to be an impediment to satisfactory management of the global software engineering effort, the acknowledgment of the overt cost of effort in dealing with the inadequacies of existing systems only exacerbates the situation. Figure 1.2 illustrates a universally acknowledged figure of between 60 and 80% of total project costs as being associated with the post-implementation phase of a system's existence. This clearly means that significantly more effort is being expended in repairing (and, to be fair, *evolving*) existing systems than in developing new ones.

It is our contention that real productivity in the development of software can only be achieved when this post-implementation maintenance effort is reduced. CASE tools and 4GLs may be used for both initial product development and ongoing product maintenance. Regrettably, improvements in productivity gained by the use of CASE tools and 4GLs in the design and development phases of the process are lost when post-implementation effort is so resource consuming. Furthermore, we believe that most post-implementation maintenance is due to poor user requirements specification—this is illustrated in Table 1.1. It may be argued that CASE, for example, can improve user

FIGURE

1.1

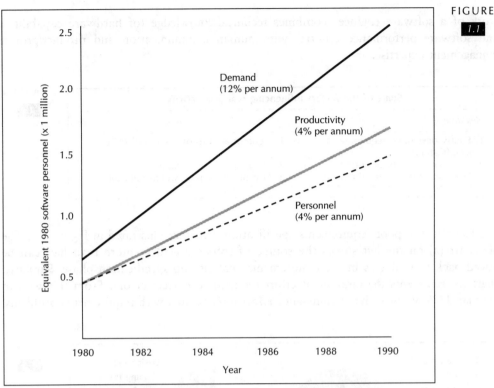

The disparity between demand and supply of software (Case, 1986)

FIGURE

1.2

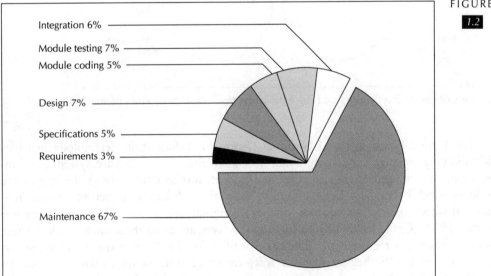

Approximate relative costs of software process phases (Schach, 1990)

requirements specification, and that prototyping using 4GLs can better define that specification in terms of the user's view, but on their own these tools will not necessarily reduce the need for post-implementation maintenance. The synthesis of the user requirements and the eventual system is still due to the skill of the software engineer. The work of a software engineer combines technical knowledge (of hardware capabilities and software performance criteria) with human communication and product/project management expertise.

Some of the factors influencing real productivity	
Negative	Positive
1. Poorly developed requirements specifications.	1. Appropriate use of CASE tools/4GLs.
2. Focus on quantity of output.	2. Focus on process/product quality.
3. High maintenance requirements.	3. Use of prototyping where relevant.

TABLE

1.1

The effect of poor requirements specification is further illustrated in Figure 1.3. The pie chart (a) on the left shows the source of software errors—more than half can be traced back to problems in the requirements analysis and specification phase. Similarly, chart (b) represents the amount of effort required to correct errors. From this we can see that 82% of corrective maintenance effort is associated with requirements problems.

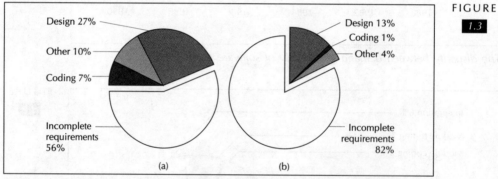

FIGURE

1.3

Software errors (a) their source and (b) their correction effort (from Finkelstein, 1989)

The United Kingdom-based National Centre for Information Technology provides the following message concerning software engineering: '. . . software system development **can** be managed to time, quality and budget, just as effectively as the rest of the business—and if there is a key message in the entire software engineering process, it is that **software engineering enables quality**' (original emphasis) (National Computer Centre, 1988). Case (1986) defines high quality systems to be those that are defect-free and meet the user's requirements. The concept of 'defect-free' is perhaps rather ambitious for most systems. We believe that for software to be truly of high quality it must be functionally predictable and performance acceptable. It should also be ergonomically fashionable and effective. Standards such as ISO 9000, discussed in detail in Chapter 5, provide guidelines for such quality process management.

THE NEED TO APPLY ENGINEERING PRINCIPLES TO SOFTWARE AND ITS IMPROVEMENT 1.4

Efficiency and effectiveness are two engineering principles that relate to product development in any domain. They are particularly appropriate to the production of software. Software, when considered as a set of products, must be developed efficiently and effectively. This is obvious when we consider the above comments about productivity and quality. Software engineering is concerned with the efficient production of programs that are effective in terms of their performance and function. It could be argued that on the other hand, *information engineering* is concerned with the efficient development of data structures and their effective definition. This apparent dichotomy is illustrated in Figure 1.4. In many respects it is difficult to distinguish between software engineering and information engineering, since many systems can be described as 'data centred', although there are claims in support of the latter being as much a discrete sub-discipline of computing as software engineering (Finkelstein, 1989).

The need to 'engineer' the software process has long been recognised. Recently, the area of software process modelling, dealt with in Chapter 2, has emerged as an increasingly more formal, or at least disciplined way of doing this.

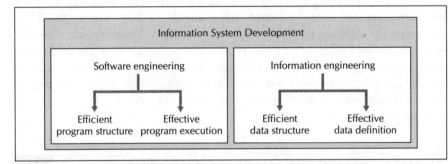

FIGURE 1.4

Engineering to attain satisfactory levels of productivity and quality in information systems

THE NEED FOR INFORMED AND COMMITTED MANAGEMENT 1.5

Tools and techniques for producing high quality software come and go as they are influenced by other aspects of technology. This is particularly true of 4GLs in respect of the advent of relational databases and cheaper mass storage, not to mention faster processors. The same is true of CASE in relation to screen graphics capabilities. As mentioned, none of these tools can be effective in securing high product quality unless the software engineer is highly skilled, highly disciplined and well managed. At least as important is the software developer's *attitude* to the need for high quality. This is true also for management.

There is an attitudinal imperative for all those involved in the software process on which high quality inevitably rests. The time and cost expenditure required to ensure adequate user requirements specifications, and to provide an environment for the efficient and effective production of software, means that management *must* understand the need for a solid foundation prior to embarking on the actual development of any software. There still exists the notion among some managers that unless programs are being written, the development team is not actually getting the job done. Business pressures and the need to strive for the competitive advantage that can be gained from the implementation of a new information system (IS) are often the driving force behind management's desire to see the completion of a project. This attitude in a sense is still held by some software engineers themselves, who maintain that so long as a program works . . . it works! Unfortunately, it can also be difficult to maintain and user-hostile.

The purpose of this book is to positively influence software engineers and others involved in the software development and management processes to recognise that high quality is essential. In many cases this may require an 'attitude shift'. It could be argued that there is an attitudinal imperative in the software development and management process in order for high quality products to emerge.

SOFTWARE STAKEHOLDERS   1.6

It is important in practical situations to remember that there are several different stakeholders involved in software development and use, and that their concerns, interests and points of view differ. Books about software engineering are typically written from the producers' or developers' point of view. It is equally important, however, to keep the consumers (customers and users) in mind. After all, the systems are designed for them. They determine the ultimate success or failure of a system. Producers are typically concerned with the ease and efficiency of the production process. Users are concerned with functionality, usability, quality and value for money of the software product. Producers who do not take consumers' concerns very seriously are risking failure, as are consumers who do not take production difficulties and problems into account. These roles are illustrated in Figure 1.5.

SOFTWARE IMPROVEMENT INITIATIVES AND   1.7
PARADIGMS

As noted earlier, the continuing software crisis is of massive proportions in economic, professional, business and social terms. Many researchers, industry professionals, and entrepreneurs have tried, and are still trying, to find ways of dramatically improving software and its production. The search for a 'silver bullet', some ultra-smart computer-assisted package which will once and for all kill the software werewolf, goes on . . . and on. However, as Fred Brooks (1975) said, 'There is no silver bullet', and as Turski (1978) said, 'There is a simple solution to every difficult problem—and it's wrong!'.

Though there is no magical software silver bullet, there are well-founded incremental approaches to software improvement involving commitment, education, persistence and professionalism. The more important of these initiatives are considered in some depth in Chapter 5.

PRODUCTIVITY, QUALITY AND MATURITY   1.8

While hardware productivity, in terms of processing power per dollar, continues to increase dramatically, software productivity lags pitifully behind, with inflation snapping

FIGURE
1.5

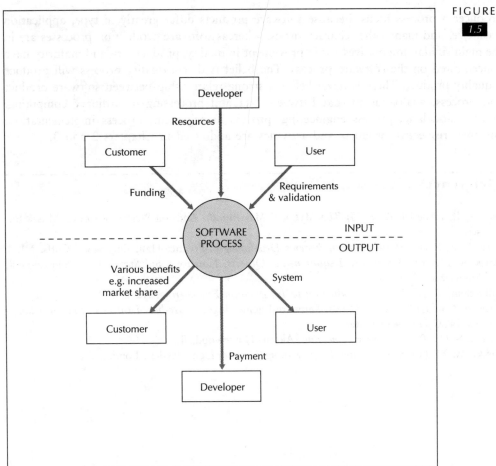

One view of the roles of software stakeholders

at its heels. The potential gains from even a small increase in software productivity are in billions of dollars, hence the many different efforts to achieve such an increase.

Productivity and quality are related. Fortunately in software the relationship is positive. In many cases improved quality can also result in improved productivity. The basic reason for this is that doing it right in the first place is less costly than having to fix it later. The rationale underlying the *measurement* of both productivity and quality is described in Chapter 10. Unfortunately most of the world's software-producing organisations are too immature professionally and managerially for them to be able consistently to produce high quality software efficiently. The issue of organisational maturity is discussed further in Chapter 5.

SOFTWARE PROCESSES AND PRODUCTS   1.9

The software customer wants high quality software **products** at reasonable prices. The software producer wants a well-engineered and managed software production **process** that will consistently produce software of at least the quality the customer demands, in an efficient and cost-effective manner. Thus the consumer has a product focus and the producer a process focus. Because software products differ greatly in type, application area, size, and many other characteristics, whereas software production processes are in the main similar, imperatives for improvement in quality, productivity and maturity have concentrated on the software process. The belief is that a quality process will produce a quality product. There is nevertheless a strong relationship between software product and process, analogous to that between data and processing in ordinary computing. Process modelling, process engineering, process management, process implementation, and their respective products and activities are addressed in Chapters 2 and 3.

References

Brooks, Jr, Frederick P. (1975) *The Mythical Man-month*. Addison-Wesley, Reading, Massachusetts.

Case, Jr, A. F. (1986) *Information Systems Development*. Prentice-Hall, Englewood Cliffs, NJ.

Davis, A. M. (1993) *Software Requirements: Objects, Functions and States*. PTR Prentice-Hall, Englewood Cliffs, NJ.

Finkelstein, C. (1989) *An Introduction to Information Engineering*. Addison-Wesley, Sydney.

National Computing Centre (1988) Software Engineering: *A Case-based Introduction for Managers*. NCC Ltd, Manchester.

Schach, S. (1990) *Software Engineering*. Aksen, Homewood, Ill.

Turski, W. M. (1978) *Computer Programming Methodology*. Heyden, London PA.

CHAPTER 2

Process definition and engineering

THE SOFTWARE PROCESS FRAMEWORK

2.1

The traditional approach

2.1.1

Software engineering textbooks have typically used a **software development life cycle (SDLC)** (Figure 2.1, page 10) as a unifying framework within which to describe the **software development process**. This SDLC framework (sometimes called a waterfall model) is typically referred to as *the* SDLC, as if there were only one, which is not the case. Figure 2.1, which is one of the better diagrams of this type of model, is adapted from Boehm (1981).

There are several steps or **phases** in this particular SDLC:

■ **System feasibility**

This initial phase is sometimes known as the **feasibility study**. It aims to establish the technological, economic and social feasibility of the proposed **system**—its ability to meet the needs of the customer or client and user in a cost effective manner. There are limits, of course, to the extent to which feasibility can be established at this initial stage for truly innovative projects without actually doing some exploratory development. Feasibility can be **validated** in the sense of obtaining customer or client acceptance of proposed functionality and the agreement of appropriate experts about technical feasibility and likely costs. Once feasibility is established and accepted, the next phase can begin.

■ **Software plans and requirements**

Requirements are the functions and features of software desired by the customer. These are validated by obtaining the customer's agreement in writing that the requirements do indeed describe what is wanted. Software **planning** is concerned with questions such as: How much? How long? What **resources** and **skills** will be needed? When? Software

9

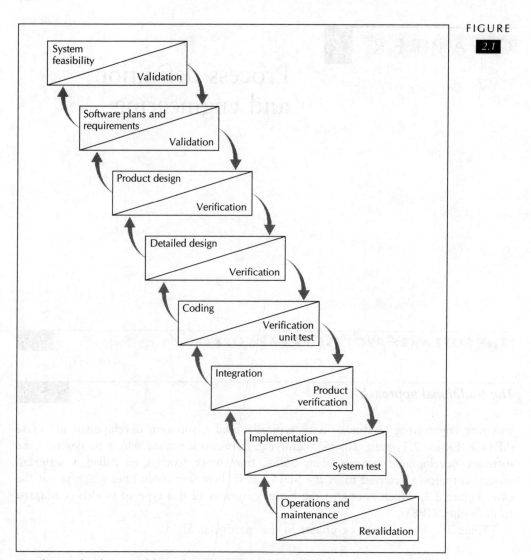

FIGURE

2.1

A software development life cycle (SDLC) (Boehm, 1981)

planning involves **estimating, scheduling** and **budgeting**. Plans are developed from requirements and are validated in the sense of obtaining the agreement of customer, management and also, as appropriate, experts, particularly as to cost and schedule. These issues are covered in greater detail in Chapters 3 and 6.

■ Product design and detailed design

Software requirements are concerned with 'what' is wanted. Design is concerned with 'how' to meet the requirements. In this particular SDLC, design is divided into two stages: product design, which is akin to architectural design for a building; and detailed design, which is more akin to engineering drawings, wiring diagrams, interior decorating instructions, etc. Design documents are **verified** in the sense that they are checked against requirements and it is established that they meet all, and only, the agreed requirements. Consistency between the product design and the detailed design is also established.

■ Coding

This phase is also known as **programming**, or sometimes **implementation**. However, in this particular SDLC the term *implementation* is used in a different sense. The designs are converted into programs which can be executed by computer systems. Programs are verified in the sense that it is demonstrated that they do indeed implement the detailed design. Complete **proof of correctness** of programs is, however, difficult, time consuming, and can also be itself error-prone. Programs are therefore tested using suitable **test data**. The testing of individual programs or program parts is called **unit testing**. One of the advantages of rigorous conceptual modelling is that development tasks can be broken into units. Because these units inevitably become portions of program code, they can then be tested as discrete entities, in addition to testing their interfaces.

■ Integration

Up to this stage we have only tested the individual programs. They must now be put together and integrated into the complete **information system** (IS) or **product** that the customer requires. The integrated product is then verified against the product design.

■ Implementation

The software is now put into operation for the first time. This may involve **data file creation** or **conversion**, operator and user **training, parallel running** with an existing system until all the teething problems have been sorted out, and other matters relating to the actual use of the system in practice. The system as a whole is tested in actual use. Implementation usually includes **acceptance testing**. The system is accepted when the user and the developers agree that it meets the requirements, which are often embodied in a contract.

■ Operation and maintenance

The last phase covers the normal **operation** of the system, in some cases for many years. During this time, problems will arise that require correction. Improvements, enhancements and other changes will also be necessary to cope with evolving needs and a changing operational environment. Operation and **maintenance** is often the longest and most costly phase, particularly if the term *maintenance* is understood to include **enhancement**.

Other aspects of the traditional approach   2.1.2

It will be noted that the example SDLC in Figure 2.1 contains feedback paths between phases. Frequently **defects** in the products of an earlier phase, such as design, are discovered in a later phase, such as integration. The feedback paths allow a return (possibly in a number of steps) to the appropriate earlier phase in order to remedy the defects and then to propagate any consequent changes downstream. In a sense the feedback paths make the SDLC a cycle or, more precisely, a set of nested cycles, or **iterated** phases.

    In some similar informal SDLC **phase models**, there are one or two additional steps prior to feasibility. Typical preliminary steps are **business need** and **concept**. There will be definite business or organisational needs or problems, together with a reasonably well-founded idea that the software of a suitable computer-based system may provide a solution. There is often also a final step, **retirement**, to indicate the ultimate withdrawal or demise of the software.

Some SDLC versions show the last phase leading back to the first, thus completing the cycle. In one sense this is valid, because users of an operational system often require enhancements either to make more effective use of existing data within the system, or to meet changing business needs. In another sense it is invalid because it has become customary to regard only major enhancements as new development. Minor enhancements, of which there are frequently a great number, are more often regarded as **adaptive maintenance** (Lientz and Swanson, 1980).

Deficiencies in the traditional approach   2 . 1 . 3

The traditional use of the SDLC is a convenient structural fiction, or at best a partial truth. It is a gross over-simplification of what actually happens in software development. All the activities shown in the SDLC do occur in software development, but not in the clear-cut manner that the SDLC diagrams imply. There are also many other activities, as well as **products**, involved, which are simply not shown.

■ There is no single SDLC

There is no such thing as *the* SDLC. The use of the definite article *the* implies that there is only one SDLC, or at least that there is a standard, or normal SDLC. This is not so. There are a number of basically different software development processes and an almost infinite number of variations on these basic themes.

■ Deficiencies in the waterfall model, with and without feedback

The SDLC shown in Figure 2.1 is an example of what is commonly called the **waterfall model** of software development. Strictly speaking it is an example of the **waterfall model with feedback**, since there is a feedback path from each step, or phase, to the previous one. The origin of the term *waterfall model* is illustrated in Figure 2.2 which shows the waterfall model without feedback. There is a forward flow, as in a waterfall, from one phase to the next. The inadequacy of the waterfall model without feedback is sometimes shown by depicting it as a series of large leaky reservoirs with water gushing from each one down to the next, or out of holes in the sides. Half-drowned developers make futile attempts to swim upstream against the flow in order to plug one or two of the leaks!

The waterfall model without feedback is quite unrealistic in that it implies that each phase can be completed and checked (validated, verified or tested) before the next phase is started. This does not happen in practice with real-life systems. Invariably defects in the products of earlier phases are discovered in later phases. There are two basic approaches to fixing these defects. The best approach is the iterative one which feeds the defect information back to the earlier phase, as indicated in the waterfall model with feedback. However, the approach all too often adopted is to fix the problem in the phase in which it is detected, rather than returning to fix it in the phase in which it occurred. There are serious disadvantages in the latter approach.

FIGURE

2.2

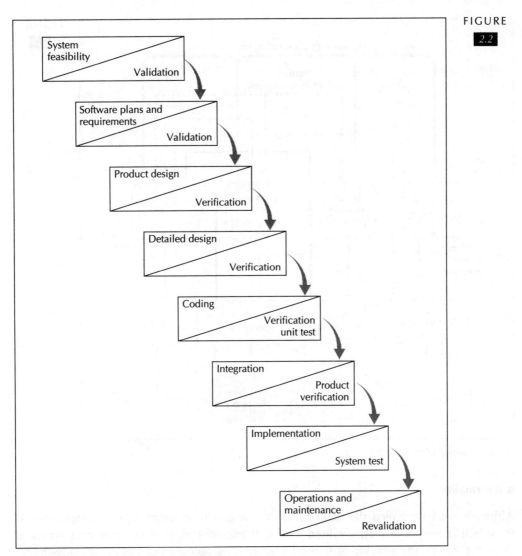

Waterfall SDLC model without feedback

Consider an example. A design defect is discovered during coding (programming). If it is fixed in the coding phase then:

(a) the design defect may not be corrected in the design documents, so someone referring to them at a later time will be misled;

(b) the time and effort expended in what is sometimes facetiously called 'deferred design' will be recorded as coding time and effort, rather than design time and effort, thus giving a false picture of the phase distribution of the development work.

Figure 2.1 is somewhat misleading in that it only shows feedback to the previous phase. However, the previous phase has feedback to the one before it and so on so there is, in effect, feedback to any previous phase. A more formal model, such as that outlined in Figure 2.3, would show this explicitly.

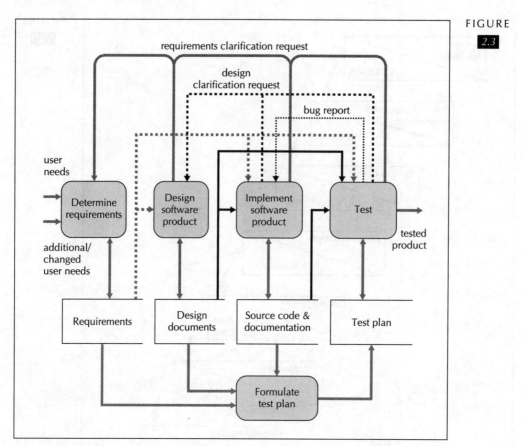

FIGURE
2.3

A more formal phase model

■ Informality

Although we have called the SDLC a *model*, it hardly deserves such a designation. It is, at best, a very informal, idealised model. It excludes many development activities, it does not depict any development products, and, as pointed out above, it omits many of the data-flow paths between activities.

Figure 2.3 depicts a simplified phase model rather more formally than usual in **data-flow diagram** form. The **activities** are represented by round-cornered boxes, the **data flows** by arrows, and the products by **data stores** (open rectangles) or by data flows (for example, 'tested product' and the unlabelled data flows into and out of data stores). This model uses a common and well-understood notation (the data-flow diagram) and can be elaborated in standard ways in order to define, for example, the detailed data contents of all data flows and data stores.

■ Overlapping phases

As one would expect, in a development of any size the software system being developed is typically broken down into **subsystems** and other smaller **components**. Progress on some of them will be faster than on others. For example, in a business application the design of the transaction subsystem may be well ahead of the design of the management reporting subsystem. Naturally, programming can and will start on the transaction subsystem before it starts on the management reporting subsystem. Even within a subsystem, a similar situation may occur, some components being ready for the next phase before others. This situation, coupled with the feedback between phases, means that in practice there is often considerable overlap between phases, almost to the extent that the strict phase-based model is quite misleading.

■ **Changes**

What is also not shown in the traditional SDLC is the continual stream of **change requests** that occur during the development of real-world systems. Not only does the user discover new or omitted requirements, but also business or other needs change during the development period. To be properly incorporated in the final system these changes also need to be propagated through all the development phases.

■ **Software development is a network with feedback**

Given overlapping phases, feedback, and a continual stream of changes, many phases of a software process may occur simultaneously. In fact, as indicated in Figure 2.3 which only contains a few of the necessary development activities, software development is a network of activities with feedback. There are examples of the software process being represented with network-oriented **PERT** or **CPM** charts (see Section 3.6). However, these have generally been unsatisfactory because of their inability to represent iteration or feedback in the process. We do not mean to imply that PERT and CPM charts are not useful, indeed essential, tools for software project management. The point is that they cannot accurately model the activities of the software development process.

SOFTWARE PROCESS MODELLING   *2.2*

The term **software process** refers to the entire process of software production and evolution from the initial concept through definition of requirements, design of software products, programming, implementation, operation, maintenance and enhancement, to eventual retirement of the software. It should be clear from our analysis of the deficiencies of the traditional approach to modelling the software process that more accurate or more formal **software process models** are needed. Such models can only be constructed using suitable modelling notations.

Modelling the software process   *2.2.1*

It is not within the scope of this text to review research in software process modelling. Indeed, that is a daunting task because the boundaries are not well-defined and overlap other major research areas, such as **software engineering environments (SEE)** or **software development environments (SDE)** (see Chapter 9) and **software configuration management (SCM)** (see Section 4.3). We therefore approach the area selectively, bearing in mind the purpose for which we require software models, that is, for the understanding and management of the software process.

What constitutes a model is seldom made explicit when models are presented or discussed. Frequently diagrams are used, for example data-flow diagrams, but the detailed semantics and database support that are needed to make such diagrams precise are not included in informal model descriptions. This can make the question of what is included in, or excluded from, a model difficult to resolve in some cases. Usually, however, a little thought will settle most such matters. When we describe models, we usually concentrate on their main features, without including all their tedious and usually rather obvious attendant details. We will follow this common practice.

Software process modelling requirements $2.2.2$

Software process modelling requirements have three related parts. We need first to consider the purposes for which we wish to model software processes and their components, that is, the 'why'. Secondly, we need to consider the aspects and objects of the software process that we need to model, that is, the 'what'. Finally we need to consider 'how' we are going to model the 'what'.

We will attempt to be as simple as we can, bearing in mind the overriding requirement for models to serve software management needs. We do not mean to imply that a simple approach for management is always necessary or possible, though it is often desirable. We seek simplicity only to the extent that it is consistent with effective management of the software process. It is perhaps worth noting in passing that one of the reasons for the waterfall model being popular is that it models a process thought to be manageable, even though that process is a gross over-simplification of more difficult-to-manage actual software processes. The term *manageable* is used informally in this context with implications of a quantitative basis for management based on measurable activities and products. Simplicity is relative to the complexity of the process we are modelling. Since the software process is very complex, it is likely that simplification which is not simplistic will be able only to clarify and structure, not remove, its inherent complexity.

■ Management requirements that software process models should satisfy

We stated that our first concern is with the 'why', rather than the 'what' or 'how' of software modelling. The overriding purpose is software process understanding and management. This leads to some consequent requirements, mostly in the 'what' category.

(a) Modelling levels

Management of a complex process such as software development requires managers and developers to take both general and more detailed views of the process. This implies a need to model the process at both a macro level, to provide a framework for the process, and at lower levels, in order to handle the details of individual activities and products. Models that allow **refinement, explosion,** or **elaboration** will generally be necessary.

(b) Understanding, understandability and simplicity

The software process is one of the most complex of human activities. The mere understanding of it is a major problem. One could argue that what we cannot model, we do not understand. By this criterion our understanding of the software process is limited. Thus there is a need for models that help us to a better understanding of this complex process. For management purposes the models have to be understandable by both managers and developers, so excessive formality and complexity are avoided where possible. A related and more difficult management requirement is simplicity and the need to avoid getting bogged down in endless complex details. Managers must be able to see the wood as well as the trees.

(c) Enaction

If software process models are to be used in the management of software development, we must be able to use them to direct or control development. Developers must interact continually with the process model they are using. One way to achieve this is to implement software models on computers and have developers work with the models in a **computer-aided** manner.

We need software process models that can be **enacted** by project managers and developers. The term **enaction**, rather than *execution*, is used to highlight the embedding of human and computer-aided human activities in the models. We will apply the term *enaction* to both software processes and software process models. The rationale behind the adoption of the term *enact* rather than *execute* or *interpret* is explained in the introduction to the Proceedings of the 4th International Software Process Workshop (Tully, 1988). 'The organising committee was anxious to preserve the concept that the mechanism for "running" process models is a symbiosis of human being and computer, and at the same time not to hint at particular roles for either partner. Enactability simply means that human beings involved in the software process receive computer guidance and assistance in what is an extremely complex activity'. The need for enaction thus relates to the inherent complexity of the software process. Only by the computer-aided enaction of such complex human–computer processes are we likely to be able to control the processes in detail and keep track of what actually happens within them.

Why is the word **enaction** used, instead of the more common (predominantly American) term **enactment** in this context? *Enact* and *enaction* are similar in language construction to *act* and *action*, whereas *enactment* is different. *Actment* would be a rather unnatural English word. There appears to be no very good reason to prefer the unnatural construction *enactment* over the more natural and euphonic *enaction*. Therefore, we prefer the term *enaction*.

(d) Flexibility (dynamic modelling)

A software process is not fixed. It may vary dynamically, over time, from environment to environment and from application to application. It may also vary during enaction. It is therefore necessary that software models be suitably flexible and extensible, facilitating additional modelling as and when this becomes necessary.

(e) Metrication

Metrication is intimately related to management. DeMarco (1982) said in relation to software development: 'You can't control what you can't measure'. It is thus a requirement of our models that they should be capable of metrication, so that we can account quantitatively for what happens during the enaction of the software process.

(f) Other management requirements

The primary purpose of software models in this context is to provide a meaningful and effective framework for the understanding and management of the software process. This implies the ability to define and measure activities and products. The management requirement also has implications for model **granularity**. The size of the model elements should be appropriate to the level of management; not too big or control may be difficult, not too small or effective measurement may be impossible.

Boehm and Belz (1988) note that for management purposes we also need to model **objectives, milestones,** products, **responsibilities,** approach/activities and resources. It may not be necessary, however, to model these as separate entities. Objectives could be considered **attributes** of activities, and responsibilities also attributes of activities, and possibly of products as well (using a responsible-agent attribute, for example). The recording of resource consumption is included in our measurement requirement, and must be related to the activities that consume the resources, and/or to the products for which the resources are consumed. Resource availability is a **constraint** that may be recorded in the database associated with a model, and may (for example, as an 'available resources' data store) be explicitly represented in a model.

The above requirements are not necessarily all compatible. In particular, the requirements for understanding in detail (which are likely to produce a complex model) and for flexibility of modelling (the process model may change in unforeseen ways) may be incompatible with some of the other management goals, such as simplicity and ability to plan with confidence.

■ What do we need to model?

Bearing in mind the management requirement for simplicity where possible, the things of interest in the software process that we need to model include the following:

(a) Products

These include both intermediate and final products, if indeed evolving software products can ever be called final. It is important to model products, for example requirements and design documents, because they are inputs to, and outputs from, software activities and include the final software products themselves, and their components. Products can be measured, for example they may have one or more **size, complexity** and **quality** measures. They represent software **work in progress,** components, assemblies or finished products and are part of the software **value chain** in which each activity adds value to the developing product, or set of products (Boehm and Papaccio, 1988). They also fit the **factory paradigm** of software production in which software engineering is regarded as analogous to the engineering of production processes that manufacture products in factories (Humphrey, 1991).

(b) Activities

Activities consume resources and in most cases lead to the development of products, though non-productive activities are obviously possible, for example where an activity is abandoned and nothing of any **utility** is produced. In general, however, even work which appears to be non-productive, for example investigating what turns out to be a blind alley, may produce something, for example a brief statement or report that a particular approach is in fact a blind alley. Effort spent on such activities may be logged as 'investigation', perhaps within 'design', depending on the particular model.

(c)   Events

Events may be thought of as action **triggers**. An obvious example is the project start event. Other examples are approval to produce a detailed proposal as the result of a feasibility study, requirements acceptance by the user, or completion of design verification against requirements. Events take place at particular points in time and are important occurrences on the **project time-line**. Some may be regarded as **milestones**. Now that information systems are weapons in the **competitive advantage** arsenal of many businesses, and **time-to-market** may be of great importance for a software product, the recording of critical events is clearly of considerable importance. We should remember, however, that software development phases often overlap in practice, so the relationship between events and activities may be more complex than would appear at first sight.

(d)   Decisions

Though events may include **decisions**, we distinguish decisions from events to highlight their role as **branch** points in the software process. An obvious place where decision points occur is in **risk management**, where decisions are made either to take **risk reduction** action, such as **prototyping** (see Section 6.4), or not. Decision points are important because the path through a model may be changed and different activities and products may ensue.

(e)   Other and alternative modelling elements

There are other alternative modelling elements, for example **states**, such as **under test**, and **transitions**, such as from **under development** to **under test**, which may be caused by events, such as *coding complete*, and may involve **inputs**, such as *test data*, and be accompanied by **outputs**, such as *test results*. We will not consider them further in this section because they do not seem to be quite as natural to the software manager as the elements identified above. They will be considered later in this chapter when we consider software process modelling notations. Some further comments on what else we may need to model, and why, were noted above under the subheading 'Other management requirements'.

SOFTWARE PROCESS MODELLING NOTATIONS   2.3

This section is concerned with *how* software processes are modelled. Once again our treatment of software process modelling notations is selective and related to our purposes of modelling for understanding and management.

■ Informal diagrams

As noted in Section 2.1, most software process models have been, and still are, described or illustrated using a variety of informal diagrams and verbal commentaries constituting 'the software development life cycle' (SDLC). Typically, informal diagrams illustrate variants of the well-known waterfall model, but recently more sophisticated models, such as the spiral model (see Section 2.4) have also been depicted using suitable informal diagrams.

There is a wide variety of informal notations. In the main they take the form of process networks. Products, in spite of their importance, are seldom explicitly represented in the informal diagrams themselves. Thus, although they are a useful aid to the exposition of the software process, informal process diagrams are unsatisfactory as software process description notations. This is not surprising because they are not intended for this purpose.

■ Process–product graphs

These are graphs (or networks—we are not concerned with formal mathematical definitions at this point) in which activities, products, and their relationships, are represented in a number of different ways. Figure 2.3 (page 14) shows a process–product network in data-flow diagram form based on a simple waterfall model of the software process, with iterations looping back to all previous activities, as well as the input of new and/or changed user needs. Some would say that this representation is not as readable as the SDLC waterfall model and provides no additional information on the process. We consider, however, that this is a far more realistic representation of the interaction between components (products, activities and so on) in the process.

■ Dynamic modelling notations

We investigate **system dynamics** approaches to software modelling in Section 2.4. System dynamics models can be expressed in the notations of **continuous system simulation** or in informal diagrams that can be elaborated into continuous system simulation diagrams or programs.

■ Process programs

The title of one of the more influential early papers in the process programming field 'Software processes are software too' (Osterweil, 1987) succinctly describes the basic idea behind **process programs**. Figure 2.4 is an example of a process program excerpt taken from Boehm (1988). This is part of a high level process program which uses a number of development products and calls a sequence of more detailed activities. Good examples of process programs are difficult to find. Indeed the literature on process programming contains much discussion of the concepts, but few actual process programming examples, though a number of large process programs have been written. As noted in Section 2.2, process programs are enacted rather than executed, in recognition of the fact that the processors are largely human.

Boehm and Belz (1988) make some interesting comments on the difficulties they encountered in applying process programming (using an **Ada-PDL** (product or program design language)) to the **spiral model** (see Section 2.4), including such questions as:

- What are the **semantics** of process programs?
- What should be formalised and what need not be?
- How are **data representation** and **visibility** issues to be resolved?

FIGURE

2.4

```
        with
                Life_cycle_plan,
                Risk_management_DB,
                Management_plan,
                Objectives_DB,
                Constraints_DB,
                Alternatives_DB,
                Risk_issues_DB;
        procedure Refine_life_cycle_plan
        is
                . . .
        begin
                Refine_plan_objectives;
                Refine_milestones_and_deliverables;
                Refine_responsibilities;
                Refine_approach;
                Refine_resources;
                Validate_refined_plan;
        end Refine_life_cycle_plan;
```

Example of an excerpt from a process program (from Boehm, 1988)

- How is change of the process during its enaction to be handled?

Process programs are clearly more expressively powerful than process–product graphs and can readily include events and decisions, as well as activities, products and other necessary data. At this stage of their development, however, they seem to raise almost as many problems as they solve. The usefulness of process programs will no doubt increase, and their potential appears to be considerable, but they would seem to be too complex for routine management use. Their main role may be that of an underlying formalism which may underpin more informal and understandable models.

■ Object-oriented notations

Process programs can be either **procedural** or **object oriented**. The latter can be represented at the design level by suitable **object-oriented design** notations (see Section 7.6). Figure 2.9 (see page 27) is an example of such a model.

■ Entity process modelling

In contrast to the essentially activity-based or functional view of process programming, Humphrey and Kellner (1989) propose a more product-oriented model made up of **entities**, such as code **modules** or user manuals, **states**, such as *non-existent, undergoing development, developed, running tests, analysing problems, passed testing,* and **state transitions,** for example from *running tests* to *analysing problems* or to *passed testing*. In order both to illustrate the technique and to enable it to be compared to the other models discussed in this section, an **entity process model** for the entity Product Design is shown in Figure 2.5. The product design entity in the figure has five states, non-existent (*none*), being designed (*designing product*), *on hold*, *product designed* and product *verified*, all represented by boxes. The state transitions are represented by arrows labelled with the events that trigger the transitions. Thus, when the requirements are available, we can start designing the product.

When new requirements or design clarification requests are received, we will have to redesign the product, or at least consider the possible need for redesign. If during

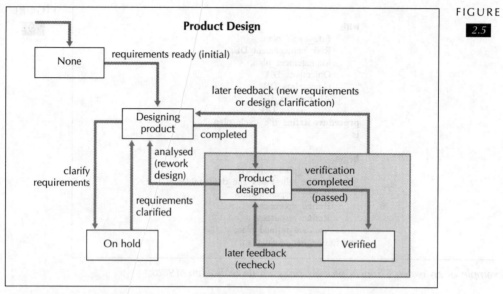

Entity process example

design it becomes clear that the requirements need clarification, we will have to put the design (or at least that part of it we are concerned with at the time) on hold while the requirements are clarified. In analysing, inspecting, or attempting to verify the designed product we may uncover problems requiring design **rework**. Later feedback, such as a program **fault**, may require us to recheck the verified design. Other entity process models would be constructed for every entity of importance, in order to complete the development picture.

The entity process model provides rather different and valuable insights into the software process. In concentrating on states and events, it gives a complementary view to that of process–product networks.

■ Entity–relationship (E–R) modelling

Entity–relationship (E–R) modelling, or **entity–relationship–attribute (ERA) modelling** is often used to describe the nature and structure of the data for software process models, that is, the data dimension of a model or family of models. This is as valid, and as partial, as the use of process networks, giving a **data-centred** rather than **functional** view. More detailed discussion of the E–R model appears in Section 7.4.

■ Other process modelling methods

A variety of other process modelling methods include **behavioural**, **rule-based**, **goal-based**, and **knowledge-based** approaches. See Madhavji (1991) for further discussion of these methods.

SOFTWARE PROCESS MODELS   2.4

Software process models are distinct from software process modelling notations, some of which can be applied to many models, whereas others relate to specific models. For ease of understanding, the software process models included below have been described either using self-explanatory informal notations or in words. Complete treatment of the models is not attempted. For example, there are many prototyping models, but only one, Boehm's spiral model (Boehm, 1988), has been included. The selection has been based partly on variety so the five models described should present a wide range of basically different views of the software process.

■ The waterfall model with iterations

This has already been covered and is represented in various forms in Figures 2.1 to 2.3.

■ Lehman's models

Lehman's **E-process** model, referred to in Lehman (1989), is notable for its emphasis on system evolution, system interaction with the environment, and the explicit inclusion of verification and validation. Figure 2.6 is a diagram of Lehman's E-process model. He notes that 'software must evolve, undergoing continuous adaptation and change. It must be treated as an ever-to-be-adapted organism, not as a to-be-produced-once artifact.' He also observes that not only does the environment influence the system, but the system embedded in it also changes the environment, which in turn changes the embedded system, and so on, so that there can in general be no information systems that do not evolve. Lehman's models are essentially variants or refinements of what we have referred to as the waterfall model with iterations. However, the emphasis on continual change

FIGURE
2.6

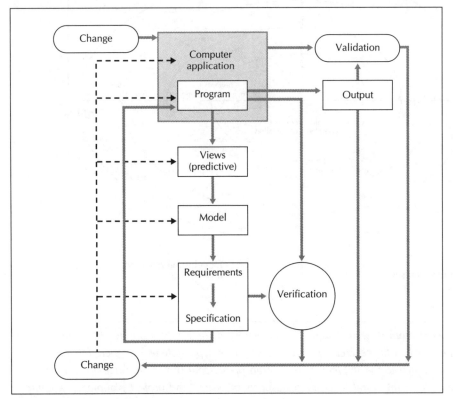

Lehman's E-process model

underlines the need for a model with feedback and/or iterations if the impact of change is to be understood.

■ The spiral model

The spiral model, originally developed by Boehm, is designed to include both risk management and iterations within the software life cycle, specifically in relation to prototyping. Figure 2.7 is a diagram of the spiral model (Boehm, 1989). The spiral model is notable in that it makes many management issues explicit, something which is not done in the previous two classes of models. In particular, the following processes are included: determine process objectives, alternatives, constraints; evaluate process alternatives; identify and resolve process risks; develop and verify next-level process plans; analyse risks. Verification and validation are also emphasised, but feedback from them to earlier activities is implicit. Figure 2.4 is an excerpt from a process program

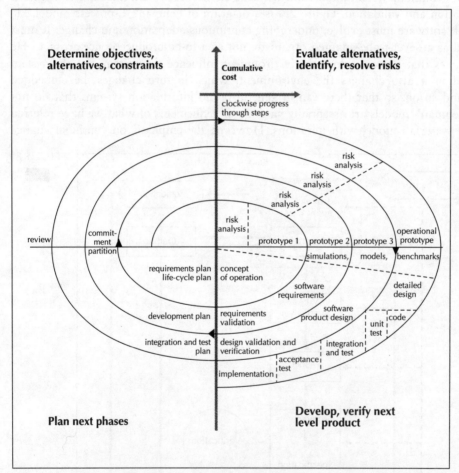

FIGURE
2.7

The spiral model (from Boehm, 1989). The software process progresses outwards from the centre of the spiral, with the creation of successive prototype systems (numbered 1 through 3 in the figure) leading to the implementation of an operational prototype (final system). Each iteration or cycle in the spiral incorporates aspects of system and project planning, feasibility analysis, process management, system development and process/product evaluation.
(© 1989 IEEE)

of the spiral model that illustrates the preceding points. The spiral model is based on project management experience. The granularity of the model for management purposes may therefore be approximately right. It can be formalised to a considerable degree as a process program. The spiral model is thus a contender as a realistic state-of-the-art process model for software project management in appropriate situations.

It is clear, however, that the spiral model, as represented in Figure 2.7, and even as augmented by verbal descriptions, is still very schematic and incomplete. The diagram has limitations and merely conveys the key ideas and concepts of the model. Further elaboration and formalisation is needed in any practical application of the spiral model, or indeed of any of the other models described.

■ System dynamics models

System dynamics involves the modelling of a process as a continuous system varying

FIGURE

2.8

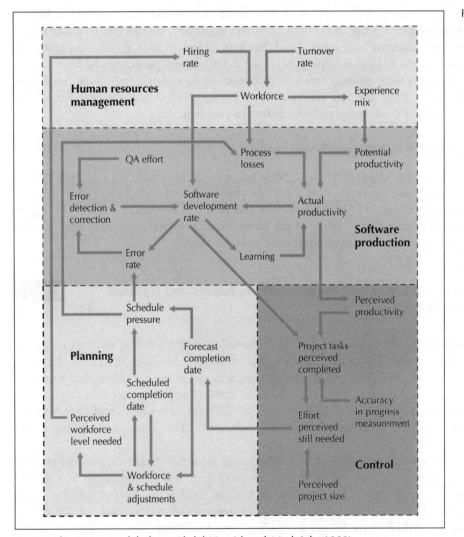

System dynamics model (from Abdel-Hamid and Madnick, 1989)

over time. It is usually done using a suitable continuous system-modelling software package. A specific system dynamics model of software project management developed by Abdel-Hamid and Madnick (1989) attempts to model some of the forces that influence the rate of software production and hence **software productivity**. In particular, the influence of **schedule pressure** (to get the job done more quickly) on productivity and rework is modelled, as are the relationships between work rate, real progress, perceived progress and reported progress, the last of these being influenced by bias and delay.

The published model of Abdel-Hamid and Madnick (Figure 2.8) is very much a macro-model in which the conventional phases of software production are not separately represented. Software production is seen as a single activity whose production rate is influenced by a number of different factors such as schedule pressure, perceived project size, hiring rate, turnover rate, work-experience mix, and so on. In this form the model is useful for examining certain aspects of the software process as an aid to understanding those particular aspects.

There is no reason in principle why different phases influenced by different factors could not be modelled using the system dynamics approach, though the resulting model would be quite complex and might be difficult to calibrate to a specific environment. Though the system dynamics approach is useful for certain purposes and throws new light on some aspects of the software process, such a single paradigm modelling technique cannot meet the full set of wider software project management needs. For example, it does not adequately model software products.

■ Product-centred and object-oriented models

Product-centred and object-oriented models are models in which development objects (often products) and operations on them are identified and modelled. Figure 2.9 is a **Booch diagram** (Booch, 1994) illustrating a **generic** form of such a model. This figure is generic in the sense that it refers to the **abstractions** product/component and activity, rather than to specific products, components or activities.

Relationships between process modelling notations and software process models   `2.4.1`

It is appropriate at this point to relate the software process modelling notations we have introduced in Section 2.3 to the software process models we have described above.

Of the models described, the system dynamics model is the exception. It is modelled using analogue techniques, that is, continuous system modelling, used in this case to balance dynamically the effects of a number of different rate inputs and to investigate the effects when the rates vary relative to each other. This type of modelling is not suited to any of the other software models.

The other models can all be represented using informal diagrams, process–product networks, process programs and entity process modelling. These models can be regarded as representative of most of the software process models in current use, or under investigation. Thus for our purposes we can regard the use of any or all of the above-mentioned three more-formal software process modelling notations as appropriate.

This does not mean that the notations are equivalent. They have quite different

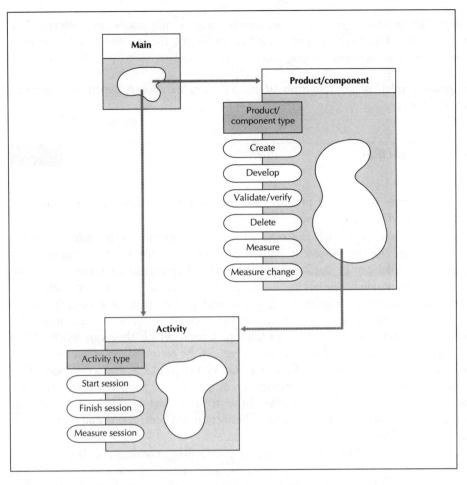

Booch diagram of product-centred process program, (Booch, 1994)

emphases and give different views of the process being modelled. In many ways they are complementary:

- Process–product networks emphasise processes and products, or products and processes, depending on users' preference and choice of notation. They are particularly good for taking the broad view, though they can be refined to levels of considerable detail. They model concurrent processes naturally but imprecisely. They do not represent event-driven processes particularly well.
- Process programs emphasise processes, process logic, products and (if desired) product structures in pseudo programming language terms, using, for example, Ada PDL (product design language) or some special-purpose language. They are particularly good for detailed logic, though representations of high-level processes are naturally used during **top-down development**. Using **real-time** programming features, they can model events and **concurrency**. The precision of expression is comparatively high, but the ease of understanding is much less immediate than it is for graphical notations.
- Entity process models emphasise events, states and state transitions. They are good

for depicting products and for representing certain milestones and intermediate events precisely. Processes are not described explicitly, though events refer to their beginning, end, suspension, or ongoing status.

An appropriate model, or combination of models, can be chosen depending on one's modelling purposes.

Process model enaction   2.4.2

This section examines the role of process model enaction, first from a conceptual and then from a practical point of view.

Conceptually, process model enaction provides a mechanism by which process models can be used for management and measurement of software development. A software process model can be used not only to define, but also to structure, direct and record software development by having it enacted by the developer under the direction of the workbench on which the model is implemented. Enaction of a suitable model has great advantages for management. If the model is clearly understood and agreed by developers, its enaction can provide a framework within which they can work. Their activities can be clearly identified and resource use can be recorded and directly related, at or near the time of use, to specific model activities, products and components. A suitable software process model can provide a comprehensive framework for development and enaction can provide traceability through the model of developer effort and its effects. In concept, the role of process model enaction is a central one and its potential advantages are considerable.

From a practical point of view, enaction is still largely experimental. We will refer to one of a number of experiments in process model enaction. Boehm and Belz (1988) briefly record some findings from a process program experiment with the spiral model. Their observations are noteworthy, including '. . . the process programming experiment led to a revised process program better reflecting the realities of Spiral Model application. In particular, it identified the importance of early process requirements, architecture and design activities and the appropriateness of the Spiral Model risk-driven approach in guiding these activities.' They identified some unresolved issues in the enaction of process programs but, more importantly, they demonstrated the feasibility of enacting a process program and the role of enaction in clarifying features of the process model being enacted.

In principle, any process connected with software development, or even more general processes, such as **IT strategic planning**, can be modelled using process programs, and enacted. The more general the activity and the less precise its details, the more enaction will lean towards, and depend on, the developer who will supply the semantics of enaction. The more well defined the process being enacted, the less developer dependent it will be.

We make a final point regarding enaction. All working software developers are enacting some software process, whether they are aware of doing so or not. It could be said that as developers, we do not completely understand what we are doing if we cannot model it. If we are to improve what we are doing we must understand the software process we are enacting. To do this we must model it.

THE SOFTWARE PROCESS CYCLE 2.5

It should now be clear that software engineering is not merely the application of engineering principles to the development of software products. It is also the application of engineering principles to the development of the processes used to develop software products. We are concerned not only with product development itself but with how we undertake product development. This has been recognised in the drive towards software improvement and software quality. The catch phrase is: 'Only a quality software process will consistently produce quality software.' There is a need, therefore, to widen our horizon from software product engineering to software process engineering.

The Redwine model 2.5.1

Figure 2.10 illustrates what we have called the Redwine Model, since it is adapted from a diagram by Sam Redwine.

FIGURE
2.10

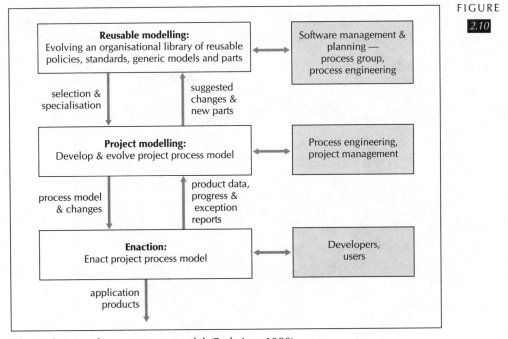

The Redwine software process model (Redwine, 1989)

It is the function of process management, aided by process engineers, to develop the process model. In practice this may often take the form of selection of a process model from a small set of standard alternatives. The model may then have to be tailored in specific ways to suit the characteristics of any particular development project. It may also have to be changed during development if unforeseen circumstances arise. As noted above, development by enaction of a defined process model lends itself to measurement of the development. Thus software product and process data can be collected, associated with specific activities and products, and fed back for management information, for process modification if necessary, and ultimately for process improvement.

Though there are differences, there are also many similarities between software projects, particularly within the same **application domain.** It is therefore appropriate for the essential elements of common process models to be reused. A process group under the software management and planning function is responsible for process engineering. This group builds up an evolving library of reusable software policies, standards, generic process models and parts of models from which an appropriate selection can be made and then specialised, or tailored for each particular project. Experience with actual software development projects will result in suggested changes to the generic models, new generic components, or even whole new generic models.

The Madhavji model   2 . 5 . 2

Madhavji (1991) gives a comprehensive framework for software process modelling which he calls the **process cycle** (Figure 2.11).

FIGURE
2.11

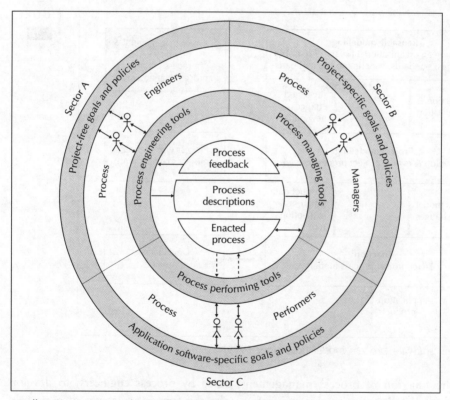

Madhavji's process cycle (Madhavji, 1991)

At Sector A, which corresponds to Redwine's reusable modelling level, is the **process engineering** function. This function has project-free (that is, *generic*) goals and policies. Appropriate **process engineering tools** are used by **process engineers** to produce **process descriptions** or models from the generic process libraries that they maintain. For these libraries to grow and for the generic processes kept in them to improve, appropriate **process feedback** data comes from completed projects.

At Sector B, which broadly corresponds to Redwine's project modelling level, is the project or **process management** function. It could be argued that process management is only a part of the software project management function, but it is such a large part that we do not distinguish between them at this stage. The concern here is with project-specific goals and policies. The process descriptions (from process engineering) describe or model the process being managed. The **process manager(s)**, including primarily the project manager, use appropriate **process managing tools**, interfaced to the specific software process being used in the project to provide the necessary information to manage the process effectively. The actual development data comes from the specific **enacted process**, whose enaction produces the application products. It is also the responsibility of the process manager(s) to feed back information about the process so that changes can be made if necessary, and also so that lessons learned from the project can be abstracted and incorporated as appropriate in the generic process engineering libraries.

At Sector C, which corresponds to Redwine's enaction level, **process performers**, that is, developers, use **process performing tools** (such as **CASE**) to develop the actual application software products, such as **application programs**, documentation, etc. Here **application software-specific goals and policies** are appropriate. The process performers interact with the process they are enacting, which in essence tells them how and when to use the process performing tools.

The Madhavji model is a cycle in the sense that it is depicted as a circle and contains feedback.

Another perspective   2.5.3

Since the concepts in this section are fundamental, we will consider them from yet another perspective, following Tate (1993). We consider some of the main components of an implementation of a model similar to the Redwine and Madhavji models. The concreteness of an implementation architecture may help some readers to a better understanding of the significance of the various levels in the models.

Referring to Figure 2.12 (on page 32), the developer interacts with both the process model, through the enaction application, and the CASE tools for application development. The process model is concerned with what to do; the CASE tools are concerned with doing it. A development record keeps track of what happens during each development session.

Other parties concerned with software and software process development include process engineers who study and abstract generic software processes for later reuse, and managers who monitor and control software development. The managers interact with project management tools which in turn interact with the enaction application and its development record. Through model assessment and evolution, managers, developers and process engineers can also be instrumental in changing software processes, either during a project or as a result of *post mortem* analysis. Since managers, developers, and process engineers are involved, different views of the process model and its enaction are necessary. Process engineers are concerned with generic software process models and model parts from which appropriate specialised models can be tailored and **instantiated***

---

* Defined in Collins English Dictionary (1983*): To represent by an instance.*

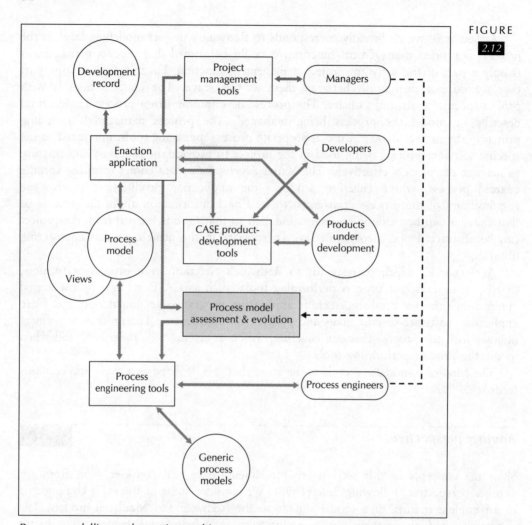

FIGURE
2.12

Process modelling and enaction architecture

for particular projects using process engineering tools. They are also concerned with the abstraction of generic process models from successful projects and the evolution of models based on experience.

Software modelling in practice

2.5.4

It may be considered by some that software process modelling is a research-oriented or 'pie-in-the-sky' activity. In one sense it is. In practice, software modelling of the more formal kind described in this section is still rare and may well remain so for some time. This does not preclude the relevance of software process modelling. It is entirely relevant because every software engineer is involved with process models, either implicitly or explicitly. The structure we describe is therefore a fundamental and essential framework for better understanding of software processes and hence for their improvement. Its conceptual importance can scarcely be overestimated.

SOFTWARE PROCESS SELECTION
2.6

Given that there are a number of different software processes in current use, and an infinite variety of possible software processes that could be used, how do we select the particular software process which is appropriate for a particular development?

In practice the decision is most often straightforward. The two most likely courses of action are the following. First, we may use a process that the organisation regards as standard for the particular application domain. Second, we may use a software process that has been previously tested in the specific application context, possibly incorporating some improvements based on previous experience.

Important issues affecting software process selection are considered below.

Application domain
2.6.1

There are a number of general, and many special, application domains. Rather than attempting to give a precise but dry definition of an application domain, we give a few examples.

■ Data-centred systems

Data-centred systems, common in business applications, are centred on one or more databases containing business information. They are concerned with *data* processing rather than data *processing*. Unless they have very special characteristics, many common business applications, such as human resource management, payroll, accounting applications, inventory control, and so on, are in this general class. Characterising it in some detail, this class has the following distinguishing features.

(a) *Data centred*

The main activities are keeping database(s) up to date and extracting information from them as required. Module data dependencies tend to be through the database, or through a handful of parameters, rather than through a data-flow network.

(b) *Few major object classes*

Most, if not all, of the modules that interact with the database can be regarded as instances of just a few **object classes,** such as **menus, screens** and **windows** (all **user interfaces**), database **updates** or **reports.** These objects inherit their shared behaviour from more general objects of each class, which are then tailored to fit each specific instance.

(c) *Simple state transition control mechanism*

Inter-module control flow is typically through menus, and can be represented as state transition diagrams.

(d) *Comparatively low procedural complexity*

This characteristic has several aspects. First, application specific manipulation, logic or calculation represents a relatively small proportion of the total job. However, since this part is specific and contains little that can be inherited or delegated, it may represent a rather larger proportion of the total effort. Second, procedural modules are in general independent of each other and are called from, or embedded in, the database manipulation object instances.

Figure 2.13 gives a simplified diagram of the application class in a schematic data-flow diagram form. The interaction process represents a menu, screen or window. The processes P1 to P5 represent embedded or called logic-modules to meet application-specific needs. These are seldom more than a handful of lines. Note that the main process types, A, B and C, are not connected directly by data flows, but interact with the database(s). This is an oversimplification in that the menu-like control structure, which is not shown, effectively passes activating information from one process to the next. Also, it is sometimes convenient to pass some transient variables from one process to the next. This is best shown on a modified state-transition diagram. The system structures of greatest interest are the data model and the control state-transition diagram, not the data-flow diagram.

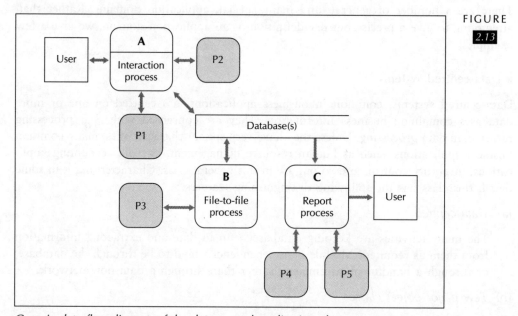

FIGURE

2.13

Generic data flow diagram of the data-centred application class

■ **Real-time systems**

Real-time systems must operate in **real time**, that is, they must keep up with and react in a timely manner to events of interest in the environment to which they are interfaced. Characteristics of most real-time systems include the following:

(a) Parallelism and inter-process communication

Real-time systems often contain a number of different communicating processes which run simultaneously. (We should note here, however, that concurrent processing does not necessarily imply real-time operation.) Process operations depend on each other and must be synchronised. They are called **cooperating sequential processes**. Terms such as **rendezvous** are also used to indicate 'meetings' between communicating processes. A message source, or **producer**, and a message sink, or **consumer**, are examples of two interacting processes.

(b) States and events

States and events are natural modelling elements in real-time systems. For example, out-of-service, idle and busy may be states of a telephone line. In state *idle*, a call event may cause a transition to state *busy*.

(c) Direct real-world interfacing

Real-time systems may have interfaces, usually through **transducers**, to real-world instruments or devices, such as air-speed indicators, altitude indicators, aircraft attitude indicators, controllers for flaps, and so on.

(d) Messages, signals and control data

Concern is mainly centred on messages, signals, and control parameters rather than files of data.

■ Systems programs

Systems programs are concerned with the control of computer resources such as **memory, ports, channels, buses** and **disk space**, so as to provide computer **hardware**-related services to computer users. They include **operating systems, device drivers, input/output control systems (IOCS), communications controllers, compilers,** and the like. They either concern directly, or centre around an operating system **kernel** which provides the basic set of services they use. They share many of the characteristics of real-time systems but have a terminology of their own, including **stacks, queues, interrupts, masks, registers,** and so on, which relate specifically to computer resource allocation and control.

■ Life/mission-critical systems

These are typically real-time systems and are often **embedded** systems in the sense that they are embedded in, and form an essential part of, some other system such as an aircraft, a spacecraft or a life-support system. They share the characteristics of real-time systems but they have the additional requirement of extra-high reliability. This requirement will not only affect the care with which the software is developed, but also affect the software process itself, which is likely to include additional stringent verification and validation activities. An example is a **fly-by-wire** system, capable of flying an aircraft automatically, including landings and take-offs.

The term *mission-critical* has recently been adopted by some business information systems (IS) people to describe applications which are essential to the success of a business enterprise and thus to the accomplishment of its mission. This has somewhat devalued the term, though a more critical approach to some business systems is not inappropriate.

■ Scientific/engineering systems

Scientific/engineering systems are primarily concerned with scientific and engineering calculations. They frequently involve computations using **arrays** or tables, which are often quite large, and the evaluation of complex formulae. Frequently sophisticated numerical methods or statistical methods, or both, are used. It used to be said that these applications were high on computation, but low on input and output. However, this is often not the case. Frequently a substantial majority of the program instructions in scientific/engineering systems will be concerned with input, output and, in some cases, with databases of substantial size.

■ Spatial information systems

Spatial information systems is a term now widely adopted by those working in the area of **geographic information systems (GIS)**. GIS are extant products used to solve particular problems in land surveying or cartography, installed and operational across a wide variety of application locations. They grew out of traditional data collection, storage and processing techniques employed by land surveyors and geographers to meet a perceived need for automation capabilities, which themselves were driven mostly by a change in demand by users of cadastral (legal land description), topographic and demographic data. GIS functionality has evolved to provide efficient methods for mass data storage, map coordinate digitisation, scanning and image processing, relational database technology, and highly interactive non-procedural programming capabilities. For example, a super-set of **SQL** (structured query language) is commonly used as the interface programming language in these systems.

So much has the GIS area (and the wider research domain of **spatial information systems (SIS)**) been influenced by software engineering methods and information technology generally, that the term **geomatics** has emerged as a new label for this field (Sallis and Benwell, 1993), and also for some professional bodies (such as the previously titled Canadian Institute of Surveyors). Some university departments have changed their names to use this term. In part, this is a direct reflection of the influence of **informatics** generally, and software engineering principles in particular, on the way in which spatial information systems are designed and built.

GIS are used by central and local government for the storage and processing of location-oriented data, especially demographic, cadastral, environmental and other land-related data. Examples include databases of the locations of all the services such as water pipes, sewers, gas mains, electrical and telephone lines, and so on. GIS are also used for rating systems, service utility and maintenance systems, traffic management and emergency services systems. Increasingly they are being used for other location-oriented data such as epidemiological research, inventory systems and organisation planning applications. For further reading, Burrough (1986) is recommended.

■ Expert systems

Expert systems are one class of **knowledge-based systems**. An expert system is software which uses the experience-based knowledge of experts to make judgements similar to those that human experts would make. There is an early phase of **knowledge acquisition** during which a variety of methods are used to draw out the experience-based knowledge from the participating experts, and to formulate this knowledge in some suitably structured way. A **knowledge base** is then built that stores the expert experience as a set of **predicates, rules,** or similar constructs which represent facts and the kinds of connections or deductions that experts can make from the available evidence. Frequently an **expert system shell** (or generic skeleton program) is used which supplies standard knowledge entry, knowledge-base management, and **inference** mechanisms, and only lacks the knowledge on which to work.

■ Other application domains

There are a great many other application domains including, for example: **office automation,** which includes **word processing, desk-top publishing, electronic mail** and **multimedia** office information processing (that is, the processing of sound and image data in addition to conventional coded data); business or general calculations (using **spreadsheets); electronic data interchange (EDI)** which implements some business transactions electronically without paper documents; financial analysis; **image processing** for dealing with medical and other image data, for example, infra-red satellite photographs; **computer graphics; CAD/CAM (computer-aided design** and **computer-aided manufacturing);** production control; **point-of-sale** systems; data communication systems; and many others.

Other application domain considerations 2.6.2

Many application domains have special software tools, or domain-specific generic packages, which provide many of the general functions within the domain. An expert system shell and spreadsheet software are examples of generic but domain-specific tools. Such tools are good for general use within their particular application domain. They may have very little or no application outside their domain.

Other application domains use more general tools, such as general purpose programming languages, for example, **COBOL** for general business applications, **FORTRAN** for engineering applications and **Ada** for real-time applications (particularly for the US Department of Defense).

Some application domains allow **end-users,** that is, just about anyone, to use or even to develop particular applications. The best examples are word processing, where the end-user employs word processing software to produce and process documents, and spreadsheet software with which users can do complex calculations and even develop complex calculation-based information systems.

Application domains do not always have well-defined limits; they may overlap and some more specialised application domains may be embedded in other more general application domains. Some integrated systems may span several application domains, for example a modern manufacturing company may have an integrated set of application systems including data-centred business systems, office automation, production control and CAD/CAM.

It should thus be clear that quite different software processes will be applicable to different application domains. Some, such as word processing, may need no explicit software process at all. Others, such as life/mission-critical systems will need a very comprehensive and well-defined process if we are to place our lives in the hands of the software they produce.

Development methodologies

There are a number of **development methodologies** which are essentially general prescriptions or recipes for developing information systems, often using some dominant **paradigm**. Development methodologies may cover all or part of the development process. They usually include a collection of related techniques and products. They may also specify parts of a software process in some detail or, attempting to appeal to a wider range of developers, claim to be adaptable to many software processes.

The use of the term *methodology* warrants some comment. The word originally meant 'science of method', but it has come to mean 'body of methods used in a particular branch of activity'. It is in the latter sense that it is used in software engineering. We will not go into detail about methodologies. That topic will be covered more thoroughly in Chapter 7. However, an example may help focus our ideas.

Perhaps the most widely used methodology today is the so-called structured methodology (see Section 7.5), which is an amalgam of **structured systems analysis, structured design** and **structured programming**. It is a rather permissive and somewhat eclectic methodology, including the use of data-flow diagrams, data models and a **data dictionary, structure diagrams**, structured textual descriptions of procedures (sometimes called **structured English** in English-speaking countries) and a variety of other techniques. The main paradigm, typically associated with structured development, is **top-down functional decomposition**; activities and the data flows between them are successively refined or broken down from major functional areas into smaller and smaller functional components, until at the bottom level the procedures can be described by succinct structured text and the data flows are typically single records or small groups of data elements.

In the structured methodology, construction of data-flow diagrams is an early activity. As the data-flow diagrams are refined in greater levels of detail, entries are made in the data dictionary. When the data-flow diagrams are complete, two activities can take place. The bottom (most detailed) level processes can be defined, using a variety of appropriate techniques including structured English. An appropriate data model, for example, a **relational model**, can be built by structuring the data in the data stores. Once all the processes are defined, structured design can start. This produces program structure charts from which programs can be produced.

The structured methodology, as briefly described above, prescribes a network of steps and a set of products covering much of the requirements and design phases of the waterfall model. The methodology can therefore be regarded as a refinement of this part of the model. As such, it specifies a particular software process model.

There are many variations of structured methodology, some elaborately formulated, such as **SSADM** (**structured systems analysis and design method**) (Ashworth and Goodland, 1990) which is widely used in the UK, and others local to particular organisations and environments, or even to individual developers.

Other methodologies and approaches similarly help to refine or more closely define the software process of which they are a part.

Tools, CASE and environments

The large number of computer-based aids to software development vary from individual tools, through CASE (computer-aided software engineering) packages which contain a more or less integrated set of development tools, to **software engineering environments** which aim to provide more or less complete support for some or all of the software process.

■ Tools

Perhaps the most common and popular collection of software tools are those associated with the **UNIX operating system**. These include **editors** for manipulating text files (for example, *vi*), **compilers** (such as the C language compiler, *cc*) and programming language **preprocessors** (such as the C language program checker or verifier, *cpp*), pattern matching or selection (such as *grep*), **lexical analysers** and **compiler construction** tools (such as *lex* and *yacc*), and software configuration management tools (such as *make*). Some authors have used the expression *the UNIX environment* to indicate the extent of the collection of tools available with UNIX. This is not the sense, however, in which the term *environment* is used in this section.

■ CASE

CASE packages are typically proprietary, and are marketed as a means of improving software development by providing graphical, filing, documentation and other computer-based aids to software specification, design and programming. Because a substantial proportion of development work can be done using such a package, the term **workbench** is often used to designate the computer or terminal, together with the CASE software, on which that work is done. Some CASE packages include planning aids, and some include maintenance or re-engineering aids. **Re-engineering** or **reverse engineering** is the recovery of information in a form acceptable to a CASE package from existing, non-CASE software.

A typical CASE package supporting structured development would include a data-flow diagram editor, a data-model editor, a program structure diagram editor, a data dictionary, a **database schema generator** and a **code generator**. Other diagramming tools, such as organisation charts or planning aids, may also be provided.

For marketing reasons, many CASE suppliers claim that their packages can be used with a variety of different development methodologies and software processes. For this reason they are often reticent about the specific software process implications of their packages. In many cases, however, CASE users soon discover that there are many constraints built into CASE packages. To take a specific example, a user may wish to perform data modelling before drawing data-flow diagrams. With many conventional CASE packages for structured methods this may be rather more difficult than doing the data-flow diagrams first. In practice, many CASE packages have required or preferred sequences of activities which, in effect, define or constrain some part of the software process.

A distinction is sometimes made between ordinary, or 'vanilla' CASE and integrated CASE, or I-CASE, though the degree of integration of a CASE package is difficult to quantify. At the unintegrated end of the scale, one has a loose collection of CASE tools, each of which may have a different interface and keep different files. At the integrated end of the scale, one has a common interface, a repository of important development data with which all tools interact, and relationships between the tools such that changes in any one product that affect other products result in all relevant updates being done.

It is to be expected that the more integrated a CASE package is, the more constraints it places on the software process.

■ Environments

A software engineering environment, or software development environment, is a much more all-encompassing support framework for the software process. As an example, we can consider the Arcadia environment described by Kadia (1992). Arcadia is an integrated software support framework including:

(a) Process definition and enaction

This includes process programming facilities and support for changes in process models and programs to meet changing process requirements, providing visibility into project and product status.

(b) Software object management

An object may be any software thing, whether a process object or a product, for example, a process model description, a data model, a piece of documentation, a process program module or an application program code module. Arcadia treats software objects as instances of **abstract data types**.

(c) User interface development system

This allows different user views of objects to be created rapidly, in order to meet the needs of different development roles, for example, manager or developer, and also to cater for changing needs within any specific role.

(d) Measurement and evaluation

A subsystem for making both static and dynamic measurements of software processes and the products they build.

(e) Language processing

Support for the programming part of the software process through generic, tailorable programming-language processing facilities.

(f) Analysis and testing

Broad-based support for the quality assurance function.

(g) Component composition

This puts all the software and software process pieces together in a flexible, but **inter-operable** manner, so that they can work together effectively while still providing acceptable flexibility and extensibility, for example, the inclusion of new tools, and changes to existing ones.

The Arcadia project is a major research project involving many researchers from academia and industry. It illustrates the convergence between software process modelling and software development environments.

Project management issues

Software process selection can also be influenced by project management issues. Consider, for example, a competitive situation in which time-to-market is a crucial factor. In such a case, an abbreviated software process with maximum parallelism and phase overlap may be selected, together with 'crashing' of critical activities, even at the expense of high costs and a possible reduction in some aspects of quality. On the other hand, if reuse and extra high reliability are project goals, a process may be selected which is suitable for use with an object-oriented methodology incorporating thorough verification and validation including, for example, formal code reading.

Risk management

In a sense, risk management is a project management issue. We treat it separately, however, because it provides an excellent example of the way in which project characteristics and goals can influence the choice of a suitable software process. If, for example, user requirements are ill defined and user acceptance is problematical, a prototyping approach is appropriate in order to 'buy knowledge' about requirements. In such a case a software process based on the spiral model may be appropriate in order to reduce the risk of user non-acceptance. If, on the other hand, the requirements are well defined and stable, a more conventional waterfall process model may be more appropriate.

Exercises

2.1 Obtain a number of different SDLC representations from software engineering, software analysis and design, or software project management textbooks. Abstract their common features and list their differences. Comment on the practical difficulties of applying them to real software development situations.

2.2 What data collection and reporting problems are associated with the waterfall model with feedback? How would you overcome these problems in order to get a reasonably accurate record of the time and effort devoted to each development activity? Comment on the likely cost of your solution.

2.3 If change (requirements volatility) is so characteristic of software, why is it ignored in so many SDLC representations? How would you include it?

2.4 Explain in detail why PERT charts cannot be used to model software processes accurately.

2.5 Choose an application domain with which you are familiar. Characterise it in as much detail as you can, for example, in a manner similar to the characterisation of data-centred systems in Section 2.6.

2.6 Distinguish between software process, software development methodology and CASE. Explain the relationships between them and the nature of the constraints they place on each other.

2.7 Explain why there is tension between the need for integration in environments and CASE on the one hand, and the need for flexibility and extensibility on the other hand. Give examples.

References

Abdel-Hamid, T. K. and Madnick, S. E. (1989) 'Lessons learned from modelling the dynamics of software development'. *Communications of the ACM,* Vol. 32 No. 12 pp. 1426–38.

Ashworth, C. and Goodland, M. (1990) *SSADM: A Practical Approach,* McGraw-Hill, Maidenhead, England.

Boehm, B. W. (1981) *Software Engineering Economics,* Prentice-Hall, New York.

Boehm, B. W. and Belz, F. (1988) 'Applying process programming to the spiral model' in *Proc. 4th International Software Process Workshop.* C. Tully (Ed.) Moretonhampstead, Devon, UK (11–13 May 1988).

Boehm, B. W. and Papaccio, P. N. (1988) 'Understanding and controlling software costs', *IEEE Transactions on Software Engineering,* Vol. 14, No. 10, pp. 1462–77.

Boehm, B. W. (1988) 'A spiral model of software development and enhancement', *IEEE Computer* pp. 61–71.

Boehm, B. W. (1989) *Software Risk Management,* IEEE Computer Society Press, Los Alamitos, California.

Booch, G. (1994) *Object-oriented analysis and design with applications,* 2nd ed., Benjamin/Cummings Redwood City, CA.

Burrough, P. A. (1986) *Principles of Geographical Information Systems for Land Resources Assessment,* Clarendon Press, Oxford.

DeMarco, T. (1982) *Controlling Software Projects: Management, Measurement and Estimation* Yourdon Press, New York, NY, USA.

Humphrey, W. S. and Kellner, M.I. (1989) 'Software process modelling: Principles of entity process models', *Proc. 11th ICSE* (Pittsburgh, PA, May 1989) pp. 331–42.

Humphrey W. S. (1991) 'Software and the factory paradigm', *Software Engineering Journal,* pp. 370–76.

Kadia, R. (1992) 'Issues encountered in building a flexible software development environment: Lessons from the Arcadia project', *ACM SIGSoft Software Engineering Notes,* 17(5) (Dec 1992), pp. 169–80.

Lehman, M. M. (1989) 'Uncertainty in computer application and its control through the engineering of software', *J. Software Maintenance,* Vol. 1 No. 1, pp. 3–28.

Lientz, B. P. and Swanson, E. B. (1980) *Software Maintenance Management: A Study of the Maintenance of Computer Application Software in 487 Data Processing Organizations,* Addison-Wesley, Reading, MA.

Madhavji, N. H. (1991) 'The process cycle', *Software Engineering Journal* (Sept. 1991), pp. 234–42.

Osterweil, L. (1987) 'Software processes are software too', *Proc. 9th ICSE,* (Monterey, CA, 30 March–2 April 1987), ACM 2–13.

Redwine, S., Jr and Riddle, W. (1989) 'Software reuse processes' ACM *SIG Software Engineering Notes* 14(4), pp 133–135.

Sallis, P. J. and Benwell, G. L. (1993) 'Geomatics: the influence of informatics on spatial information processing', in Barta, B. Z., Hung, S. L. and Cox, K. R. (Eds) *Software Engineering Education* IFIP Transactions A-40, Elsevier Science B. V. (North-Holland), Amsterdam, pp. 199–208.

Tate, G. (1993) 'Software process modelling and metrics: A CASE study', *Information and Software Technology,* Vol. 35, No. 6/7.

Tully, C. (Ed.) (1988) Representing and enacting the software process, in *Proc. 4th Int. Software Process Workshop,* (Moretonhampstead, Devon, UK, 11–13 May 1988) reprinted as *ACM SIGSOFT Software Engineering Notes,* Vol. 14, No. 4 (June 1989), pp. 46–56.

CHAPTER 3

Process management principles

THE NEED FOR PROCESS MANAGEMENT   3.1

Why management of developers is difficult   3.1.1

For all but the smallest software development projects, groups of development personnel are required, normally under the control or supervision of project managers. As is the case in almost any group-based endeavour, communication and coordination within each group is of vital importance if the development process is to be carried through to a successful conclusion. Ensuring adequate paths of communication is an increasingly difficult task as the size of a project group grows. If lines of communication are required between every individual in a group of n people, then there is a total of $n(n-1)/2$ separate interaction paths. For a small group, this may be a manageable number—for example, a group of three people generates three lines of communication. However, a group of eight personnel, not an overly large number for many development projects, results in twenty-eight distinct paths of communication. Maintaining common knowledge and understanding over such a network can therefore become close to impossible. This concept of conflicting understanding is illustrated in Figure 3.1 (see page 44).

Process managers must also contend with the widely varying characteristics and personalities of the individuals in each group. Project personnel will have different degrees of ability for certain development tasks, they will have different skills and levels of experience, and they will have different attitudes towards others. All of these factors need to be considered when personnel are (a) assigned to project groups, and (b) assigned to particular roles and activities within those groups. (See Figure 3.2 for an illustration of the factors that contribute to individual differences.) The impact of these attributes on the effectiveness of team activities increases non-linearly as the size of the group grows. To further complicate the task of personnel management, software development is still in part a creative endeavour, in spite of recent advances in process automation and process support. Therefore if standards for both product and process are not

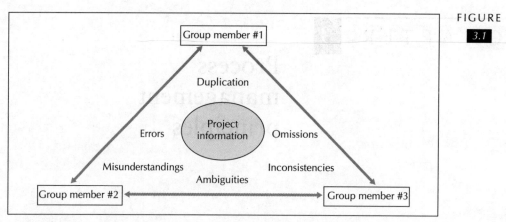

Issues affecting communication and coordination in development

FIGURE

3.1

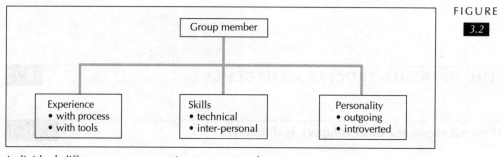

Individual differences among project group members

FIGURE

3.2

developed and enforced, it is almost certain that individuals will perform their respective activities differently.

Why management of software is difficult

Irrespective of whether it is more or less difficult than management in other disciplines, management of the software process is an often frustrating and problematic task. This is in spite of the fact that information technology in general, and software in particular, is widely recognised as a vital component in the function of most organisations. A number of diverse factors contribute to this apparent conflict. Some of them are shown in Table 3.1 and are then discussed in detail.

Factors influencing the effectiveness of process management	
Evolving requirements	System size and complexity
Developed from scratch	Few measurement methods
High demand for systems	Meaning of requirements
Changes to current systems	Developed by people

TABLE

3.1

(a) Requirements for information systems support evolve

Software is developed and used in a dynamic environment—as the functions of organisations change, *their requirements for information systems support evolve.* This would not be a significant problem if change was gradual or could always be anticipated. However, the reality is that businesses and other organisations are constantly evolving, particularly at the operational level. It is therefore not uncommon to find that system requirements change markedly over the life of a development project, before the software system has even come into use. Similarly, the functionality of systems can become outdated in a very short period, leading to a requirement for system maintenance or redevelopment.

(b) Software is still developed from scratch

Despite growing awareness of the concepts of software reuse, a significant amount of *software is still developed from scratch* to fulfil specific requirements. One would hope that some degree of reuse is encouraged and undertaken within software development departments or software houses. Outside these organisational boundaries, however, a very large amount of repeated effort must be expended developing functionally similar (if not equivalent) systems. Another important consequence of this approach is that instead of plugging pre-tested system components together, each must be developed anew with an inherent possibility that errors will be introduced. Finally, maintaining consistency in both methods and techniques is made all the more difficult when each new product is developed in virtual isolation.

(c) Demand for systems has grown

As organisations have become more aware of the potential of software in terms of supporting and advancing the effectiveness of their operation, the *demand for systems has grown* at an enormous rate. Managing and prioritising the software process so as to deliver systems in a timely manner has become increasingly difficult as a result. Although the 'software crisis' occurred due to the lack of productivity-enhancing tools and methodologies, the boom in demand for application systems, together with the backlog of system requests (stated and unstated) was also a significant cause. In a real sense the software crisis, which began in the 1960s, has continued to the present day.

(d) Changes to systems already in use

Changes in the organisational environment also lead to requests for *changes to systems already in use.* Thus an information systems manager's job is made even more difficult, with the need to consider maintenance proposals as well as requirements for new systems.

(e) Size and complexity of the requested systems

Just as the demand for new and revised systems has increased in volume terms, so has the *size and complexity of the requested systems* also grown. This has consequently placed greater pressure on developers and project managers to ensure that the process delivers systems that are not only supplied on time but also provide the increasingly complicated functionality with a high degree of quality.

(f) Management without proven methods of measurement

Engineering is founded on quantitative measurement—many 'desirable' attributes of software processes, however, are difficult to measure in this way. Given that measurement is a precursor to effective planning and control, *management without proven methods of measurement* is fraught with difficulties.

(g) Maintaining the intent and meaning of the requirement

Software products are abstract entities, from the relatively rich (but ambiguous) natural language representation of a requirements specification, through to the sparse (but precise) digital implementation of machine code. As a system is transformed from specification to implementation it becomes increasingly abstracted from the original expression of a system need. *Maintaining the intent and meaning of the requirement* through the various levels of abstraction, generally using a variety of notations that do not always enable a direct mapping from one to the other, is therefore by no means a trivial task.

(h) Software is developed by people

Software is developed by people whose differing attitudes and characteristics can, if uncontrolled, have a significantly detrimental effect on the quality and effectiveness of both the process and the product (as discussed earlier in this section). Further-more, software is normally developed by **groups** of people. Apart from the communication problems that this introduces, it also imposes a managerial require-ment to ensure that duplication of work is avoided and that consistency and standards in the process are maintained.

Given such conditions, it is hardly surprising that management of the software process can, if unchecked, deteriorate into a set of reactive and remedial procedures or, worse still, virtual chaos. Crisis management is all too common in the software business. Thus, as discussed in Chapter 2, the software process itself must be constantly monitored and improved if software systems are to fulfil their potential.

Approaches to managing software development   3 . 1 . 3

The likelihood of a successful outcome in a development project is influenced greatly by the management methods employed. All other things being equal, dynamic, realistic and proactive management is far more likely to result in a system delivered on time, within budget, and up to the required standards of quality, than a management attitude and approach that is static or reactive.

Perhaps the most widely used approach to software development management is through the organisational structure of teams. Although there are newer methods for task division, such as individuals or groups taking functional responsibility for specific aspects of a system, the team approach continues to be popular. A typical team leader (or project leader) would be a senior programmer/analyst with proven technical and leadership qualities. Teams vary in size, but between five and seven members is not unusual. It may be that the teams are further subdivided into those who write code according to specifications/designs passed to them from the team leader through another layer of intermediate level programmer, or those at the intermediate level may be responsible for writing module interface programs, or for program testing. Subdividing development tasks, such as those that are essentially analysis, design, programming or testing in nature, helps to determine the most effective mix of expertise within the team. Given that different development tasks are sometimes taking place simultaneously (and across more than one project), it is often important to have a mix of expertise within teams. The extent to which this kind of team mix is necessary is usually a function of the size of the development portfolio of the organisation. Figures 3.3 and 3.4 illustrate from two different perspectives the skill requirements at various stages of a basic software process.

FIGURE
3.3

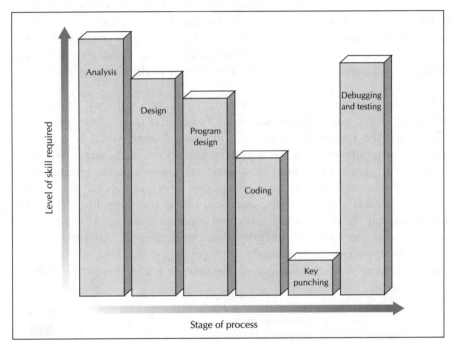

Skill requirements at various stages of a 'waterfall-type process' (Bell et al., 1987)

FIGURE
3.4

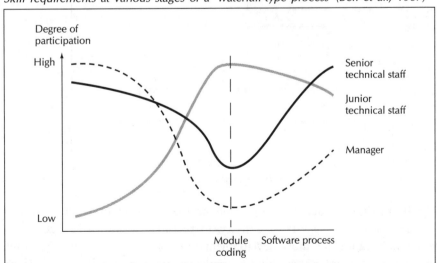

Participation variations throughout the software process (National Computing Centre, 1990)

With regard to the management of teams and projects, team leaders need to be aware of the following dangerous assumptions (National Computing Centre, 1990):

- the productivity of project personnel is constant, and can be set and controlled by management;
- the output of a software project is directly and measurably proportional to the effort applied to the project;
- project time schedules can be compressed arbitrarily.

Adoption of these expectations will greatly increase the probability of project failure. In relation to the first assumption, productivity will vary markedly across individuals and projects for a variety of reasons, including the size and complexity of the tasks involved, the development process employed, and the abilities of project personnel. Any attempt to 'control' such an attribute will almost certainly fail. (This does not mean that it should not be *measured* and monitored. This issue is dealt with in greater detail in Chapter 10.)

Bell, Morrey and Pugh (1987) suggest that there are two common methods of organising software project teams: *functional teams* and *project teams*. Functional team members all carry out the same type of work. In this model there would be a team of analysts, a team of programmers, a team of testers, and so on in the organisation. In the project team model, expertise is mixed, so some are analysts, some programmers, and some testers. A further individual or even a team may be responsible for the software library. This would include reuse libraries, and subroutine and copy libraries of file structures. It may be that the database administrator assumes this role, or some person in the team responsible for database integrity. Since management skills vary across individuals who may appear to be technically appropriate for this task, choice of the responsible person is crucial to the success of the proactive and innovative reuse of development components.

FIGURE

3.5

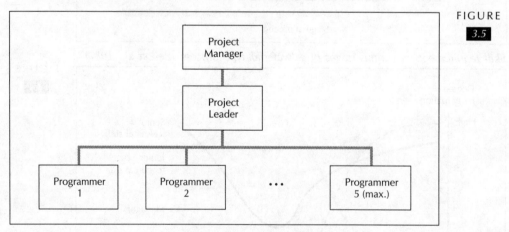

A common team structure for small- to medium-size projects

Rakos (1990) provides a detailed discussion of the selection of team structures according to project size. He suggests that the two structures, as shown in Figures 3.5 and 3.6, are not uncommon for most development organisations. (It should be noted that the structures shown are essentially for implementation only—thus there is no consideration of the roles of analysts or designers.)

FIGURE

3.6

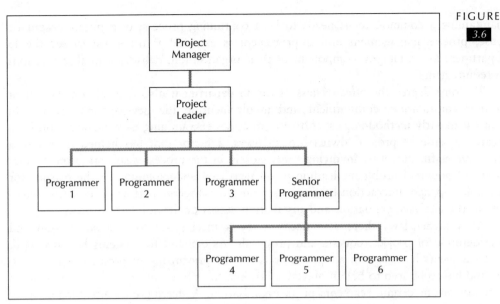

An appropriate team structure for larger projects (after Rakos, 1990)

Given that supervision of more than five programmers is not feasible for most project leaders, it is important that adequate decomposition of the team and the project be undertaken, extending the reporting and responsibility hierarchy (see Figure 3.6).

The responsibilities of each participant in Figures 3.5 and 3.6 are as follows:

- Project Manager—provide leadership, coordinate communication, plan and control the software process;
- Project Leader—lead technical activities, solve system difficulties, ensure quality;
- Senior Programmer—coordinate programming effort, liaise between Project Leader and programmers, initiate system testing;
- Programmer—write and test code.

At a much higher level, the system dynamics model of Abdel-Hamid and Madnick (1989) described in Chapter 2 provides a useful illustration of the *interdependence* of management activities within the software process. Thus although planning, control and resource management tasks may occur discretely and in apparent isolation, their impact on other management subsystems may be wide ranging. It is therefore essential that the consequences of management decisions be considered in this respect.

Organisational and political issues

3.1.4

Effective process management has an impact not only on those directly involved in software development but also on the organisation as a whole. For many years, investment in information technology was granted almost grudgingly, with management often questioning the value of the return on that investment. Alignment of the IS function with the goals and objectives of the organisation, coupled with the increased effectiveness of IS departments, has led to significant improvements in the cost effectiveness of the software development department, though much still remains to be done. However, maintaining a common focus needs to be a continuing process; in a purely pragmatic sense, process management and improvement is essential if users are to see the IS department as an integral component of their organisation, delivering quality solutions to requirements.

To some degree the effectiveness of the IS department also depends on the extent of user consultation, commitment and involvement in the development process. In contrast to early methodologies, software processes encouraging user participation have created a sense of project 'ownership' in users, a factor that has helped to ensure a more successful outcome. Involving users closely in the process also makes them more aware of potential problems, leading to an increased understanding of the reasons for schedule slippage. Interaction between users and developers must be particularly extensive in the analysis, validation and installation stages of the software process.

At a higher level there also needs to be a mechanism for the submission and consideration of project requests and proposals. As demand for systems has increased, IS departments have had to adopt methods for the prioritising of projects. This has to be (and has to be seen to be) an objective process, so as to ensure that the IS department does not favour certain segments of an organisation. A steering committee made up of functional unit managers and representatives of the IS department may be an appropriate body for this task.

A considerable amount of research into the effectiveness of steering committees has been carried out, particularly as they relate to project selection criteria and the mechanisms for choosing one application over another for inclusion in the IS portfolios of large organisations. The most recent paper, and one which makes reference to other work on the topic, is that by McKeen, Guimaraes and Wetherbe (1994), giving a comparative analysis across eight industry types of portfolio selection mechanisms. The strategic advantage of using steering committees to determine applications for computer project development highlights yet again the need for both user and developer participation in the resource allocation process of organisations where success of new systems is to be observed. In previous work by these authors (1985) the point that resource allocation is to a large extent the result of internal political processes is made. Such processes rely heavily on participation by all individuals who may be influential in the selection so that all understand the implications of their choice.

The reasons for project failure

3.1.5

Many reasons for project failure are not technical but it is extremely difficult to separate the purely technical aspects of a perceived system failure (or success) from the human or environmental aspects. In any case most technical objects are the result of some human involvement. Nevertheless, it is clear to us that the main reasons for project failure have to do with people and are mainly managerial or organisational behaviour problems. Thus, ineffective process management contributes directly to project failure. Many of the symptoms of ineffective management have been discussed above—some are now reiterated by way of a summary:

- insufficient communication and reporting between users and developers;
- differing expectations of system functionality;
- development in isolation of business aims and objectives;

- failure to assess risks, costs and benefits;
- poor estimation of costs and duration;
- development without adequate change procedures;
- short cuts in development taken in reaction to schedule constraints;
- poor coordination among developers.

A PROCESS MANAGEMENT FRAMEWORK · 3.2

The management of software processes is much like the management of any other complex project-based activity such as the construction of a bridge or a shopping complex. The major activities are described briefly as follows.

■ Project setup

The project is established as a separate and distinct venture, usually within a larger organisation. The scope of the project is defined, as are its relationships to the environment organisation(s) with which it interfaces. The general level of resources (people, equipment, support, etc.) is decided, together with the major constraints (time, money, etc.). Quality requirements are set and other appropriate standards are selected. At this stage also, a suitable generic software process is selected which can be specialised at later stages to fit better the particular application to be developed. Risk analysis may be appropriate in software process selection.

■ Planning

There is inevitably some overlap between planning and project setup in the sense that a good deal of initial planning has to be done during the setup stage. Planning involves **estimation** of the time, effort and other resources needed to meet requirements. If resources are inadequate, then either they should be increased or the requirements should be reduced. **Risk analysis** and planning for **risk management** are also appropriate. All the various development tasks, their relationships and dependencies, the resources they will need, when they will need them, and who is responsible for each, are set out in the plan.

■ Task allocation

The planned tasks are allocated to those who have to perform them. This may seem obvious, but because many of the tasks are highly complex and because of the communication difficulties noted in Section 3.1, it is essential that those who carry out the tasks know precisely what is expected of them and that their specific agreement is obtained. In particular, the developers must be familiar with the parts of the defined software process that they are following.

■ Control and support, both managerial and technical

Once the tasks are allocated, they must be carried out. This involves the ongoing management activities of control to make sure that they are actually being done and the provision of support where necessary; for example, where staff are inexperienced, where additional education or on-the-job instruction is necessary, or where specialist skills are needed.

■ Monitoring

Progress, quality, risk management, resource consumption and cost must be monitored against the plan. Where there are significant differences, appropriate action must be taken, either to remedy the situation, or to modify the plan. Measurement of the software process and its products is clearly necessary if it is to be properly monitored.

The steps of planning, allocation, control and monitoring form a loop which is continually repeated. Project status or progress meetings are held at least monthly, but often fortnightly or even weekly.

■ Project post mortem

At the end of a project a *post mortem* should be held so that the organisation concerned can learn from its hard-won experience. It is helpful (and, more importantly, financially valuable) to know what went right and why, and what pitfalls to avoid in future. To preserve this experience in a formal manner, some of it can be fed back into the software process engineering function.

In the following sections we concentrate on several of the more difficult project management activities: estimation, risk management, project planning, project monitoring and control.

PROJECT ESTIMATION   3.3

The complexity and variety of software and of the software process make the management of software development both complex and difficult. Many different activities and skills are involved. They must be planned and scheduled over an extended development period, seldom much shorter than a year, and sometimes two or more years for larger projects. To plan a software development project effectively and to schedule the availability of the required skills at the appropriate times it is necessary to have a good estimate of the software size, how much it will cost, and how long it will take to develop. Software size estimation seeks to answer the first of these three key questions: How much software are we going to develop? Software cost estimation, which is normally based on software size estimation, seeks to answer the last two of these three questions: What is it going to cost to develop that much software? and, How long is it going to take?

Because software development is a labour-intensive activity involving teams of highly-skilled computing professionals, people costs make up by far the largest variable cost component of software development expenditure. For this reason it is common practice to concentrate on effort estimation. **Effort** in this sense is the developer person-power devoted to the software process. It is typically measured in person-months (abbreviation pm), this being a measure of the time integral of the number of personnel employed on a project over the duration of that project. People costs can be obtained from effort by applying suitable employment costs, often divided into skill categories and burdened with appropriate overheads.

Schedule estimation is the forecasting of both development duration and salient milestones in the development process. The term *software cost estimation,* sometimes shortened to *software costing,* is frequently used to include schedule estimation. This is not only convenient but also appropriate in the sense that 'time is money' in software exploitation, and opportunity costs are often associated with delivery delays.

Our purpose is to review cost estimation research and practice, in order to understand, classify and appraise the various approaches that have been adopted and determine their strengths and weaknesses. Since much research in this area is based on models, most of the review is concerned with the nature and adequacy of the models themselves, particularly their performance in practice.

The main approaches to cost estimation   3 . 3 . 1

We are concerned with macro-models for software effort estimation, that is, our primary concern is to estimate the cost of a development project as a whole, rather than, for example, of a single computer program. Two of the main approaches for doing this are:

(a) *Methods based on history and experience*

   (i) Expert judgement—consult one or more experts—but what do you do when they disagree? One method of resolving conflicts is to use a Delphi technique (Boehm, 1981).

   (ii) Bottom-up—this is perhaps the most commonly used approach. Break the project down into its separate activities using a work breakdown structure; for example, estimate the time for each activity and add them all.

   Though these methods are very common, they are also commonsense and so will not be further described.

(b) *Methods based on theoretical or statistical models*
   Some of the main models will be described in some detail in the following subsections.

The major models   3 . 3 . 2

The purpose of this subsection is to provide a conceptual basis for the study of software costing models. We therefore introduce only the salient features of some of the most important models. Before doing this, however, we briefly consider the general cost estimation process shown in Figure 3.7.

It will be noted from Figure 3.7 that size estimation is a separate process requiring both product specifications, sometimes referred to as functional specifications or requirements—what the application must do—and other size drivers, for example programming language, which may affect software size. Software size is usually measured in **KSLOC** (thousands of source lines of code) or **KDSI** (thousands of delivered source instructions), though occasionally function metrics are used, such as **function points** (Zwanzig, 1984) or function weight (DeMarco, 1989). Frequently function measures are converted into lines of code measures using either published tables (Jones, 1986) or environment-dependent factors based on local conditions and measurements. Size estimation is often treated as a process separate from cost estimation and a number of standalone size estimation

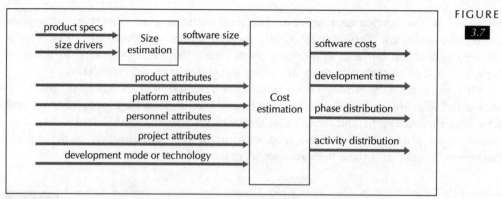

FIGURE

3.7

The general cost estimation process

tools are available. Some commercially available cost estimation tools include size estimation tools; others do not.

In addition to size, a number of other **cost drivers**, that is, factors known or thought to influence cost are assessed. Following Boehm (1981), these are traditionally grouped into product, platform, personnel and project attributes, but other categories and factors are sometimes used. Cost drivers vary in number from a handful to 30 or more.

Different application domains, development modes and development technologies may affect software cost. For example, straightforward in-house business developments are different from contracted safety-critical real-time applications. Most models, unless they are designed for just one type of development, also require the input of development mode or technology information, usually chosen from a small menu of categories which affect the parameters of a particular model. A development mode may be a very broad classification, in which case there will be only a few modes, say 3, or it may be characterised in some detail, in which case there may be 10 or more different modes. Alternatively the technology may be represented by a parameter which takes a numeric value, allowing both wider and finer choice, but at the same time making that choice more difficult.

■ COCOMO

The most influential and most widely used cost estimation model is Boehm's COCOMO (COnstructive COst MOdel) (Boehm, 1981). It assumes a conventional waterfall software development process and is based on an exhaustive analysis of a 63-project data set, consisting of projects in several different programming languages, of several different project types from business to systems programming, the projects being completed between 1968 and 1979. COCOMO is the basis of a large number of derivative models with many variations and extensions. Figure 3.8 presents the general structure of COCOMO and its derivatives. Size estimation, as noted above, is not in fact a part of COCOMO. It is included to give a more complete picture of the context of COCOMO.

The software size estimate (in KDSI) is used as the primary input to the effort estimation process, which consists of two steps. In the first step a **nominal** effort for that size and development mode is computed. In COCOMO the following three development modes are recognised:

- **organic**—typically corresponding to developments up to 50 KDSI in size within stable, forgiving, relatively unconstrained environments;

FIGURE

3.8

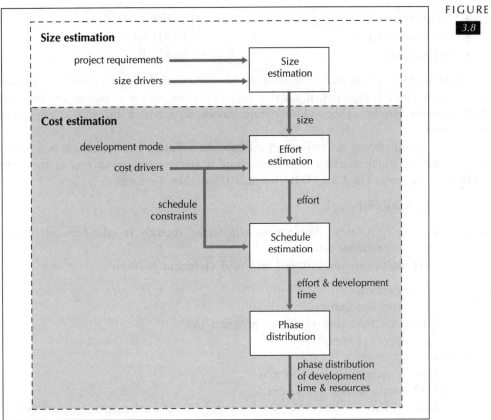

General structure of COCOMO and its derivatives

- **embedded**—typically ambitious, unfamiliar, unforgiving, tightly constrained developments of any size;
- **semi-detached**—intermediate in characteristics between organic and embedded, typically below 300 KDSI in size.

There are three levels of COCOMO models; basic, intermediate and detailed. Basic COCOMO uses size as its only cost driver. Intermediate COCOMO has 15 other cost drivers, or **effort multipliers**, as well as provision for component level estimation. Detailed COCOMO provides for a more detailed product breakdown into a system-subsystem-module hierarchy as well as phase-sensitive effort multipliers. Experience has shown that basic COCOMO is too simplistic and that detailed COCOMO gives no better results in general than intermediate COCOMO. The following description of COCOMO therefore refers mainly to the intermediate COCOMO model, which is the one most commonly used in practice.

A **nominal effort estimate,** usually in person-months, is calculated using a formula of the form:

Nominal effort = $a(\text{KDSI})^b$

The standard values of a and b for the three COCOMO development modes are:

- organic: $E_{nom} = 3.2\ (KDSI)^{1.05}$
- semi-detached: $E_{nom} = 3.0\ (KDSI)^{1.12}$
- embedded: $E_{nom} = 2.8\ (KDSI)^{1.20}$

Note that under this approach, diseconomies of scale (related to b) increase with greater development mode complexity. If suitable project history data is available, the nominal effort formula can be calibrated to obtain values of a and b fitted to a particular environment.

In the second step of the estimation process, the nominal effort estimate is adjusted up or down by taking account of the effects of a number of cost drivers in the form of effort multipliers. The COCOMO formula thus takes the form:

Effort = $a(KDSI)^b E_1 E_2 \dots E_n$

where n is 15 in COCOMO, but has been increased recently to take account of new factors, such as component reuse.

The effort multipliers are grouped into four classes as follows:

- *Product attributes*
     RELY—required software reliability
     DATA—database size relative to program size
     CPLX—product complexity.
- *Computer attributes*
     TIME—execution time constraint
     STOR—main storage constraint
     VIRT—virtual machine volatility (or instability of implementation platform)
     TURN—computer turnaround time.
- *Personnel attributes*
     ACAP—analyst capability
     AEXP—applications experience
     PCAP—programmer capability
     VEXP—virtual machine (that is, implementation platform) experience
     LEXP—programming language experience.
- *Project attributes*
     MODP—modern programming practices
     TOOL—use of software tools
     SCED—required development schedule (that is, compressed or extended).

Each cost driver is rated on a 4, 5 or 6-point scale. The 6-point scale is: very low, low, nominal, high, very high, extra high. The 4 and 5-point scales have points missing at one or both ends of the 6-point scale. The effort multiplier values associated with the scale points for each of the 15 effort multipliers are given in Table 3.2.

Note that the effort multiplier values all have a nominal or normal rating to which a value of 1.00 is assigned. This is convenient, in that in the absence of other knowledge, nominal values can be used as defaults. The effects of the effort multipliers vary from a possible 20% range for language experience to a possible 236% range for product complexity. Quite detailed guidelines are given in Boehm (1981) on how to rate the various cost drivers.

The effects of cost drivers are all in expected directions, except perhaps for SCED, where any compression below, or extension above, the normal development time results

TABLE
3.2

COCOMO effort multiplier values for different ratings						
	Ratings					
Effort multipliers	VL	L	N	H	VH	EH
Product attributes						
RELY required software reliability	0.75	0.88	1.00	1.15	1.40	
DATA database size		0.94	1.00	1.08	1.16	
CPLX product complexity	0.70	0.85	1.00	1.15	1.30	1.65
Computer attributes						
TIME execution time constraint			1.00	1.11	1.30	1.66
STOR main storage constraint			1.00	1.06	1.21	1.56
VIRT virtual machine volatility		0.87	1.00	1.15	1.30	
TURN computer turnaround time		0.87	1.00	1.07	1.15	
Personnel attributes						
ACAP analyst capability	1.46	1.19	1.00	0.86	0.71	
AEXP analyst experience	1.29	1.13	1.00	0.91	0.82	
PCAP programmer capability	1.42	1.17	1.00	0.86	0.70	
VEXP virtual machine experience	1.21	1.10	1.00	0.90		
LEXP programming language experience	1.14	1.07	1.00	0.95		
Project attributes						
MODP modern programming practices	1.24	1.10	1.00	0.91	0.82	
TOOL use of software tools	1.24	1.10	1.00	0.91	0.83	
SCED required development schedule	1.23	1.08	1.00	1.04	1.10	

in an increase in project effort. The concept of **nominal development time** is an important one with a number of theoretical and empirical overtones related to **nominal project profiles**. The latter are based on the **Rayleigh distribution,** a skewed bell-shaped curve which was shown by Norden (1958, 1963) to give a good approximation to the labour distribution for many types of research and development activities. In the COCOMO context, the Rayleigh distribution takes the form:

$$P(t) = MM * (1/t_d^2) * e ** -(t^2/2t_d^2),$$

where t is time measured in months from the start of the project;

$P(t)$ is the number of personnel required at time t, that is, the person-power utilisation rate at time t;

MM is the total effort required for the project in person months;

t_d is the month in which the project achieves its peak effort, that is, where $P(t)$ is a maximum.

COCOMO cuts off the left and right tails of the Rayleigh distribution, the left tail being concerned with plans and requirements which are assumed to precede development and the right tail being concerned with activities such as maintenance, which succeed integration and test.

The effort estimate (MM) is the main input into the schedule estimation process. The term schedule estimation is commonly used to refer to the process of estimating the development time for a software project because effort distribution or scheduling assumptions are built into the models. It follows that it is common practice to use the term *schedule* both to mean development time (T_{DEV}) and to imply an underlying scheduling model. The **nominal schedule** is typically calculated using a relationship of the form:

Nominal schedule = c (MM)^d

The standard values of c and d for the three COCOMO development modes are:

- organic: $T_{DEV} = 2.5 \, (MM)^{0.38}$
- semi-detached: $T_{DEV} = 2.5 \, (MM)^{0.35}$
- embedded: $T_{DEV} = 2.5 \, (MM)^{0.32}$

The relationship between effort and schedule is not quite so simple, however, since a certain amount of schedule compression or extension can be specified. The maximum compression permitted in COCOMO is to 75% of the nominal schedule, with an effort penalty of 23%. The schedule compression and extension, given as percentages of nominal (T_{DEV}), allowed for in COCOMO are:

VL	75% of nominal	23% more effort
L	85% of nominal	8% more effort
N	nominal	MM estimate
H	130% of nominal	4% more effort
VH	160% of nominal	10% more effort.

There is a complex relationship between schedule change and required effort because the shape of the Rayleigh curve changes, and with it the effort distribution over the project. Also, schedule compression is known to be difficult and, beyond a certain level, which COCOMO puts at 75% of nominal, is thought to be impracticable.

Development time and effort are input to a phase distribution process which uses a standard set of (waterfall model) development phases, as follows:

- Product design
- Programming
  - Detailed design
  - Code and unit test
- Integration and test.

The proportion of effort and time in each phase varies with project size and development mode. COCOMO project sizes are small (2 KDSI), intermediate (8 KDSI), medium (32 KDSI), large (128 KDSI), and very large (512 KDSI). In addition to the above phases, a preliminary plans and requirements phase is also recognised, though not included in the COCOMO effort (MM) and duration (T_{DEV}) estimates. Plans and requirements are estimated to take an additional 6–8% of effort and 10–40% of development time, depending on the size and development mode of the project. For example, for a medium-size organic project, the effort and schedule distributions by phase are:

	Effort%	Schedule%
Plans and requirements	6	12
Product design	16	19
Detailed design	24	} 55
Code and unit test	38	
Integration and test	22	26

Plans and requirements are outside the phases normally estimated because they have to be completed in most cases before reliable estimates can be made. Note also that in the middle of the effort–time curve, where effort is greatest during detailed design and code and unit test, 62% of the effort is expended in 55% of the scheduled time in this case. At earlier and later phases, however, percent effort is less than percent schedule as manpower builds up or decreases. This is in accordance with the Rayleigh distribution.

We now make specific mention of one important development of COCOMO, Boehm's Ada-COCOMO (Boehm, 1989) which is intended for estimation in new (object-oriented) Ada development environments, including significant reuse of software components in some cases.

■ Ada-COCOMO

Ada-COCOMO has the following process model milestones:

- Software requirements review (SRR)
- Preliminary design review (PDR)
- Critical design review (CDR)
- Unit test completion (UTC)
- Software acceptance review (SAR).

The first and last of these correspond to milestones SSR and FQT in the US DoD standard DoD-STD-2167A. The Ada process model is a more disciplined one than previous COCOMO process models, resulting in a changed phase distribution of effort. A greater proportion of time and effort is expended up to PDR and CDR. There is a smaller proportion of time and effort devoted to code, integration and test. There is also less effort overall, and reduced diseconomies of scale. Boehm recognises, however, that the transition from traditional software processes to the more disciplined Ada process will not occur immediately and may only be partial. His Ada–COCOMO model, therefore, allows for partial transition to the Ada process model in the embedded mode, as follows:

$$\text{Effort} = a(\text{KDSI})^{1.04 + b} \, E_1 E_2 \dots E_n$$

where $b = 0$ for full use of the Ada process model;
           $b = 0.16$ if the Ada process model is not used at all; and
           $0 < b < 0.16$ for partial use of the Ada process model.

The b factor is broken down into three additive terms relating to design thoroughness by PDR, risk elimination by PDR, and requirements volatility. Because b is a sum of this type, it is usually denoted by Σ. Non-use of the Ada process model has less effect for organic and semi-detached modes. The Ada–COCOMO models can be summarised as follows:

Mode	Effort	Schedule
Organic	$\text{MM} = 1.9 \, (\text{KDSI})^{1.01 + 0.25\Sigma} \, E_1 E_2 \dots E_n$	$T_{\text{DEV}} = 3.0 \, (\text{MM})^{0.38 + 0.2\Sigma}$
Semi-detached	$\text{MM} = 2.35 \, (\text{KDSI})^{1.02 + 0.625\Sigma} \, E_1 E_2 \dots E_n$	$T_{\text{DEV}} = 3.0 \, (\text{MM})^{0.35 + 0.2\Sigma}$
Embedded	$\text{MM} = 2.8 \, (\text{KDSI})^{1.04 + \Sigma} \, E_1 E_2 \dots E_n$	$T_{\text{DEV}} = 3.0 \, (\text{MM})^{0.32 + 0.2\Sigma}$

The effort multipliers are also modified in Ada–COCOMO. There are 18 of them, new ones being:

RUSE—required reusability of code produced

VMVH—virtual machine volatility of host
VMVT—virtual machine volatility of target
SECU—classified security application.

VMVH and VMVT replace the original COCOMO VIRT. The values of the multipliers have also been changed so that there is:

- less effect for high reliability and complexity;
- larger analyst influence and smaller programmer influence;
- larger language experience influence;
- larger tools and turnaround time influence;
- no schedule stretch effort penalty.

There are also new instruction counting rules which include reuse effects.

■ Other COCOMO versions and variants

There are a large number of independent implementations of COCOMO, many of which have a number of minor differences, mainly in their adaptation to particular environments. These may include modified cost-driver effects, additional or fewer cost drivers, additional or different development modes and/or calibration of the effort and schedule scaling equations to different environments, resulting in different values for the parameters a, b, c and d. The complete details of these variations are difficult to obtain and tedious to describe, so we have only summarised them. Those that have the most effect in general are calibration of the scaling equation parameters a, b, c, d to different environments. The latest versions of most COCOMO variants also contain either Ada–COCOMO implementations or variants.

■ Putnam's model

Putnam's model is based on the Rayleigh curve, together with several other related concepts, such as **difficulty** and **technology** (Putnam, 1978; Putnam and Fitzsimmons, 1979; Putnam et al., 1984; and Putnam and Putnam, 1984) which are briefly explained below. Its original derivation used data collected in the mid-1970s. We will not go into the derivation of the model, but will concentrate on its main features. The basic effort macro–estimation model, sometimes called the *software equation*, is

$$S = C K^{1/3} t_d^{4/3},$$

where S is the number of delivered source instructions;
K is the life-cycle effort in person-years;
t_d is the development time in years;
C is a technology constant.

In the Putnam model, the development time, t_d, is the time at which the person-power utilisation rate is a maximum. The effort to this point is 39.45% of the total life-cycle effort for the project (including maintenance). The technology constant C can be as low as 610 or as high as 57 314, covering a proposed spectrum of 20 discrete values. High values of C correspond to high productivity development technologies.

The difficulty metric:

$$D = K/t_d^2,$$

is important in deriving the basic effort estimation model and therefore in determining software effort and schedule. Based on an investigation of some 50 US Army projects, Putnam found a relationship between software productivity P, and difficulty D, of the form:

$$P = c \, D^{-\frac{2}{3}}$$

where c is a constant, absorbed into the technology factor C. This relation is used in the derivation of the basic Putnam macro-estimation model.

The most controversial aspect of the Putnam model is obtained by solving the software equation for K, obtaining:

$$K = t_{d}^{-4}(S/C)^{3}$$

The resulting fourth power trade-off law between effort and development time is described by Boehm (1981) as 'rather radical'.

The Putnam model is built into the software product SLIM (Software LIfe cycle Methodology) which includes a number of other associated estimation facilities and a large number of cost drivers. Essentially these contribute to, or modify, the technology constant C. The maximum compression of project schedule permitted by SLIM is approximately 86% of nominal.

The Jensen model (Jensen, 1981, 1984, 1985, 1987) is similar in many respects to that of Putnam, but has a less radical trade-off between effort and development time t_{d}. Jensen's software equation is:

$$S = C \, t_{d} \, K^{\frac{1}{2}}$$

where C is a basic technology factor involving 13 cost drivers which are somewhat different from Putnam's. This leads to a second rather than a fourth power trade-off between t_{d} and effort, namely:

$$\text{Effort} * t^{2} = \text{constant}$$

JS2, JS3 and SYSTEM-3 are commercial versions of the Jensen model.

The appropriateness of the Rayleigh distribution to software development has been questioned by Parr (1980) who observed that most projects do not start from the origin, with zero manpower, and follow a learning curve upward from there whose slope is related to Putnam's difficulty metric. They can start some distance up the effort rate axis because preliminary work on requirements, for example, has been done, and staff are already familiar with the project's tools, requirements and methods. Parr's person-power distribution curve is of the form:

$$\text{Staff}(t) = b \operatorname{sech}^{2}\left(\frac{at + c}{2}\right)$$

which is similar in shape to the Rayleigh distribution but not constrained to pass through the origin. There is some evidence that the Parr model is a better fit than the Rayleigh curve to some data sets (Basili, 1980).

nt analysis (FPA) approach

n points are also described from a different point of view (that of
ner than estimation) in Chapter 10.

FPA approach is fundamentally a sizing approach, it also forms the
basis ____ ure cost estimation in some environments, particularly for business
applications. The FPA approach (Albrecht 1979; Albrecht and Gaffney, 1983; Zwanzig,
1984) is fundamentally different in concept from approaches based on lines of code, or
delivered source instructions, in that it is based on the input of a **product function** rather
than a product size to the effort estimation process. Function points are an indirect
estimate of system function, based on an analysis of system inputs and outputs, including
files and interfaces. FPA uses a set of rules to identify an individual function as one of
the following: input, output, inquiry, internal file (or entity), or external interface. A
further set of rules is then used to rate the complexity of each function as low, average,
or high. Function complexity depends on the number of data elements, files (or entities),
and record types (or relationships) involved. The relationship is illustrated by the
following complexity matrix for input transactions:

Data elements

		<5	5–15	>15
Files/	<2	L	L	A
entities	2	L	A	H
	>2	A	H	H

The complexity levels are low (L), average (A), and high (H). Though this matrix
may give the impression of objectivity in FPA, the rules for identifying transactions are
complex and subject to interpretation in unusual instances. Moreover, there is provision
in the counting rules for an FPA assessor to change the complexity up or down by one
level, based on experience and judgement. Thus, FPA has some subjective aspects.

Individual function point ratings are then assigned, depending on function type and
complexity, according to the following classification matrix:

Complexity

	Low	Average	High
Input	3	4	6
Output	4	5	7
File/entity	7	10	15
External interface	5	7	10
Inquiry	3–4	4–5	6–7

Inquiries are separated into an input and an output part and are given the complexity
rating of an input or an output, depending on which of the input or output parts has
the higher rating.

The sum of all the individual function point counts gives the total unadjusted or
raw function point count for a system. This is then adjusted up or down by a maximum
of 35%, depending on 14 overall **system adjustment factors**, rated on a 6-point scale.
These include such factors as data communications, distributed function, complex
internal processing, on-line updating of master files, critical performance constraints,
design to facilitate change, ease of use, and so on. Some can be classed as size drivers

(or functionality modifiers), for example, ease of use by the end user, whereas others, for example, complex internal processing (corresponding to Boehm's CPLX) and critical performance constraints (corresponding to Boehm's TIME and STOR) are more in the nature of cost drivers.

Finally, a relationship is established between function points and effort, analogous to the relationship between size and effort used in COCOMO and most other models. The validity of the FPA approach depends on the strength of this relationship, that is, its 'goodness' of fit. In most cases, however, a simple linear relationship is used. A productivity factor, developer days per function point or function points per developer month, is used to derive effort from function points. Scheduling relationships, like those of COCOMO, are either not used or not described in the literature.

Though function points are conceptually different from SLOC (or DSI) measures in that they attempt to measure software function rather than software product size, for certain application types, particularly in information systems and data processing, function points are also used as a size measure. This is because in these application domains, function points can typically be estimated more easily than SLOC from requirements or specifications and also because function points and SLOC are highly correlated in this case. The conversion of function points to SLOC for input into the effort estimation process is typical of cost models which use FPA inputs.

■ **FPA variants**

There are a number of variants of the FPA approach, the most important being that of Symons (1988) who proposed an input–processing–output model which splits the functionality of the kth transaction into three parts:

- input, measured by the number of input data elements, I_k;
- processing, measured by the number of entities referenced or accessed, E_k; and
- output, measured by the number of output data elements, O_k.

Symons Mark II function points are then computed using a formula, such as:

$$\Sigma_k(0.44I_k + 1.67E_k + 0.38O_k),$$

where k indexes all transactions. Symons also proposed a number of changes to the system adjustment factors of FPA. Though Symons' Mark II function points may appear to be more objective than traditional, or Albrecht, function points, there are still some difficulties in unambiguously identifying transactions to be counted in the above manner.

Cost estimation in practice 　　　　　3.3.3

Having examined some of the main cost estimation models, it is now appropriate to summarise the findings of empirical studies concerned with the use of the models in practical or test situations. First we need appropriate model comparison criteria.

■ **Model evaluation and comparison criteria**

There are two major concerns in the evaluation of costing and scheduling models: accuracy and consistency. Accuracy has been the traditional criterion for model evaluation, but recently researchers at IIT Research Institute have introduced the important concept of consistency, which they have used in a recent study (IIT Research Institute, 1989).

Accuracy in this context is most commonly measured by either or both of MMRE or PRED(level). MRE is the magnitude of the relative error and is frequently just called the error. The MRE for an estimate is obtained by dividing the absolute value of the difference between the estimate and the actual, by the actual. MMRE is the mean magnitude of a set of relative errors; it will frequently be more simply called the average error. PRED(level) is best explained with an example. In reference to a set of estimates made using a particular model, PRED(0.25) = 75% means that 75% of those estimates are within 25% of actual.

It is not a simple matter to define suitable evaluation criteria for software cost estimation models. Conte et al. (1986) show that no one criterion is satisfactory on its own, and suggest a combination of:

$$\text{MMRE} \leq 0.25 \text{ and } \text{PRED}(0.25) \geq 0.75.$$

Their criteria have, however, very seldom been met in practice, and then only in models very carefully fitted after completion of development, and with full hindsight knowledge of software size and other important variables.

We follow the IITRI (1989) definition of consistency. An adjustment for systematic bias is made as follows. For each estimate, the percentage of actual to estimate (that is, the reciprocal of estimate to actual) is calculated. The highest and lowest resulting percentages are discarded 'to achieve a truer sampling of percentages'. A mean value of the remaining percentages is computed and applied to all of the given model's effort estimates. The relative error for each project is recalculated using the adjusted efforts. The resulting 'unbiased' estimates can then be evaluated in the normal way using MMRE and PRED, those with the best MMRE and PRED values being the most consistent.

■ Summary of empirical research

The following sections summarise the main findings of a large number of reported empirical studies or comparisons of the use of cost estimation models in practical or test situations.

(a) Diseconomies of scale

The value of b in the COCOMO model determines the shape of the effort–size curve and whether it indicates economies of scale ($b < 1$) (higher productivity with greater size) or diseconomies of scale ($b > 1$) (lower productivity with greater size). Calibration studies in substantially different environments give a wide range of values for b, from 0.59 to 1.20. However, most values cluster around 1. A recent analysis by Kitchenham and Kirakowski (1991), which reviewed previous studies, concluded that in almost all cases, b was not significantly different from 1 at the 0.05 significance level, so the size–effort relationship could be considered to be linear.

(b) Environmental, cultural and application domain differences

Many studies note the need for calibration of models to environments. In some of these, for example, Miyazaki and Mori (1985), Funch (1987), Marouane and Mili (1989) and Marwane and Mili (1991), the model parameters are very different from those of

COCOMO and the differences in development modes much more marked. Most of the studies also indicate substantial development environment differences, at least between the development environments and data sets of the empirical studies and the reference environments and data sets on which models such as COCOMO are based (Conte et al., 1986; Acosta and Golub, 1987; Kemerer, 1987; Martin, 1988; IIT Research Institute, 1989; Desharnais, 1988; Mermaid, 1991). It therefore seems that it is the development environment that matters rather than the development mode, and that models need to be calibrated for effective use in each different environment. It is also suggested by the MERMAID studies that relatively few cost drivers are important in any particular environment and that these are likely to differ from one environment to another.

(c) Cost driver and similar adjustments

Under this heading we include effort multipliers, FPA influence factors, and the like. Several studies indicate that such adjustments, whether for COCOMO, FPA, or for other commonly used models, make little difference (IIT Research Institute, 1989; Kemerer, 1987; Marwane and Mili, 1991). The whole question of cost drivers is a difficult one. Subramanian and Brelawski (1989) have shown that the COCOMO cost drivers are not independent and the MERMAID studies (Kitchenham and Kirakowski, 1991) have shown that the FPA influence factors are not independent. A problem with so many separate cost drivers is that users may tend either to ignore them, in which case some important influences may not be allowed for, or alternatively provide settings for a large number of cost drivers on the basis of imperfect knowledge, which may just introduce noise. It is arguable either that cost drivers should only be set at other than nominal or standard levels as the result of a careful risk analysis, or that 'standard' costs should first be established, using standard cost-driver settings and deviation should only be permitted on the basis of a strong and well argued case. In any event a standard cost and a deviation with reasons may be more useful than just a single adjusted cost estimate. Note that a standard cost may not have all cost drivers set at nominal. A few may be different, for example, TURN may be low in an on-line development environment.

(d) Effort–time trade-offs

The validity of the Rayleigh curve as an effort distribution over time, and the cost–time trade-offs of most models that indirectly depend on it, have been questioned. There is convincing evidence for some bell-shaped curve as the ideal effort demand pattern, but usually there is a rather flat top to the curve in practice, simply because the effort supply is not as resilient as the demand, and tends to have a maximum below the ideal. Several studies, particularly Conte et al. (1986), Jeffery (1987), and MERMAID (1991) have not supported the Putnam time–cost trade-off. Indeed, Jeffery's work did not support *any* time–cost trade-off. This factor, so fundamental to some models, may be environment dependent. It is also evident from the MERMAID (1991) study that some cost-driver factors are conducive to schedule compression, and some are not.

(e) Data quality

The data sets used to validate or compare the models show great variability, not only in project size and type but also in productivity defined as lines of code per person-month. Even where a data set, for example, from a single organisation engaged in one line of business, might be considered fairly homogeneous, there are usually productivity variations of more than an order of magnitude. In spite of efforts to quantify most aspects of a project affecting cost, and to collect data consistently, both the quality and the completeness of the data for estimation purposes must in most cases be questioned. In particular, abnormal or atypical projects appear to be present in most data sets without the reasons for the abnormality being effectively recorded. Some method of data collection during a project which records relevant information about abnormalities (for example, massive iterated rework in several process phases) near the time they occur would seem to be desirable. Robert Park's observations in his 'open letter to cost-model evaluators' (Park, 1989) make a number of very pertinent points concerning the mismatch that frequently occurs between the formats, and even the definitions, of project data as collected, and the formats and definitions of estimation data as required by costing models. As he states: 'This violates a fundamental principle of estimating—that the tool for data collection should be the same as the tool used for estimation.'

(f) Disappointing results

The results in general are disappointing. Using Conte's suggested criteria that an acceptable estimate should have an MMRE ≤ 0.25 and a PRED(0.25) $\geq 75\%$, only a few sets of very carefully fitted *ex post* project estimates, such as those of Conte's generalised COPMO model (Conte et al., 1986), manage to meet these criteria. Most sets of estimates, even after calibration, and applied *ex post* to completed projects, come nowhere near these criteria of acceptability.

Estimation and software process modelling 3.3.4

From the point of view of top-down estimation, most of the estimation models described support the waterfall development life cycle. Some, particularly COCOMO, do allow for incremental development, but none specifically allow for prototyping or for flexible software development life cycles. From another point of view, since the primary output of the models is a single estimate of cost and duration for a project as a whole, we can regard them as being in a sense independent of the software development life cycle. However we look at it, all the models described take a very simplistic view of the software process. Fundamentally they regard it as a single entity, or perhaps a set of subprojects or increments, which for costing purposes obey some relatively simple set of relationships between cost, time, and possibly staff level, as well as being subject to a number of other influences which are typically modelled as multipliers, adjusting values up or down from some average, or nominal, cost or time. It seems likely that such simplistic models reflect too few of the complexities of actual software development.

User opinions of software estimation 3.3.5

Since software cost estimation is clearly both an important and difficult area, it is useful to canvass opinions as to the causes of poor estimation. The following is a summary of user opinions of causes of inaccurate estimates, based on a study of business application development (Lederer and Prasad, 1992). It is important to remember that estimation errors, for example, in budgets, can arise either from things that might go wrong during development, or from poor estimating. In order of importance these user-perceived causes of inaccurate estimates (summarised from the Lederer and Prasad study) are:

- User requirements volatility
- Overlooked tasks
- Poor user–analyst communication
- Imprecise problem definition
- Estimate based on insufficient analysis
- Poor communication/coordination
- Inadequate estimation methodology
- Staff turnover
- Insufficient historical data
- Political pressure
- Inability to predict team capability
- Poor monitoring
- Lack of developer participation in estimation.

SOFTWARE RISK MANAGEMENT   3.4

What is risk?   3.4.1

We should first understand the meaning of *risk* in more general usage, before we apply it to software processes. Risk is defined in the *Concise Oxford Dictionary* as:

1. hazard, chance of bad consequences, loss, etc., exposure to mischance . . .
2. amount of insurance; person or thing insured or otherwise representing source of risk.

The senses in which the word is used in this book are closely related to, but more precise than, the above, as follows:

1. chance of bad consequences, either in general, for example, in the phrase 'risk management', that is, management of chances of bad consequences, or in a more specific sense, for example, in the phrase 'risk to schedule', that is, chance of bad consequences affecting scheduled completion date;
2. person or thing representing source of risk, for example, the phrase 'major risks' might refer to inappropriate requirements and user non-acceptance; the phrase 'risk management' may also refer to the management of the (risk aspects of) persons or things which are sources of risk.

We will not use the word *risk* in either of the senses 'exposure to mischance', 'amount of insurance', or 'person or thing insured'. Exposure to mischance, or **risk exposure**, is something which is normally quantified, as follows:

Risk exposure = (probability of bad consequences) × (resulting loss).

For example, if a $2 000 000 software project has a 0.1 probability of being a complete failure when it is completed, then the risk exposure is $200 000. Risk exposure is the expected loss in the statistical sense of the term *expected*.

Risk management implies the ability to do something about risks.

Why is software risky?   3.4.2

Software development is, in general, riskier than many other types of projects. There are a number of reasons for this, including:

- **new/unique products;** though some software developments are similar to previous projects, a great many are not; much software is innovative and some systems are unique; there are risks in doing something new;
- **inherent evolution and mutability;** software systems are used to solve real-world problems, which are by their nature subject to continual change, even while the software systems are being developed; as noted in Section 2.4 (Lehman's E-process model), change is a fundamental characteristic of information systems; mutability adds complexity and risk to software;
- **abstract products—impact of change is seldom clear;** software is abstract, rather than concrete; unlike a physical structure, it is difficult to visualise; poor visibility into the structure of software makes it difficult to assess both the consequences of requirements and the impact of changes in requirements;
- **unclear limits of technology and tools;** precisely because software itself is 'soft', as are the software tools used to build it, it is often unclear what the limits are to information technology which includes software; sometimes, the chosen combination of hardware and software is not adequate to solve the problems within the constraints of the particular situation;
- **dependence on many different kinds of people;** software development is a complex activity involving many different organisational, professional, and technical skills; the numbers and types of people involved (managers, customers, users, analysts, developers), coupled with tight time constraints, introduce many organisational, social and communication risks.

Computing projects involve both hardware and software. Because of the fixed, stable nature of hardware in comparison to the more flexible nature of software, the less well-defined, and hence riskier aspects of a system are invariably left to be implemented in software, rather than in hardware.

Risk of what?   3.4.3

There are four main types of risk to software projects:

- Cost/schedule failure; the project costs too much or takes too long.
- Premature project termination or radical re-scoping; the project is either canned or dramatically changed, often downsized.
- Product functional failure; the functionality of the developed product is inappropriate.
- Product technical failure; certain technical requirements of the product, such as performance, are not met, or certain functionality cannot be delivered for technical reasons.

Boehm (1989) classified what he termed his 'top ten' software risks under the following headings:

People

1. **Personnel shortfalls**
    This covers many more specific risks, such as team inexperience in the application domain, development or target environment; large team size, long duration or large product size in relation to team experience; project team turnover and possible loss of critical team members.

Resources

2. **Unrealistic schedules and budgets**
    This covers cases where estimates, expectations or constraints of time and human or other resources are unrealistic in relation to requirements. Such risks sometimes arise because similar products/developments are not available for comparison.

Requirements

3. **Wrong functionality**
    The client may have an imperfect understanding of requirements, particularly where the requirements are complex; the developers may misunderstand, omit, or otherwise fail to deliver the required functionality; the complexity of communication with the client may be a contributory factor affecting this risk.

4. **Wrong user interface**
    In some cases the appropriateness and user-friendliness of the user interface may be crucial to the success of a system; in such cases the risk of not developing a suitable and acceptable user interface may be considerable.

5. **Gold plating**
    This is the understandable, but inadvisable and unnecessary desire of some developers to produce 'gold-plated' components which bear their own trademark, as it were, and provide additional features, beyond the requirements, which the developer thought might be useful and might impress the user.

6. **Requirements volatility**
    This is the risk of an excessive number of changes in requirements during development.

Externalities

7. **Shortfalls in externally furnished components**
    Purchased or contracted components may be unsatisfactory, either in functionality or in quality.

8. **Shortfalls in externally performed tasks**
    Some skills may be obtained from outside the development team or organisation; these may be inadequate, or there may be imperfect communication with collaborators or subcontractors.

Technology

9. **Real-time performance shortfalls**

   Real-time applications typically have stringent performance requirements; there may be situations where these are not, or cannot, be met.

10. **Straining IT/computer science capabilities**

    Risks arise when there is a reliance on new and untried technologies, or on new and unstable development or target platforms.

Risk management goals and importance   3.4.4

It is appropriate to quote from an acknowledged expert in risk management. Paul Rook (1986) notes: *When a project is successful, it is not because there were no problems, but because the problems were overcome.*

Why is risk management important?

- Sometimes it is not, or is not thought to be important; many organisations simply accept the uncertainties—they either do not care enough to do anything about them, or do not think risk management is the answer.
- To reduce the number and severity of software shortcomings or disasters; project failures or radical re-scoping; cost and time overruns; unsatisfactory performance and/or usability.
- To reduce rework; a substantial amount, sometimes up to 50% of project effort is rework; Boehm and Papaccio (1988) noted that rework is typically concentrated in 20–30% of components.

A question that must be asked is: If risk management is so important, why is so little of it done? Excuses or reasons for not explicitly managing risks include the following:

- Good project managers do it anyway; there is no need to make a song and dance about it.
- We do not want to give management the impression that we may not know exactly what we are doing; admitting that there are risks might give this impression.
- Management is suspicious enough about software already—mention of risk may be used as ammunition to shoot down projects.
- Risk management is an overhead that is difficult to justify—it is only needed in some projects.
- We should concentrate on software improvement, and reduced risks will follow.

Managing software risk   3.4.5

Software development is a difficult and unpredictable business. Risk management involves assessing and controlling potential software problems (risks). Basing our treatment on AFSC (1987) (Figure 3.9) and on Boehm (1989), we note that risk management includes the following activities:

Risk assessment—what is the risk situation?
- Risk identification. What can go wrong? How and why? (What are the potential risks?)

Risk analysis—what are the risk specifics and their implications for this project?
- What is the specific nature and possible effect of each risk?
- Which are the worst risks? Which ones can we do something effective about?

Risk control and monitoring — doing something about it
- How will we deal with the risks? Formulate a plan.
- Carry out the plan.
- Is our risk control plan working? Do we need to change it?

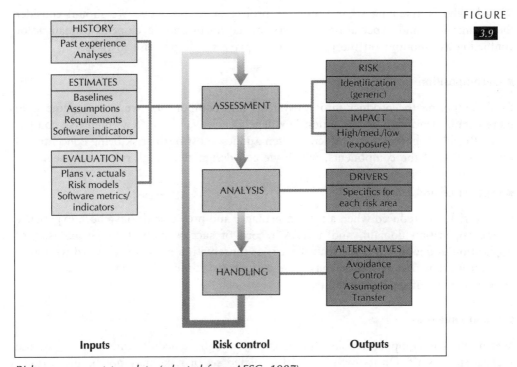

FIGURE

3.9

Risk management template (adapted from AFSC, 1987)

Risk identification: What can go wrong?

3 . 4 . 6

It is not always the case that the main risks associated with a project will be obvious to the project manager, the customer, or others who are vitally concerned with the progress and success of the project. In order to ensure that no important risks are overlooked, some or all of the following risk identification methods can be used.

■ Checklists

Risk checklists enumerate generic risks, or risk types that commonly occur in software development. Each risk type in the checklist should be examined in relation to the specific project under consideration. Boehm's list of top ten risk types, described earlier in this chapter, is an example of such a checklist. Organisations working in particular application domains and environments should develop their own checklists which, though still generic, are likely to be rather more specific than Boehm's top ten.

■ Decision analysis

Here we ask who sets the goals, budget, schedule and quality targets or other imposed constraints. By asking such questions, we may be able to determine whether there are political/technical conflicts or imposed solutions which may not fit the problem. Unrealistic constraints, conflicts or inappropriate imposed solutions will give rise to risks.

■ Assumptions

We ask who is assuming what about the project or its products. We should consider the assumptions and expectations of users, management and developers. Unrealistic or conflicting assumptions on the part of major players will give rise to risks.

■ Decomposition

By decomposing the product into subsystems and components, we can examine it in more detail, identifying uncertainties, key dependencies, and the (few) high-risk components. Recollect that a Pareto principle often applies, most of the risk being concentrated into 20–30% of the components, which we can designate as high-risk components.

■ Experience and track record

Clearly, risks are reduced when a project manager and project staff have both experience in the application domain, and a track record of success with the type and size of application in question. Inexperienced staff, or those with a poor track record who have not learnt from past mistakes, may pose serious risks. However, inexperience may to some extent be offset by capability.

■ Compound risks

Watch out for compound risks, for example, a tight schedule with new tools and inexperienced staff. On its own, each of a related set of risks may not be too serious, but taken together, they may be highly project-threatening and quite unacceptable. However, the reduction or avoidance of the related risks has to be handled separately.

■ Winners and losers

The introduction of a new information system can change the way an organisation operates and may subtly alter ownership of information and consequently power structures. In situations where there are winners and losers, it is not surprising that the losers may oppose the introduction of new systems in ways that increase the risk of failure.

Risk analysis—a closer look at the risks and their effects　　`3.4.7`

We attempt to answer three questions: What is the specific nature of each risk? What are the possible effects of each risk? Which are the worst risks—which ones can we do something effective about?

Table 3.3 summarises the risk analysis methods appropriate to various kinds of risk,

TABLE

3.3

Risk analysis methods (adapted from Boehm, 1989)	
Risk to:	*Methods*
Budget	Cost models, decision analysis, WBS
Schedule	Cost/schedule models, CPM, PERT
Function	Prototyping, size/function/cost models, decision analysis, cost-benefit analysis
Operation	Reliability models, hazard analysis, performance testing, human factors
Support	Quality, satisfaction studies

such as risk to budget, risk to schedules, and so on. The main methods of risk analysis are examined briefly below.

■ Cost models

Whether or not it is used for estimation, COCOMO (see Section 3.3) can be used for some types of risk analysis. Cost drivers from other models, or local environment cost drivers, can also be used if appropriate. In a sense, such analyses are in the nature of 'what if?' investigations, for example, what if the people on the project team are not as good as we would like? What is the effect on budget and schedule likely to be? An example should make clear the usefulness of cost models in this context.

Example

Consider a project for the development of an object-oriented design diagram editor. The estimated size of the diagram editor is 60K. Since the editor can be considered to be systems software, the development mode is semi-detached. We will suppose that the average cost/pm in the relevant development organisation and environment is $12K. The values of the COCOMO cost drivers for the planned development are:

CPLX	H	1.15
TIME	H	1.11
ACAP	H	0.86
AEXP	H	0.91
PCAP	H	0.86
MODP	H	0.91
TOOL	H	0.91
SCED	VL	1.23
All others	N	1.00

Using intermediate COCOMO, the estimated cost is:

$$3.0 * (60)^{1.12} * 0.87 * \$12K = 256 \text{ pm} * \$12K$$
$$= \$3072K$$

and the estimated development time is 17.4 months.

The main concern is time-to-market of the product. Factors that could adversely affect development time are:

- unexpectedly high complexity (for example CPLX actually VH 1.30, instead of just H);
- a low size estimate (for example, size may be >70K);

- execution time (performance) problems (for example, TIME actually VH 1.30);
- the loss of some experienced programmers to another project and the need to bring in less capable programmers (for example, PCAP actually N 1.00).

Using COCOMO, the individual effects of these adverse outcomes are estimated as:

	Cost increase	Schedule overrun
Higher complexity	1.3/1.15 = 13%	0.8M
Low size estimate	19%	1.1M
Execution time problems	1.3/1.11 = 17%	0.9M
Programmer capability	1.0/0.86 = 17%	1.0M

The worst case, if everything is adverse, results in a cost increase of 83% and a schedule overrun of 4.1 months.

Cost drivers and risk

The usefulness of cost models for risk analysis in this manner is, however, limited as is shown in Table 3.4. Note that the cost drivers cover only a few of the top 10 risks, and some of them relate imperfectly to the corresponding risk type.

Risk–cost-model correspondences	
Boehm's top 10 risks	*(Corresponding cost-model elements)*
1. Personnel shortfalls	(ACAP, AEXP, PCAP, VEXP, LEXP)
2. Unrealistic schedules and budgets	(SCED, Est. cost, TDEV)
3. Developing the wrong software functions	
4. Developing the wrong user interface	
5. Gold plating	
6. Continuing stream of requirements changes	
7. Shortfalls in externally furnished components	
8. Shortfalls in externally performed tasks	
9. Real-time performance shortfalls	(TIME, STOR)
10. Straining computer science capabilities	(CPLX)

TABLE 3.4

■ Decision analysis

Two different types of decision analysis are relevant to risk analysis. The first, which has been called **decision driver analysis,** is concerned with an examination of the factors influencing software decisions. For example, if decisions regarding budget, schedule and functionality have been influenced more by marketing considerations than by technical feasibility, then the risks of project failure may be higher than they would otherwise be. The second type of decision analysis involves the use of **decision trees** to examine the expected costs of alternatives with different possible outcomes. Typical alternatives for software are: build or buy; modify or redo; ambitious, conservative or compromise. Figure 3.10 is a simple example of a decision tree in this context. It should be noted that the use of decision trees in this manner is heavily dependent on obtaining realistic values for the probabilities of the various outcomes. In this simple example the expected cost of the purchase-and-modify option is lower than that of the build option, even though, if major modifications turn out to be necessary (probability 0.5), it will be the most expensive option.

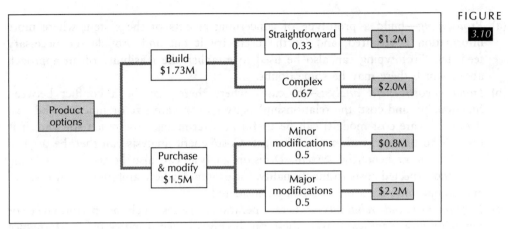

FIGURE

3.10

Simple decision tree

■ WBS

A **work breakdown structure (WBS)** is a tree-structured decomposition of any task into subtasks, sub-subtasks, and so on. It is often difficult to make reliable effort estimates for large tasks until they have been broken down into manageable and understandable components. Once one sees in greater detail the nature of a job, its components can be estimated separately with greater confidence, and amalgamated into a better effort or cost estimate for the total job. A WBS allows difficult or risky tasks to be identified that might otherwise be hidden. It is appropriate to remember the Pareto principle in this context: 70–80% of the problems will be concentrated in 20–30% of the tasks.

■ Schedule models, PERT, CPM

Risk-to-schedule is frequently a major software risk, particularly where competitive advantage or business deadlines are involved. The relationship between software development effort and schedule, and the problems associated with schedule compression, have been covered in Section 3.3. Cost/schedule models such as COCOMO, or the Putnam or Jensen models, can be used to investigate costs and, less directly, risks associated with proposed schedules. If a project history database is available, as, for example, with some proprietary software cost/schedule packages, then probabilities of achieving planned schedules with given resources can be estimated. PERT and CPM (see Section 3.6) are task network project planning tools which take into account time dependencies between tasks. They provide a detailed representation of the sequence and timing of the tasks necessary to complete a project. PERT allows optimistic, pessimistic and most likely task time estimates to be input and, as a result, can give some indication of the probability of achieving a particular schedule.

■ Analysing risks to function and operation

These are essentially user- or customer-related risks. Will the system do what the user wants effectively, efficiently and reliably? Will the user accept the system? Will the system be sufficiently user friendly? Techniques which may be appropriate for the analysis of these types of risk include:

(a) *Prototyping*—build a prototype of concerning aspects of the system where more information is required, and let the users try it out and provide the necessary feedback. Prototyping can also be used to establish the feasibility of an approach about which there may be some doubt.

(b) *Function/cost/benefit analysis*—in cases where there may be a conflict between functionality and cost, the relationships between software size or function and cost (from software cost models) can be useful in determining how much software it is possible to produce with a given budget. Cost/benefit analysis can then be used to select the most beneficial system. Decision analysis can also be useful in relating risks and expected costs to functionality, for example, where ambitious, conservative and compromise solutions are being considered.

(c) *Performance and reliability*—where operational issues such as performance or reliability pose significant risks, these can be investigated using system performance or simulation models. Where software reliability, or more generally software quality, may pose risks, specific software quality studies using appropriate models will be necessary. It may also be necessary to use a somewhat different software process, for example, the Cleanroom approach (see Section 8.6), if very high quality is to be achieved.

(d) *Support*—where large numbers of end-users or customers are involved, substantial risks may be associated with inadequate support services, or levels of support. Analysis of risks of this nature falls more into the fields of marketing and management studies.

Risk prioritisation 3 . 4 . 8

We ask two main questions. Which are the worst risks? Which risks can we do something effective about, that is, on which risks do we have some leverage? Risk prioritisation requires some way of quantifying both the risk itself and risk reduction. The following two concepts are important in this respect.

■ Risk exposure

We seek a measure of which risks are the most serious, not just in the sense of which have the highest probability of an unsatisfactory outcome, or which could cost us most, but a combination of these senses, that is, which risks have the highest expected cost. The risk exposure, re, for a particular outcome, o_i, is:

$$re(o_i) = Prob(o_i) * Cost(o_i)$$

For example, if o_1 is 'user non-acceptance' and o_2 is 'loss of project manager' then the risk exposures for a \$1M project may be:

$$re(o_1) = Prob(o_1) * Cost(o_1) = 0.1 * \$1M = \$100K$$
$$re(o_2) = Prob(o_2) * Cost(o_2) = 0.5 * \$100K = \$50K.$$

Though 'loss of project manager' is more likely than 'user non-acceptance', the effect of the latter is less, so we are more exposed to the less likely event. It is worth noting that in some cases, risk exposure could be negative, for example, loss of a poor project manager and replacement by a much better one might actually reduce project costs.

■ Risk leverage

Risk leverage measures the effectiveness of risk reduction action. It is used to answer questions such as: Is a particular risk reduction proposal worth pursuing? What is the most effective risk reduction action? Risk (reduction) leverage, rl, associated with a particular risk reduction action, a_i, relating to a particular outcome, o_j, is:

$$rl(a_i, o_j) = \left(re_{before}(o_j) - re_{after}(o_j)\right) / cost(a_i)$$

where $re_{before}(o_j)$ is the risk exposure to outcome o_j before action a_i is undertaken;
$re_{after}(o_j)$ is the risk exposure to outcome o_j after action a_i is undertaken;
$cost(a_i)$ is the cost of the risk reduction action a_i.

For example, suppose an ambitious $10M project has a comparatively high (0.25) probability of failure due to uncertain requirements and possible user rejection. However, carrying out a $100K prototyping exercise could reduce the probability of failure for these reasons to 0.05. Then the risk exposure before prototyping is $10M * 0.25 = $2.5M, the risk exposure after prototyping is $10.1M * 0.05 = $505K (assuming the prototype is discarded). The risk reduction leverage is $1.95M/$100K = $19.95. So for every $1 we spend on the prototype, we are reducing our risk exposure by almost $20, a leverage of 20:1. Leverage values in the small single digits would indicate unattractive risk reduction options, while values of 10 or more might be much more acceptable. There is, however, no absolute guideline. It depends on how serious an adverse outcome would be. The major problem with both risk exposure and risk leverage is that of getting reliable probabilities. A database of all past projects, successful or not, can be helpful for this purpose. Certainly some empirical data is required in order to forecast risk, which is why formal probability analysis is necessary to ensure high quality in cost estimation decision making.

Risks are generally prioritised by listing them in decreasing order of risk exposure. This tells us which risks most need reducing or avoiding, as well as periodic monitoring. At times, steps can be taken to reduce the effects of risk but not always. In such instances the only available course of action may be to accept a particular risk and keep it under constant review. Risk leverage is used to assess the effectiveness of whatever risk reduction action is available to us.

Risk control and monitoring   `3.4.9`

The remaining steps in the risk management process are relatively straightforward. Risk analysis has provided us with the necessary insight to formulate a risk management plan. It is then a matter of carrying out this plan and monitoring our progress. In particular, as a development proceeds, the exposure to the main risks may change. Some risk reduction or avoidance actions may succeed; others may not. For important projects, it is advisable to have contingency plans in case some major risks do lead to unsatisfactory outcomes. As shown in Figure 3.9 (page 71), the risk management process is cyclic. The frequency with which the risk situation is formally monitored will vary from project to project. A good project manager will always be aware of the main risks. However, once a month or so, a formal review of the risk situation, plans and actions will be necessary, accompanied by a brief report.

PROJECT PLANNING   3 . 5

First and foremost it must be understood that project planning is a non-trivial task. Indeed, although the word *complexity* is used liberally throughout the software engineering literature, particularly in the sense of software design or program complexity, it is no less evident as an attribute of the planning process.

The project planning task combines the software specific techniques of effort, time and cost estimating with the fundamental issues of human resource management. Essentially, it is an exercise in resource allocation, but the level of personal communication skills of those charged with this task should not be underrated. From the outset of any project, the involvement of many individuals from diverse backgrounds and with different perspectives of both the development process and the eventual system will be evident. Those responsible for project planning need to recognise this and, wherever possible, include in the planning process all those connected with the system. This means that the project planner should have first-hand knowledge of the individuals and organisational structure within which the system will operate, and in turn must create an organisational infrastructure for the project. As stated in the previous chapter, project planning should also take account of process engineering principles, in that policies, standards and generic process models developed and maintained through process improvement should be influential in the formulation of new project plans.

It should therefore be clear that project planning is not a single activity; rather, it is a descriptor for the number of tasks that must be undertaken at the outset of a project and during its evolution. Some of these constituent tasks have already been covered in earlier sections, while others are still to come. However, a summary list of the tasks concerned is as follows:

- determining the scope, objectives and constraints;
- determining processes and deliverables;
- scheduling;
- resource allocation;
- team organisation;
- cost estimation;
- risk management;
- determining methods for project monitoring and control.

The outcome of these steps is the production of a formal *project plan*. The structure of plans may vary across organisations, and even across projects within organisations. Common to *most* plans, however, are the following components:

(a) *Overview*—a discussion of the scope of the project, the definition of the problem to be solved and an outline of the project objectives. These components show the development team's understanding of the problem at hand, while establishing the system boundaries, that is, the functional domain in which the system will operate. It also provides a common basis for subsequent development.

(b) *Functional description*—a more detailed (but still high-level) discussion of the proposed system, generally following the form of a work breakdown structure (WBS) or functional decomposition.

(c) *Team structure*—a description of the personnel involved in the project, their roles and responsibilities.

(d) *Schedule*—derived from the functional description, this would normally include a time-line, a task network diagram and a correspondence chart matching personnel with project activities (see Section 3.6 for further details on these tools).

(e) *Estimates*—a discussion of the expected cost, effort and schedule associated with the project.

(f) *Risk assessment*—the identification, analysis and evaluation of the risks inherent in the project, together with recommendations concerning alternative options given risk conditions.

(g) *Resource usage*—this component should describe project requirements in terms of staff, hardware and software, and any other project-specific resources.

(h) *Methods and tools*—a description of the software process to be used in the project, including recommended subprocesses for quality assurance, configuration management and adherence to standards.

(i) *Project control*—specification of the methods to be used to monitor and control the project.

Planning occurs at a number of levels in organisations. Incorporation of an IS project infrastructure within the planning structure of the organisation is necessary if IS projects are to participate fully in goal setting and business strategy planning. This means being part of the goal setting for *strategic* (long-term) goals set up by top level management, *tactical* (medium term) goals set by middle management and *operational* (day-to-day) goals set by individuals with responsibility for achieving product throughput levels, delivery deadlines, etc. This notion of various planning levels under the widely employed hierarchical management structure is illustrated in Figure 3.11. The integration of an IS project infrastructure within these business planning levels is shown in Figure 3.12.

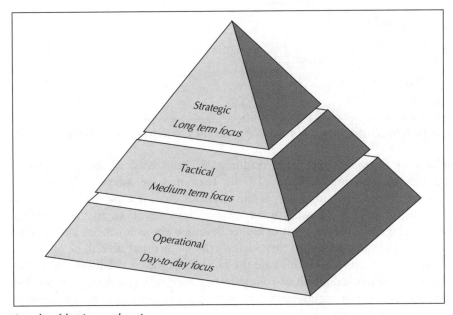

FIGURE

3.11

Levels of business planning

A second characteristic of the project planning task is that, like the system development process itself, planning is a non-linear occurrence of events; it is iterative.

Tasks need to be repeated, and previous decisions need to be revisited. Project control can only be achieved when the process of its management is monitored in an effective manner. This means that the project plan needs to be dynamic; it needs to state how the monitoring will occur and when, with some options for future decisions to be made on the basis of performance, such as when the programming schedule falls behind.

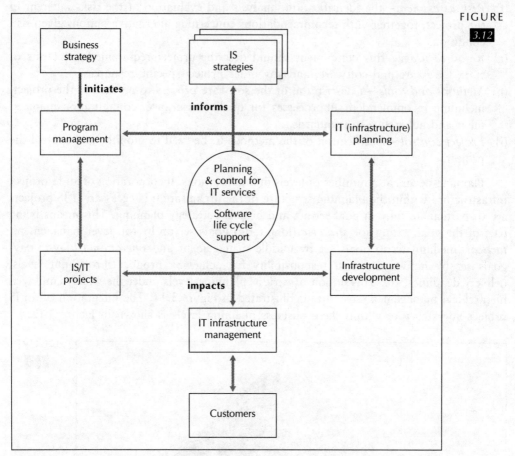

FIGURE
3.12

The interaction between IS planning and organisational structure (Johnson and Warden, 1993)

Critical success factors (CSFs) have traditionally been used in the processes of strategic and tactical planning (Rockart, 1979). They may be adapted, however, to information system project planning. IS personnel decide that, if a particular project is to attain its goals, a number of issues must receive close attention. In the simplified example shown as Figure 3.13, the goals of higher development productivity and product quality are chosen. The same personnel then identify the factors that need to be optimised if these goals are to be achieved—in this case the factors are the establishment of quality assurance (QA) procedures, adoption of robust testing methods and the use of productivity tools. Clearly there is a requirement for quantification here, in that evaluation of goal attainment can only occur if values are in place. Following the example shown once again, this might translate into goals of average output per day (for productivity) and errors encountered per test (for quality).

FIGURE

3.13

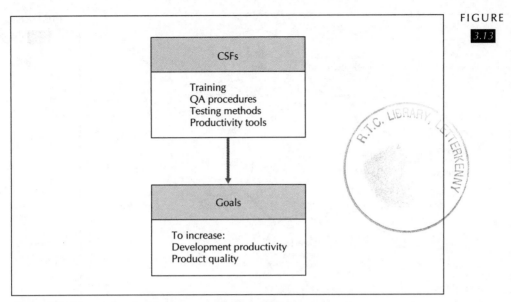

A simplified example of critical success factors (CSFs)

PROJECT MONITORING AND CONTROL   3.6

The establishment of process management principles is only worthwhile in the long term if assessment of their effectiveness is undertaken. Project plans, though clearly essential, are often found to be inaccurate—the effort and schedule estimates on which they are based may prove to be too low, extra functionality (requiring extra effort) may be requested after the formulation of the plan, or the original functionality may not have been understood in sufficient detail to enable accurate planning. Thus project progress must be tracked and documented so that:

(a) plans and estimates can be adjusted if necessary;
(b) all those involved in the project (including the users) are aware of the current status;
(c) the software process (including process management) can be analysed and improved.

Schedule   3.6.1

PERT or critical path method (CPM) charts, such as the simple example shown in Figure 3.14, are used widely in process planning. They also provide managers with concise and quantitative representations of a project's schedule, against which approximate comparisons can be made in line with actual progress reports.

Given the tasks and durations specified in the example in Figure 3.14, the critical path of the process can be determined. There are two paths in the diagram:

ABCDFG, with duration of 29 days;
ABEFG with duration of 12 days.

The *critical path* is the one that has the largest amount of time associated with it. For the network represented in Figure 3.14, the critical path is therefore ABCDFG. The duration of the critical path, at 29 days, is the minimum completion time for the entire

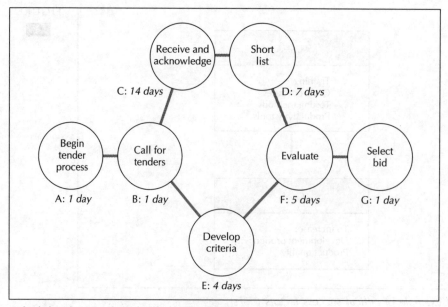

FIGURE
3.14

A high-level CPM chart for the tender evaluation process

project. Overall completion time cannot be reduced unless the time required for one or more of the activities on the critical path is reduced. Moreover, any delay in an activity on the critical path will produce a delay in completion of the project as a whole. This example is a simplified illustration of the tender evaluation process, but it is intended to make clear the elements of the CPM technique rather than dwell too much on the difficulties of scheduling. A scaling up of the diagram to illustrate more closely the complexity of the tender evaluation process would be more realistic but could lose the focus we are attempting to depict.

Four progressive schedule indicators can be associated with each task in the CPM network, based on predicted activity durations and a project start date:

(a) *Earliest start* (ES)—the first point in the schedule at which a task can be started, based on the completion of all required prior tasks.

(b) *Latest start* (LS)—the final point at which a task can be started before a delay in the overall completion schedule is imposed.

(c) *Earliest finish* (EF)—if a task is begun at the earliest opportunity (its ES) and is completed according to the estimated duration, then this point of completion is its earliest finish.

(d) *Latest finish* (LF)—similarly, progressing through the duration of a task from the LS with no delays will lead to completion at the latest finish.

The information included on the network diagram in Figure 3.14 enables us to determine these schedule indicators for each task in the project. The general algorithm is as follows:

> ES_i—Earliest start for activity i
> EF_i—Earliest finish for activity i
> LS_i—Latest start for activity i
> LF_i—Latest finish for activity i .

ES and EF for each activity: Set ES = day 0 (or to an actual date if you want to determine calendar durations) for the first task, then add the duration of the task to obtain the EF for this first activity. Examine the network diagram for any task that has predecessor activities with ES and EF values. The ES of such a task is equal to the largest of the EF values of its immediate predecessors. Its EF is then found in the usual manner (that is, adding the duration to the ES value). For the network in Figure 3.14 this procedure produces the following values:

Activity	ES	EF
A	Day 0	Day 1
B	Day 1	Day 2
C	Day 2	Day 16
D	Day 16	Day 23
E	Day 2	Day 6
F	Day 23	Day 28
G	Day 28	Day 29

LS and LF for each activity: For the last task in the network set LF = (the previously determined) EF. Then subtract the duration of the task to obtain the LS value for this final activity. Examine the network diagram for any task that has successor activities with LS and LF values. The LF of such a task is equal to the smallest of the LS values of its immediate successors. Its LS is then found in the usual manner (that is, subtracting the duration from the LF value). This process results in the following values for the network in Figure 3.14:

Activity	LS	LF
A	Day 0	Day 1
B	Day 1	Day 2
C	Day 2	Day 16
D	Day 16	Day 23
E	Day 19	Day 23
F	Day 23	Day 28
G	Day 28	Day 29

If the network of activities is kept up to date, incorporating changes and adjustments, the resultant tables of activity start and finish indicators can provide a quick reference point against which project managers can assess current progress.

These indicators can be derived automatically by project tracking software; such systems also enable 'what-if?' analysis, to test the potential effect of adjusting start dates and activity durations. Project control is also supported through the identification of potential effort bottlenecks. Given that these problems can be identified before they occur, action can be taken either to remove the problem or to adjust expectations to cope with the problem in a managed manner. This may well involve the reallocation of personnel and other resources. The PERT/CPM technique is also especially useful for assessing the likelihood of milestone achievement. Given the detailed breakdown of activities, and the fact that some may occur in parallel, some discrepancies between expected and actual durations can be expected at the individual activity level; however, significant problems in achieving major milestones on time need to be investigated and overcome if the total process is to be concluded on schedule.

In order to provide a project manager with a calendar-related schedule, the information recorded in a CPM network can be transferred to a Gantt chart representation, as in Figure 3.15 below.

FIGURE

3.15

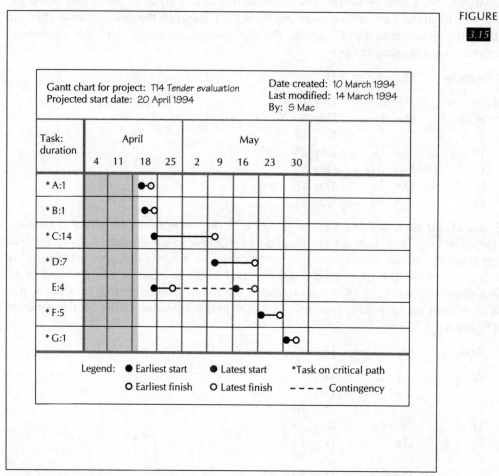

A sample Gantt chart

A more detailed insight into the progress of a project can be gained using a **status matrix**, as described by Macro and Buxton (1987). It illustrates succinctly the state of completion of currently scheduled activities by using a set of three symbols: '−' for tasks still to be commenced, '0' for those currently in progress, and '+' for those tasks that have been completed at the time of matrix production. Table 3.5 is an illustration of the status matrix. Macro and Buxton suggest that the matrix is especially applicable to progress tracking during program module development. Given a well-developed activities plan, however, it should also be a useful tool for project monitoring at an earlier stage, for example, from the end of the specification development phase.

Effective monitoring requires both continuous review and anticipation of the demands of pending activities. Individual developers also have a responsibility to alert managers to possible project delays through both formal and informal reporting. Of course there is still no guarantee that, given these tools and conditions, projects will be completed according to schedule. It does, however, provide the basis for project control, the difference between a managed process and an observed process.

Function	Develop structure chart	Derive data flows	Refine data dictionary	Measure	Walk-through
P1.1	+	+	0	–	–
P1.2	+	+	+	–	–
P1.3	+	0	–	–	–

Sample status matrix
(Adapted from Macro and Buxton, 1987)

TABLE
3.5

Cost

3 . 6 . 2

Development effort tracking is vital if costs are to be monitored and managed (if not controlled) effectively (see Figure 3.16). The cost of personnel is widely recognised as the largest component of total project expenditure.

Some developers, particularly those who have experienced the days of unmanaged development, express disdain towards effort tracking. They may have a perception that the information will be used to assess personal performance levels with a view to determining employment conditions. However, few managers worth their salt would judge the worth of individuals on the basis of raw effort figures without at least considering aspects of the tasks performed.

The likelihood of obtaining useful indications of progress, in terms of both time taken and costs incurred, depends in part at least on the accuracy of the effort records supplied. In general, a structured program of data collection is needed so that management information requirements can be satisfied. This has traditionally required that project personnel complete relatively detailed timesheets, ideally each day, or at the outside, weekly. Each timesheet entry includes information such as: the project on which the developer was working (probably a project code); the process phase, for example, requirements analysis; the specific activity, for example, data model refinement; and the associated number of hours of expended effort.

Timely and accurate completion of effort records enables managers to derive frequently updated quantitative indications of a project's status. The most obvious limitation to this approach is that development personnel can (intentionally or otherwise) forget to complete the forms, or may fill them out incorrectly. Over the duration of a large project, however, it is likely that a few unintentional inaccuracies will be of only minimal influence. Moreover, as the need for effective process management has been recognised, an increasing number of automated progress-tracking tools have become available, so that effort recording, as well as project planning and progress report generation, may be performed in a less intrusive yet more efficient manner. This is directly related to the remarks concerned with process enaction made in Section 2.2—an enactioned software process model in an automated environment greatly enhances the measurability of, for example, development effort associated with particular tasks and/or products.

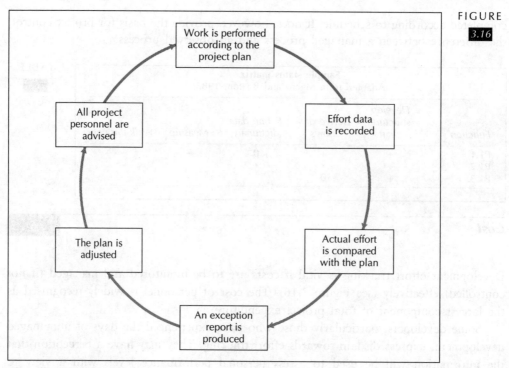

FIGURE
3.16

The effort recording cycle

Exercises

3.1 What do you think are the most critical factors in human communication?

3.2 What indications do you perceive could be collectively termed the 'software crisis'? What signs, if any, are there of the crisis being overcome?

3.3 Obtain an implementation of COCOMO. (Several are available non-commercially.) Explore and discuss the changes that occur in the resultant cost estimates, given variations in size, development mode and cost driver influence.

3.4 Can you think of other reasons/excuses for not taking risk management seriously? Can you think of good answers to these excuses, as well as the excuses of Section 3.4?

3.5 Why is software risky? Consider how we can effectively reduce the impact of Boehm's top ten risks.

3.6 Discuss the factors that contribute to project failure.

3.7 Where does software project planning fit in business planning?

3.8 How would a CPM diagram representing a software development project differ from that developed for painting a house?

References

Abdel-Hamid, T. K. and Madnick, S. E. (1989) 'Lessons learned from modelling the dynamics of software development'. *Communications of the ACM*, Vol. 32, No. 12 (Dec 1989), pp. 1426–38.

Acosta, E. O. and Golub, D. H. (1987) 'Early experience in estimating embedded software costs at AVSCOM'. *Proceedings of the International Society of Parametric Analysts Ninth Annual Conference* VI, 1, San Diego, CA, USA (May 5–7 1987), pp. 665–75.

AFSC (1987) Pamphlet 800-XX *Software Risk Management* Headquarters Air Force Systems Command, Andrews Air Force Base DC 20334-5000.

Albrecht, A. J. (1979) 'Measuring application development productivity' in *Proc. Joint Share/Guide IBM Application Development Symposium* (October 1979), pp. 83–92. Also reprinted in Jones, T. C. (Ed.) (1981) *Programming Productivity: Issues for the 80s.* IEEE Computer Society Press, pp. 34–43.

Albrecht, A. J. and Gaffney, J. E. (1983) 'Software function, source lines of code, and development effort prediction: A software science validation', *IEEE Trans. Software Engr.,* Vol. 9, No. 6 (November 1983), pp. 639–48.

Basili, V. R. (1980) 'Resource models' in *Tutorial on Models and Metrics for Software Management and Engineering,* IEEE Computer Society (Sept 1980), pp. 4–9.

Bell, D., Morrey, I., and Pugh, J. (1987) *Software Engineering: a programming approach.* Prentice-Hall, Englewood Cliffs NJ.

Boehm, B. W. (1981) *Software Engineering Economics,* Prentice-Hall, New York.

Boehm, B. W. (1989) *Software Risk Management* IEEE Computer Society Press, Los Alamitos, California.

Boehm, B. W. and Papaccio, P. N. (1988) 'Understanding and controlling software costs', *IEEE Transactions on Software Engineering,* Vol. 14, No. 10 (October 1988), pp. 1462–77.

Conte, S. D., Dunsmore, H. E. and Shen, V. Y. (1986) *Software Engineering Metrics and Models,* Benjamin/Cummings, Menlo Park, California.

DeMarco, T. (1989) 'In the land of function metrics', presentation at *Fifth International COCOMO Users' Group Meeting,* SEI, Carnegie Mellon University, Pittsburgh, PA, USA (October 1989).

Desharnais, J. M. (1988) 'Analyze statistique de la productivite des projets de developpement en informatique a partir de la technique des points de fonction', *Rapport d'activite de synthese, Programme de maitrise en informatique de gestion,* Université du Quebec à Montreal (Dec. 1988)

Funch, P. (1987) 'Recalibration of Intermediate COCOMO to recent AF acquisitions', *Third COCOMO Users' Group Meeting* Carnegie Mellon University, Software Engineering Institute, Pittsburgh, PA. (Nov. 1987).

IIT Research Institute (1989) *Estimating the Cost of Ada Software Development,* prepared for US Airforce Cost Centre (AFCSTC) Arlington, VA, 22202, US Army Cost and Analysis Center (USACEAC) Washington, DC, 20324-0200, and Ada Joint Program Office (AGPO), Arlington, VA, 22202 by IITRI, 4600 Forbes Boulevard, Lanham, MD, 20706-4324 (April 1989).

Jeffery, D. R. (1987) 'The relationship between team size, experience and attitudes and software development productivity', *Proc. COMPSAC87,* IEEE Computer Society (Oct. 1987), pp. 2–8.

Jensen, R. W. (1981) 'A macro-level software development cost estimation methodology', *14th Asilomar Conference on Circuits, Systems and Computers,* New York, IEEE.

Jensen, R. W. (1984) 'A comparison of the Jensen and COCOMO schedule and cost estimation models', *Proceedings of the International Society of Parametric Analysis,* pp. 96–106.

Jensen, R. W. (1985) 'Projected productivity impact of near-term Ada use in software system development', *Proceedings of the International Society of Parametric Analysis,* Vol. 4, No. 1, Florida, May 1985, pp. 43–55.

Jensen, R. W. (1987) SYSTEM-3 presentation at *Third COCOMO Users' Group Meeting,* Pittsburgh, PA, Nov. 1987.

Johnson, B. and Warden, R. (1993) *Software Lifecycle Support.* CCTA IT Infrastructure Library, publication of HMSO, London.

Jones, T. C. (1986) *Programmer Productivity,* McGraw-Hill Book Co., New York, NY, USA.

Kemerer, C. F. (1987) 'An empirical validation of software cost estimation models', *Communications of the ACM,* Vol. 30, No. 5 (May 1987), pp. 416–29.

Kitchenham, B. and Kirakowski, J. (1991) '2nd analysis of MERMAID data', Deliverable D3.3B from Project P2046 (MERMAID) to Commission for the European Communities ESPRIT II Program (Oct. 1991).

Lederer, A. L. and Prasad, J. (1992) 'Nine management guidelines for better cost estimating', *Communications of the ACM*, Vol. 35, No. 2 (Feb. 1992) pp. 51–9.

Macro, A. and Buxton, J. (1987) *The Craft of Software Engineering*. Addison-Wesley, Wokingham.

McKeen, J. D. and Guimaraes, T. (1985) 'Selecting MIS projects by steering committee', *Communications of the ACM*, 28 (12), 1985, pp. 21–48.

McKeen, J. D., Guimaraes, T. and Wetherbe, J. C. (1994) 'A comparative analysis of MIS project selection mechanisms', *Data Base*, (Feb. 1994), pp. 43–59.

Marouane, R. and Mili, A. (1989) 'Economics of software project management in Tunisia: Basic TUCOMO', *Information and Software Technology* 31, (5), pp. 251–7.

Martin, R. (1988) 'Evaluation of current software costing tools', *Software Engineering Notes*, Vol. 13, No. 3 (July 1988), pp. 49–51.

Marwane, R. and Mili, A. (1991) 'Building tailor-made software cost model: Intermediate TUCOMO' *Information and Software Technology,* 33, (3), (April 1991), pp. 232–238.

MERMAID: Angeliki Poulymenakou (Ed.) (1991) 'Improved models and methods', Deliverable 5.5A from Project P2046 (MERMAID) to Commission for the European Communities ESPRIT II Program (November 1991).

Miyazaki, Y. and Mori, K. (1985) 'COCOMO evaluation and tailoring', *Proc. 8th Int. Conf. on Software Engineering*, IEEE Computer Society Press, pp. 292–9.

National Computing Centre (1990) *Methods and Tools for Estimating Software Projects*. NCC Ltd, Manchester.

Norden, P. V. (1958) 'Curve fitting for a model of applied research and development scheduling', *IBM Journal of Research and Development* Vol. 2, No. 3 (Jul. 1958).

Norden, P. V. (1963) 'Useful tools for software management', *Operations Research in Research and Development*, John Wiley, New York, NY, USA.

Park, R. E. (1989) 'An open letter to cost model evaluators', *J. of Parametrics*, Vol. 9, No. 3 (October 1989), pp. 6–10.

Parr, F. N. (1980) 'An alternative to the Rayleigh curve for software development effort', *IEEE Trans. Software Engr.* (May 1980), pp. 291–6.

Putnam, L. H. (1978) 'A general empirical solution to the macro software sizing and estimating problem', *IEEE Trans. Software Engr.* (Jul. 1978) pp. 345–61.

Putnam, L. H. and Fitzsimmons, A. (1979) 'Estimating software costs', *Datamation,* Sep. 1979, pp. 189–98, and Nov. 1979, pp. 137–40.

Putnam, L. H. Putnam, D. T. and Thayer, L. P. (1984) 'A tool for planning software projects', *Journal of Systems and Software*, Vol. 5 (January 1984) pp. 147–54.

Putnam, L. H. and Putnam, D. T. (1984) 'A data verification of the software fourth power trade-off law', *Proceedings of the International Society of Parametric Analysis*, Vol. 3, No. 1 (May 1984), pp. 443–71.

Rakos, J. J. (1990), *Software project management for small to medium sized projects*, Prentice-Hall Inc., Englewood Cliffs, NJ.

Rockart, J. F. (1979) 'Chief executives define their own data needs'. *Harvard Business Review*, Vol. 57(2), Mar.–Apr. 1979, 81–93.

Rook, P. (1986) 'Controlling software projects', *Software Engineering Journal* (Jan. 1986).

Subramanian, G. H. and Brelawski, S. (1989) 'A case for dimensionality reduction in software development effort estimates', *TR-89-02*, Department of Computer and Information Science, Temple University, Philadelphia.

Symons, C. R. (1988) 'Function point analysis: Difficulties and improvements', *IEEE Transactions on Software Engineering*, 14(1), (January 1988), pp. 2–10.

Zwanzig, K. (1984) *Handbook for Estimating Using Function Points,* GUIDE Project DP-1234, GUIDE int. (Nov. 1984).

CHAPTER 4

Project management issues

PRESSURES ON THE PROJECT MANAGER

4.1

There are a number of competing demands on the time, quality and performance of project managers. Meeting time and cost deadlines is perhaps the most obvious pair. These pressures are external to the actual project and occur alongside such resource constraints as the availability of staff and the reliability and size of hardware configurations. Steering committees, for example, are a popular forum for determining the strategy and portfolio for IS developments within organisations, particularly large ones. Whatever their title, they are essentially groups of those who represent the interests of major stakeholders in the building or use of information systems. Because they are representatives, individual committee members are subject to the same pressures, and face similar difficulties to those of any other constituent representative. In effect they become like politicians and the work of the steering committee comes to reflect the character of any other political institution, with all its incumbent motivations, desperation and compromises. This group can place significant pressures on the project manager. The pressures internal to the project arise from staff (in)competence, human communication, precision and clarity of requirements specifications, and quality assurance procedures.

Boehm and Ross (1989) claim that contemporary software project management is an art, requiring skilful integration of software technology, economics and human relations. Software projects often span a long time period and involve a wide variety of individuals with different task orientations. Boehm and Ross say: '*The software project manager's primary problem is that a software project needs to simultaneously satisfy a variety of constituencies: the users, the customers, the development team, the maintenance team, the management.*' They illustrate these pressures by use of the diagram in Figure 4.1. This can be compared with the system dynamics model we have illustrated in Chapter 2 (Figure 2.8).

89

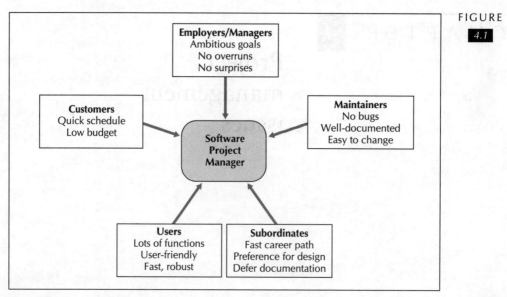

FIGURE
4.1

The software project manager's problem   (© 1989 IEEE)

Boehm's Theory–W

4.1.1

Put simply this theory means: *Make everyone a winner!* Boehm first explained his theory in 1989, reflecting previous management theories that used the letters X, Y and Z. Boehm states that a good software project management theory should be simultaneously simple, general and specific. He proposes two underlying principles for Theory–W: (1) plan the flight and fly the plan, and (2) identify and manage your risks. Table 4.1 lists the major steps of Boehm's theory (Boehm and Ross, 1989).

TABLE
4.1

Steps to Boehm's Theory–W
1. Establish a set of win–win preconditions. (a) Understand how people want to win. (b) Establish reasonable expectations. (c) Match people's tasks to their win conditions. (d) Provide a supportive environment.
2. Structure a win–win software process. (a) Establish a realistic process plan. (b) Use the plan to control the project. (c) Identify and manage your win–lose or lose–lose risks. (d) Keep people involved.
3. Structure a win–win software product. (a) Match product to users' and maintainers' win conditions.

MANAGEMENT OF IN-HOUSE SOFTWARE DEVELOPMENT

4.2

The principles of monitoring and control described above and in Chapter 3 are as applicable for the management of in-house software development as they are for contracted software. Acknowledging responsibility for software products by all involved parties, ensuring adequate interpersonal communication, and properly documented inspection procedures, are all required to ensure high quality software development.

Team management

While many small projects might only involve a few individuals, this is seldom the general case. For organisations with large IS development portfolios, a large team may work on a variety of large and small projects. Therefore even the small projects, which would typically only be dealt with by one or a few people in smaller organisations, may be handled by sizable teams in larger organisations. Gareis (1989) describes these organisations as 'project-oriented', suggesting that this brings with it new management demands:

- the professional management of single projects;
- the simultaneous professional management of a project network;
- the professional management of the relationships between the projects and the base organisation.

In small organisations, some individuals have a variety of skills that address all aspects of the development life cycle, but in larger organisations they tend to be more specialist, with the effect that some developers work only on requirements specification, while others work only on programming or testing. Regardless of the particular functions of individuals, the management task is to ensure cohesion and integration of effort and ability across the entire IS portfolio as a means of ensuring quality. This includes the application of standards and internal development procedures (see Chapter 5) but it is also largely dependent on the attitudinal imperative incorporated in the management culture. Figure 4.2 is perhaps a better depiction of the networked relationship between individuals and phases of the software process than merely tagging each phase with an individual or group's work function. In effect, then, each participant in the process interacts (directly or indirectly) with every other participant across the node connections on the network.

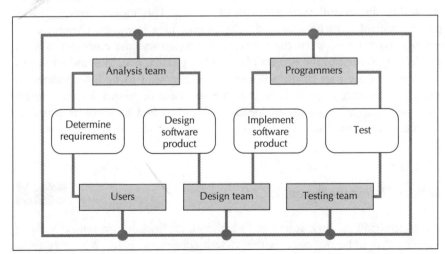

FIGURE

4.2

Communication and management network during development

Organisations that contract out their software development need to ensure that these elements are taken into account in the formulation of a working relationship between themselves and their provider. This will effectively be incorporated in any contract that is written, but probably needs some form of memorandum of understanding between the contracting organisation and the contractor (provider) in order to ensure that it is appropriately understood.

Management of change   4.2.2

One of the most difficult aspects to manage in the development process is change in software products. Change management needs to be seen as a distinct set of procedures parallel to the software process and yet part of it. As with all management considerations, compared with the so-called technical tasks, one must be seen as intimately related to the other. If this attitude does not exist, antipathy between the two functions grows. This simply means that both technical and management personnel need to understand and 'own' each other's tasks and functions. Figure 4.3 illustrates this in practical terms where the steps in change management are seen applying to process stages, while product development is ongoing.

MANAGEMENT OF CONTRACTED SOFTWARE   4.3

It is difficult to manage any resource that is not immediately available or observably present, but the management of off-site software development is particularly difficult in that product progress is only finally assessable when functional components can be demonstrated. True, code can be read, and programming structure and style assessed, but only the working software offers proof of accomplishment. This means that the project plan, if it is to incorporate contracted software, must call for deliverables in various forms and at specific times during the development process. Structured walk-throughs of program code, demonstrations of operational modules, and software documentation all need to be assessed and critically examined in terms of their quality and suitability within the overall system design objectives. This monitoring process is essential if project control is to be exercised. The project plan becomes, therefore, the basis for creating a contract between the software developer and the customer who in this case is seen in the persona of the project planner. Safeguards, penalties and strategies in the case of failure on the part of the software developer need to be incorporated in the project plan. Merely complaining later that the software developer let the project down is not enough. Potential for failure needs to be identified as early as possible, which means monitoring and building adequate disaster avoidance strategy into the project plan.

Software configuration management (SCM)   4.3.1

Quality in the production of any software, whether done locally, or remotely by a contractor, requires that it be managed within a well-considered plan. Whatever techniques are used for individual projects, the principles of what is often called *software*

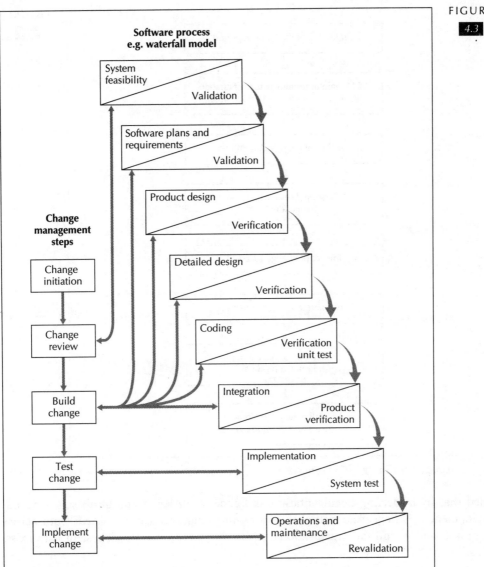

Change management and the software process (adapted from Johnson and Warden, 1993)

configuration management (SCM), or some similar philosophy, is needed. Ratcliff (1987) provides a thorough coverage of this management approach. These principles require that throughout its development, all aspects of the process are visible to those who require to view any of the system elements, such as programs. All such elements should be traceable back from how they exist now to what they were developed from (for example, programs traced back to design specifications) and a high degree of integrity should exist between all elements of the system under development, so that an up-to-date and complete baseline configuration view can be obtained at any time. Consequently the management of change is an integral component of SCM (see Figure 4.4).

Active monitoring is the key to project control. This is the basic tenet of the now famous Fagan Inspection Method first published in 1976 (Fagan, 1976). Fagan main-

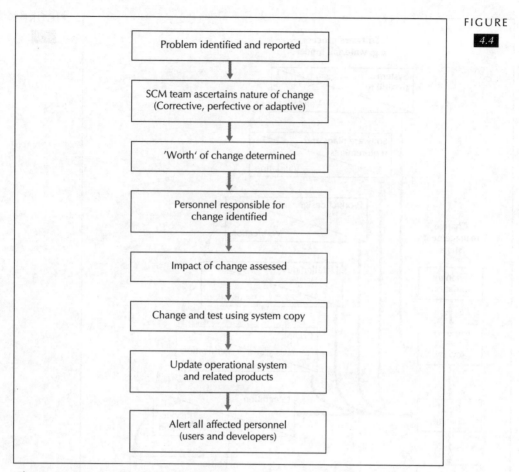

FIGURE
4.4

Change management in the SCM sequence

tained that by inspecting documentation and code at all levels and at all stages during development it is kept clear, self-explanatory, unambiguous and consistent both across the project and within the organisational goals where the operational system is to exist.

Requirements statements

4 . 3 . 2

The process of requirements analysis, whether for in-house or contracted software development, is described in detail in Chapter 6. However, certain aspects of the process are of particular importance for tender-based development. Some of these issues are discussed below.

Gilb (1988) describes a general hierarchy of requirements, as shown in Figure 4.5. The individual requirements that make up each of the three partitions in Figure 4.5 need to be identified and included in a requirements statement, with particular emphasis on the functional requirements and on any resource constraints. The functional requirements describe critical features that *must* be delivered as part of a solution if a contract is to be considered as fulfilled. In general there is no avenue for partial fulfilment—either a function is supplied (in full) or it is non-existent. Limitations on resource usage (such as processor time and storage) also need to be communicated clearly in the requirements

FIGURE
4.5

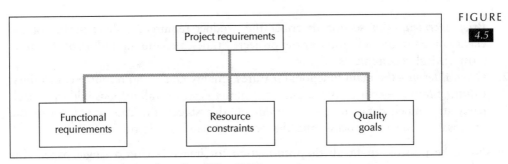

Project requirements hierarchy (after Gilb, 1988)

statement, together with performance requirements, such as those related to response time. Issues concerning time scales and cost restrictions are naturally of particular importance to prospective suppliers. The final partition, quality goals, defines many of the non-functional system requirements. These should be delineated in measurable terms, with specific indications of what the client considers to be the lowest acceptable level for each. For example, if one of the quality goals is minimal weekly downtime, this should be bounded by quantitative limits—say, no more than 10 minutes per week, and no more than 30 minutes in a calendar month. Measurable definitions are especially important for those requirements that together make up the delivered system in the context of contract fulfilment.

Requirements that are 'measurable' are also more likely to be delivered, as the selected supplier has clearly defined goals on which to base his or her development (see Table 4.2; also see Section 7.1). The evaluation of proposals, discussed in greater detail in the following section, is also made more straightforward with quantified requirements—these requirements are the very criteria against which the proposals can be compared.

Comparison of requirements	
Common measures for:	*Not so easily measured:*
System performance	Product quality
Project duration	Modifiability
Project cost	Portability

TABLE
4.2

Another important issue that should be addressed in a requirements statement is any need for integration with existing hardware and software configurations. As this is a form of limitation, this may be most appropriately included in the resource constraints segment of the document. Any such requirement should be tempered, however, by the consideration that the document is one of requirements, not of solutions; severe configuration restrictions may create a degree of reluctance among potential suppliers.

The degree of detail in the requirements statement should generally be high, certainly higher than if the development were to be undertaken in-house. This is necessary if the client expects potential suppliers to provide (albeit first-cut) schedule and cost projections, with little if any further interaction with the client.

The specific form of requirements statements for contracted development varies from organisation to organisation. A number of examples used by NASA, the US Department of Defense and the IEEE are given in Davis (1993). Some characteristics, however, are common to most examples:

1. *Brief overview*—this section describes the product required, a short profile of the client company, an indication of the projected timescale, and an outline of the (few) most critical requirements.
2. *General terms*—the main functional features, quality goals, and resource constraints.
3. *Contract terms*—general restrictions on contract type, overall responsibilities of each party (too much detail here is irrelevant at this stage), the date and form of the proposal submission process, and the projected date of selection.

(It should be possible to fit all the information for items 1–3 on a single page. This 'vital' information is the initial basis for a supplier's decision to submit a proposal. More detailed information, such as the following, is then attached to the cover page.)

4. (a) Detailed functional requirements—current.
    (b) Detailed functional requirements—projected.
    (c) Detailed resource constraints.
    (d) Detailed quality goals.
    (e) Detailed company profile.
    (f) Forms for proposal (if applicable).

Tendering and proposal evaluation   4.3.3

The procedure for inviting proposals is generally of two forms: general tender, and selective tender.

A general tender is announced to the public, most often through major newspapers and specialist computing publications. As a result, any supplier who feels so inclined can submit a proposal. An advantage of this approach is that a large and varied selection of proposals might be received, giving ample scope for effective discrimination and selection. One of the disadvantages of this procedure, however, is that some of the proposals will probably be of far too low a standard—but each must be examined, requiring a significant investment of time.

The selective tender is often preferred by large organisations and/or by companies with very specialised requirements. In this approach the client company determines in advance the suppliers it considers might be interested and able to supply the required system. A requirements statement is then sent to each prospective supplier. This clearly reduces the possibility of the client being overwhelmed by proposals; on the other hand, it may result in a particularly innovative or cost-effective solution from a newly-established organisation being passed over. Thus there is something to be said in favour of both approaches.

Irrespective of the tendering method adopted, it is likely that at least a few of the proposals received will clearly fail to meet one or more of the critical functional requirements outlined in the statement. These should be put to one side for subsequent consideration if a suitable proposal cannot be chosen from the remaining selection. (These apparently failing proposals should never be discarded out of hand—in fact, components of several proposals when assessed together may have a considerable degree of merit, and an integrated contract across a small number of suppliers might be a particularly cost-effective solution. In general, however, a single supplier, or at least a prime contractor, is normally preferred; thus the remainder of this section concentrates on the evaluation of sole-supplier proposals. An overview of this process is shown in

Figure 4.6.) At this stage, only those proposals that demonstrate the capability to supply the critical functions should remain. The evaluation process is then a matter of determining the proposal that most closely matches the previously stated quality goals and which can adapt to the resource constraints imposed. If these requirements and constraints have been stated in quantitative terms, then some degree of objectivity can be applied in the evaluation.

Particularly in cases where a large number of proposals appear to meet all critical requirements, a simple but relatively effective assessment approach can be used to reduce the number of potential suppliers. For each proposal, the degree to which each stated requirement has been addressed and solved/fulfilled can be 'marked', often on a 0–10 scale, but perhaps on a scale from –10 to 10 (negative effects can occur where a solution to one requirement actually reduces the effectiveness of the solution to another requirement). A total mark can then be calculated for each proposal, providing a first-cut indication of proposal 'value' based on common criteria. At the very least, this might be useful in determining a 'short list' of a few highly promising proposals from a much larger original selection. If no useful proposals are found, it may be necessary to widen the tender round, to consider the components of a number of single proposals (as mentioned above), or to improve and re-release the requirements statement with more information included and perhaps less restrictive initial constraints.

Once an initial selection has been completed, a somewhat more rigorous assessment can be performed with those proposals deemed acceptable. One approach is simply an extension of that described above, with those requirements considered more important being assigned a higher weighting. The mark allotted to each requirement (as in the procedure described in the previous paragraph) is then multiplied by the associated weighting factor, to give a final total that considers the relative contribution of each requirement to the overall system value. If this approach is implemented in an automated manner, most logically in a spreadsheet-type format, the actual calculation can be performed very quickly; moreover the impact of weighting adjustments on overall values can be assessed easily in an interactive setting.

FIGURE

4.6

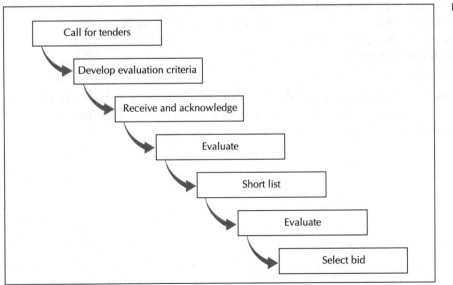

Project tender evaluation

This procedure is not without drawbacks. Most important is its lack of sensitivity to system costs. A proposal that undertakes to deliver every requirement to the requested degree (or better) would, under the above approach, receive a 'perfect' mark, and would be the logical choice based on this criterion. The same proposal, however, may have an associated cost projection that is totally prohibitive to the client. Thus an evaluation method that includes some consideration of cost may be preferred. One such approach involves the assignment of dollar values by the client to each requirement in the statement, followed by an assessment of each proposal against this cost scheme. Each time one of the requirements is not addressed sufficiently in a proposal its associated cost is added to a running total. Similarly if a particular specification in a proposal is suggested as fulfilling a requirement at more than the client-allocated value, the difference between the two values should be added to the same running total. By this method, the proposal that results in the lowest running cost total is the logical choice.

Both the weighted mark and costing approaches incorporate a significant degree of subjectivity, so the methods are by no means flawless. Furthermore, the costing-based approach is probably excessive for small- to medium-sized systems, owing to the effort required for its use. However, these and other similar methods do produce partially objective results that may be used for proposal comparison—they are certainly to be preferred over guesswork, or purely heuristic decisions. In all likelihood, some combination of mark-based, costing-based and heuristic-based techniques is used in most cases to select the successful bidder.

One final point, not directly associated with evaluating the functionality or cost of a proposal, may have an overriding influence on the eventual selection outcome—the standing, track record and maturity of the supplier organisation. To this end, information concerning the following organisational issues may be required as part of a submitted proposal:

(a) company history;
(b) financial base;
(c) use of current technology (products and processes);
(d) development team skills and experience;
(e) any ISO9000 process quality or CMM process maturity assessments;
(f) managerial policies and experience;
(g) previous contract work;
(h) contract conditions.

Consideration of such issues may help the client to avoid the temptation of choosing the lowest-cost solution option based on that fact alone, only to find that the selected supplier falls into bankruptcy six months into development.

Exercises

4.1 How does a model of system dynamics relate to the pressures on a project manager?

4.2 What makes Boehm's Theory–W different from other methods of software project management?

4.3 How much does an attitude of openness to change affect the introduction of system development methods to organisations?

4.4 What are the measurables and immeasurables in requirements statement definitions?

4.5 List and comment on five ethical considerations in the tendering process.

References

Boehm, B. W. and Ross, R. (1989) 'Theory–W software project management: Principles and examples', *IEEE Transactions on Software Engineering* 15 (7), July 1989, pp. 902–16.

Davis, A. M. (1993) *Software Requirements: Objects, Functions and States*. PTR Prentice-Hall, Englewood Cliffs, NJ.

Fagan, M. (1976) 'Design and code inspections to reduce errors in program development' *IBM Systems Journal*, 15 (3).

Gareis, R. (1989) 'Management by projects': The management approach for the future', *Project Management* 7 (4), November 1989, pp. 243–49.

Gilb, T. (1988) *Principles of Software Engineering Management*. Addison-Wesley, Wokingham.

Johnson, B. and Warden, R. (1993) *Software Lifecycle Support*. CCTA IT Infrastructure Library, publication of HMSO, London.

Ratcliff, B. (1987) *Software Engineering: Principles and Methods*. Blackwell, Oxford.

CHAPTER 5

Software process maturity and improvement

THE NEED FOR SOFTWARE IMPROVEMENT 5.1

Most engineering disciplines are relatively mature. Engineers, whether they have been explicitly so called or not, have been constructing bridges, roads, castles, temples and other public works and buildings for thousands of years. During this century, a number of more specific and well-defined engineering professions have flourished, including civil, structural, electrical, electronic, chemical, mechanical, aeronautical and traffic engineering. In most countries, the existence of certain engineering professions is more or less officially recognised. There may be specific charters, defined membership criteria, professional governing bodies, sets of nationally and internationally accepted standards, codes of good practice, and professional ethics. However, software engineering has not yet achieved this level of maturity and acceptance. It is reaching towards it, but it still has some way to go before it attains a comparable level of professionalism.

In spite of the lack of an officially recognised software engineering profession, massive and growing amounts of software are produced each year. Many claim there to be a *de facto* software engineering profession, responsible for this production. Many new systems are produced each year, but much software production is enhancement of existing systems whose functionality is continually being extended to meet new user demands. Increasingly, software influences more and more of our lives. It controls our household appliances, helps manage our bank accounts and credit cards, controls nuclear power plants, analyses bridge and building structures, flies aircraft, monitors patients in intensive care, makes it easier for us to write books, and supports endless other personal, social, educational and administrative functions. The increasing number of life-critical or mission-critical applications of software, together with the ever-increasing impact of software on our daily lives, clearly demands a level of reliability comparable to that of other, more well-established, engineering disciplines. Yet much, possibly most, software (but fortunately not most life-critical software) is poorly structured, poorly documented, of indifferent reliability, and difficult and expensive to change. As software becomes more pervasive in modern life there is a clear and growing need for higher quality software, together with greater professionalism or maturity in software production. Software must improve.

THE CONCEPTS OF SOFTWARE PROCESS MATURITY AND IMPROVEMENT   5.2

General issues   5.2.1

The statement 'Software must improve' raises many questions. First, how do we characterise and measure good software? It is difficult to improve something unless we have a measure of 'goodness' for it. A perceptive, but somewhat glib answer to this question, following Boehm (1978), is: Good software is software that is reliable, portable, efficient, user friendly, testable, understandable, and modifiable. The answer is glib for several reasons. The qualities are very general and require careful definition themselves. The qualities are not independent and some may conflict or at least strongly interact, for example reliability/user friendliness/modifiability or efficiency/understandability/modifiability. Though all the qualities may be important to at least some degree in most situations, priorities and emphases may vary greatly from case to case. Quality may mean different things in different situations.

Thus 'goodness' of software, consisting as it may do of a number of non-commensurate qualities, may be difficult to measure and may vary from one development organisation, application domain and environment to another. For example, reliability may be paramount in life-critical systems, whereas understandability and modifiability may be more important in situations where requirements are highly volatile and changes must be made quickly to react effectively to rapidly changing market situations.

Further questions arise. Are we concerned merely with the quality of software, regardless of how it has been produced, or are we more concerned with the quality of software processes in the belief that quality processes will typically produce quality products? What is a good software process—one that produces good software or one that conforms to generally accepted principles and practices of good software production? Are the two necessarily the same? To what extent is professionalism and maturity in software production dependent on the professionalism of its practitioners and on the monitoring of their qualifications and continuing professional education? Is quality the only issue? Are not increasing productivity and decreasing risk also important?

It should be evident that, if software is to improve, all the questions in the preceding paragraph must be addressed. We must define, measure and monitor important software characteristics, such as quality, productivity and risk. We must also focus on software processes in order in turn to define, measure and monitor them, and so improve quality and productivity and decrease risk. Furthermore we must seek to improve the professionalism of practitioners through suitable education and training as well as membership and participation in appropriate professional societies.

The main approach that has been taken in order to make progress in software improvement is to adopt a **process focus** and to develop an operational definition and associated assessment procedures for **software process capability maturity**. However, this does not mean that related matters, such as software improvement or professionalism have been de-emphasised. The process focus has been adopted for the following reasons:

- As noted previously, there are multiple goals for software improvement, such as increasing quality and productivity and decreasing risk; quality itself is many-faceted and dependent on the type and purpose of the software.
- It is easier at this stage to define a generally acceptable quality assurance (QA) process than to specify acceptable software quality with similar generality.
- Instances of poor quality, or **defects**, are introduced into software by imperfect processes or subprocesses; if software processes are improved, and if they include suitable QA, then quality software products should be assured.

The word *capability* has been added to the phrase: software process capability maturity, in order to qualify the concept of maturity, and to suggest the idea of development or perfection (maturity) of software capability. As noted above, software process improvement and software process capability maturity are intimately related. Without some maturity yardstick or framework, improvement is difficult to define. With such a yardstick or framework, improvement can be characterised either as reaching the yardstick or as climbing up to some higher capability maturity level.

Approaches to software improvement   5 . 2 . 2

We consider three major software improvement approaches or initiatives.

- The TAME (Tailoring A Measurement Environment) approach of Basili and others at the University of Maryland (Basili and Rombach, 1987, 1988). This is a very general framework for characterising an environment, setting improvement goals, devising or choosing appropriate models, methods and tools for achieving them, and choosing or devising suitable metrics to assess progress towards the improvement goals.
- The ISO9000 (International Standards Organization) standards for 'Software quality management system'. These emphasise quality rather than more general software improvement, though the term *quality* is sometimes used in a sense broad enough to include other aspects of improvement. ISO9000 is a single-level, pass–fail standard, not for product quality but for the quality management system that is considered to be necessary to ensure product quality. Improvement is interpreted as progress towards, and finally meeting, the quality management system standard.
- The SEI CMM (Capability Maturity Model), developed by the Software Engineering Institute (SEI) at Carnegie-Mellon University (1993). This is a 5-level maturity scale that takes many aspects of software production into account, including quality, productivity and risk, and uses comprehensive questionnaires, or assessment instruments, administered by trained professionals, to establish the capability maturity level of a project or of an organisation. Improvement is interpreted as progress up the capability maturity ladder.

The TAME approach is a very general one that can be specialised or instantiated to fit many different situations. The accent is on *tailoring* the approach and the models, methods, tools and metrics within it to meet the particular situation. The improvement goals may be ambitious or limited. TAME can serve as a framework for either a global software improvement effort within an organisation or a more local exercise intended to solve a particular software development problem and achieve improvement in a particular area.

The ISO9000 and CMM initiatives are also rather general, but both have a process focus. In ISO9000 this is on the process of software quality management. In CMM it is on the wider software process and its management. After briefly considering TAME, we examine these two software improvement initiatives, in particular the CMM, in greater detail.

In both ISO9000 and CMM, a factory analogy or **factory paradigm** is employed. The production of software is likened to the production of goods in a factory in which products are processed from an initial unformed state through a sequence of processes that finally transform them into finished products. If the process is a good one, properly planned and monitored, the products will also be good. It is important to be aware of this underlying factory paradigm because it may not be entirely applicable to software development, which has many design characteristics in addition to its production characteristics.

TAME   5 . 3

In the TAME project at the University of Maryland, Basili, Rombach and their co-workers (1987, 1988) have developed a methodology for improving the software process by tailoring the software to specific project goals and environments. The improvement methodology is a loop with five steps:

Step 1: Characterise the environment and candidate models, methods and tools for improvement.

Step 2: Establish and quantify improvement goals and check consistency between goals and improvement agents.

Step 3: Choose first appropriate models, then appropriate methods and tools.

Step 4: Transfer the chosen technology; carry out the software project; and collect, validate and analyse data, providing on-line feedback throughout.

Step 5: Do *post mortem* analysis and recommend new improvement goals.

In TAME, metrics are chosen using the GQM (Goal, Question, Metric) paradigm. Improvement goals lead to questions which must be answered to determine whether the goals are being achieved. These questions in turn lead to metrics, which are necessary to obtain quantitative answers to the questions. An example of the application of the GQM paradigm is given in Section 10.1.

The TAME framework identifies the important steps and entities involved in software improvement. The main entities and some of the important relationships between them are shown in Figure 5.1, adapted from Tate et al. (1992). Most of these entities occur explicitly in the brief description above of TAME. Management is more implicit than explicit, however, which does not make it any less important. Model enaction is not specifically mentioned, but models must actually be used or enacted (see Section 2.4) for their validity to be established and for them to furnish defined products and processes that can be measured. In accordance with the GQM paradigm, appropriate measurement answers management's questions about the extent to which improvement goals are being achieved.

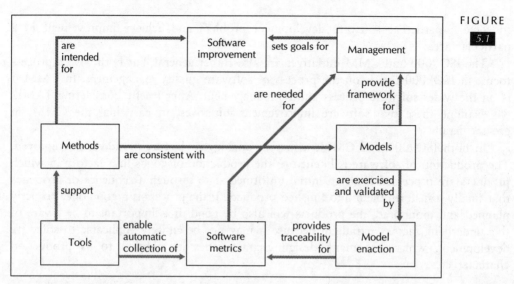

FIGURE

5.1

Main entities involved in software improvement

ISO9000 FOR SOFTWARE PRODUCTION
5.4

The ISO9000 series is a related set of standards concerned with quality systems. ISO9001 has the general title *Quality systems for design/development, production, installation and servicing*. The quality systems it is concerned with are very general indeed in their scope. The special case of software is addressed to some extent in ISO9000-3, *Guidelines for the application of ISO9001 to the development, maintenance and supply of software*. It is clear, however, on reading ISO9000-3, that the specialisation to software makes minimum concessions to what many developers feel to be the special nature of software and the special problems of its development. The ISO9000 standards are pass–fail, rather than having a number of quality system levels. They concentrate entirely on the (software) developer's quality management system, including such matters as management responsibility; maintenance of an effective system for quality management; contract review, planning and requirements control; design, programming and user documentation control; quality system document control; sub-contract control; customer-supplied information and material; configuration management; inspection and testing; corrective action; handling, storage, packaging and delivery; quality records; internal quality audits; training; and control of the development environment. An example of the extreme generality of the ISO9000 standards as applied to software is the following, taken from the Australian Standard AS3563.1–1991 which is itself closely based on ISO9001 and 9000-3:

> '*Software maintenance* If software maintenance is specified in the contract, the developer shall establish and maintain post-commissioning support procedures for the identification of maintenance and enhancement methods. Such methods shall ensure the rectification of design errors as well as addressing the implementation of enhancements due to changes in documented requirements. Standards and procedures applied during software maintenance shall be consistent with the standards and procedures applied by the developer during software development.'

As a standard to cover quality in software maintenance and enhancement, which is surely the greatest source of difficulty, frustration, effort and cost in the software industry, this is quite inadequate. ISO9000 leaves the specifics to individual organisations who should know best what is appropriate in their situation. All it attempts to do is to ensure that they go about ensuring quality in a generally accepted standard manner.

The key premise of ISO9000 is that a quality process produces a quality product. While this may be generally true, most developers can cite gruesome 'war' stories where everything was done according to the book and the result was a well-structured, thoroughly tested, quality-assured, disaster.

A criticism of ISO9000 that one often hears is that the motives for obtaining accreditation are frequently marketing rather than quality motives. In such circumstances the letter of the standard may become more important than the spirit. On the other hand, purchaser requirements that their suppliers must be ISO9000 accredited can be the necessary jolt to wake up reluctant software suppliers to the importance of quality and to impel them towards a true quality culture.

We do not examine ISO9000 in further detail. It is very largely a subset of the CMM, which we examine in much greater detail.

THE CAPABILITY MATURITY MODEL (CMM)   5.5

Our main source of information concerning the CMM is the detailed description in the set of SEI Technical Reports (1993). This has the rare and welcome annotation 'Approved for public release. Distribution unlimited'. Specific quotations concerning the CMM are from that reference unless a different source is explicitly designated.

The CMM is a 5-level model where each **maturity level** is 'a well-defined evolutionary plateau on the path towards becoming a mature software organization.' We will first characterise the five levels in general terms, then look in more detail at the structure of the CMM and some of its key areas, briefly examine the assessment process, and finally attempt a critical appraisal.

General characteristics of the CMM levels   5.5.1

■ Level 1: Initial

Since there is no lower level, this is the level of any organisation which is not at a higher level. It has been referred to as the failed level. Clearly it represents immaturity. It has been characterised as '*ad hoc*, and occasionally even chaotic.' There are few, if any, common defined processes that all developers follow. Success depends on the abilities, efforts and organisation of individuals who are not, in general, guided by sound, consistent management practices and do not work within a stable development environment. Reactive, crisis management is not uncommon. This description of Level 1 may sound absolutely damning. It is unfortunately all too true in practice for many software producing organisations.

■ Level 2: Repeatable

Level 2 is characterised by the effective use of software project management policies, procedures and processes in order that organisations may 'repeat successful practices developed on earlier projects.' Data collected from previous projects, together with a clear definition of requirements for the project to be managed, provides a basis for estimation and planning. Costs, schedules and functionality are monitored and any problems found are dealt with appropriately. 'Software requirements and the artifacts developed to satisfy them are **baselined** and their **integrity** is controlled.' This means that one starts off with a clear set of requirements and there is an effective change control system which avoids confusion when later modifications are made. Customers and subcontractors, if any, become part of the managed development. Although Level 2 is characterised by the introduction of effective project management, it is important to distinguish Level 2 from Level 4 (managed). Level 2 takes only the first steps towards complete software process management. It does not seek to change existing software development methods, merely to make good existing experience repeatable through effective project management. Software development itself is still dependent on individuals and is not clearly and completely defined.

■ Level 3: Defined

The standard software process (or set of processes) used in an organisation is defined and documented. It is no longer dependent primarily on individuals. Software process in this sense includes both software engineering and software management and is consistent with the use of the term *software process* in Chapter 2. 'The organization exploits effective software engineering practices when standardizing software processes for the organization.' An identifiable process group 'facilitates process definition and improvement efforts,'—an activity described in Chapter 2 as process engineering. Related characteristics are 'peer review to enhance product quality' and greater visibility into project progress, the former a part of, and the latter resulting from, a well-defined process consisting of measurable tasks and products.

■ Level 4: Managed

Whereas at Level 2, project management was used in order to establish some sort of stability and consistency, at Level 4 management is used to meet specific quantitative quality goals. To this end an organisation-wide process database is used to collect data from defined processes which have been instrumented with well-defined and consistent metrics. Management to achieve the desired goals is based on analysis of this data. Following well-known quality control principles, quality variations outside established limits are investigated and corrected. 'The process capability of Level 4 organizations can be summarized as measured and operating within measurable limits.' Software process dependence on the application domain is also understood at Level 4 in the sense that 'the risks involved in moving up the learning curve of a new application domain are known and carefully managed.'

■ Level 5: Optimising

The focus in this level is on continuous measured process improvement and optimisation. The organisation has the necessary data to perform cost benefit analyses on new technologies. 'Improvement occurs both by incremental advancements in the existing process and by innovations using new technologies and methods.'

Visibility into the software process   5.5.2

Increase of level in the CMM is characterised by greater **visibility** into the software process, resulting from better definition, more detailed task breakdowns and better, more automatic, and more detailed measurement. Specifically, at Level 1 there is little real visibility into the software process. What is happening is often more a matter of opinion than of fact. At Level 2, visibility is limited to project management items, for example, milestones and tasks, which may not fit as well as one would like with the imprecisely defined and often variable software processes of individual developers. At Level 3, visibility increases because software processes are now defined and standardised. Therefore we can start to measure them in greater detail and with some degree of accuracy. At Level 4, process definition and measurement are directed towards maintaining the quality of (sub)processes and their products within close limits. This requires greater and sharper visibility. At Level 5 the software process is under even greater scrutiny with a view to improving individual steps, reorganising or eliminating steps, or introducing new technologies in order to improve the process as a whole. We cannot do this effectively without a clear quantitative view of the process and all its defined parts and products.

Process variability   5.5.3

Process variability should decrease as the CMM level increases, and predictability should increase. We have noted in Section 3.3 that project estimation is frequently poor, being at best within 25% of actual no more than 75% of the time, with the bad cases mostly on the high cost and late delivery side. Repeatability, definition, and goal-oriented management all represent tighter degrees of control of the software process and consequently less variability. Optimisation implies not only low variability but improvement of quality and/or productivity.

An improvement progression   5.5.4

The writers of the CMM document warn against attempting to skip maturity levels, using what is essentially a 'learn to walk before you try to run' argument. It is claimed that the levels build on each other, each providing a foundation for those above. For example, an undefined process cannot be effectively measured and managed. The descriptions of the levels given above support this argument. The definition of the CMM levels, though logical, intuitively appealing and certainly forming a progression, is not absolute. Application domains and organisational goals differ and achieving all of Level 1 before going on to parts of Level 2, and so on, may be inappropriate in some circumstances. The question of level definition is considered below in Section 5.11.

CMM and TAME   5.5.5

In many respects TAME is complementary to CMM. From the CMM point of view, the TAME improvement methodology can be regarded as an iterative process for climbing up the capability maturity ladder. From the TAME point of view, CMM is concerned with Steps 1, 2 and 5 of the TAME improvement methodology: characterising the environment, at least from a maturity level point of view, identifying key metrics issues and setting improvement goals (the next rung on the maturity ladder), and doing *post mortem* analysis (what maturity level has been achieved?).

THE STRUCTURE OF THE CMM   5 . 6

The structure of the CMM is represented in Figure 5.2:

FIGURE
5.2

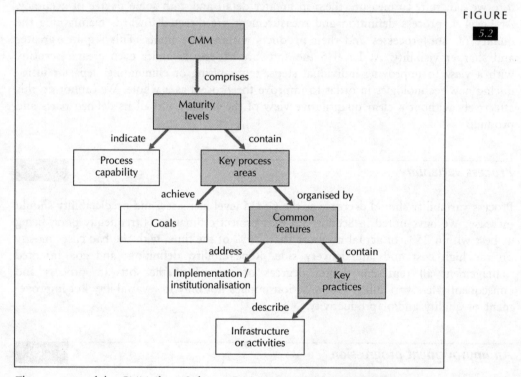

The structure of the CMM (from Software Engineering Institute, 1993)

As described above, the CMM consists of five levels (1 Initial, 2 Repeatable, 3 Defined, 4 Managed and 5 Optimised) which build on each other and form an ordinal scale indicating increasing process capability. Each level (except Level 1) contains a small number of key process areas formulated as goals whose achievement indicates that that level of process maturity has been attained. For example, the key process areas for Level 2 are: requirements management, software project planning, software project tracking and oversight, software subcontract management (if applicable), quality assurance, and configuration management. Each key process area is intended to achieve certain goals. For example, the goals for the key process area *requirements management* for Level 2 are: **Goal 1**—System requirements allocated to software are controlled to establish a baseline for software engineering and management use; **Goal 2**—Software plans, products, and activities are kept consistent with the system requirements allocated to software. The key process areas are organised into five common features (or aspects) sections: Commitment to perform, Ability to perform, Activities performed, Measurement and analysis, and Verifying implementation. The relevant key practices within each key process area are listed and amplified within the relevant common features section. For example, under the key process area *Requirements management* for Level 2, under the common feature heading *Verifying implementation* there are the following three key practices: **Verification 1**—The activities for managing the allocated requirements are reviewed with senior management on a periodic basis; **Verification 2**—The activities for managing the allocated requirements are reviewed with the project manager on both a periodic and an event-driven basis; **Verification 3**—The software quality assurance group reviews and/or audits the activities and work products for managing the allocated requirements and reports the results. Thus the key practices are briefly described and in this case, the QA infrastructure is also referred to.

THE KEY PROCESS AREAS OF THE CMM   5.7

The key process areas for Levels 2–5 give perhaps the best brief view of the CMM. They are reproduced from the publication of the Software Engineering Institute (1993) below.

■ The key process areas for Level 2: Repeatable

Requirements management

Goal 1   System requirements allocated to software are controlled to establish a baseline for software engineering and management use.

Goal 2   Software plans, products, and activities are kept consistent with the system requirements allocated to software.

Software project planning

Goal 1   Software estimates are documented for use in planning and tracking the software project.

Goal 2   Software project activities and commitments are planned and documented.

Goal 3   Affected groups and individuals agree to their commitments related to the software project.

Software project tracking and oversight

Goal 1   Actual results and performances are tracked against the software plans.

Goal 2   Corrective actions are taken and managed to closure when actual results and performance deviate significantly from the software plans.

Goal 3   Changes to software commitments are agreed to by the affected groups and individuals.

Software subcontract management

Goal 1   The prime contractor selects qualified software subcontractors.

Goal 2   The prime contractor and the software subcontractor agree to their commitments to each other.

Goal 3   The prime contractor and the software subcontractor maintain ongoing communications.

Goal 4   The prime contractor tracks the software subcontractor's actual results and performance against its commitments.

Software quality assurance

Goal 1   Software quality assurance activities are planned.

Goal 2   Adherence of software products and activities to the applicable standards, procedures, and requirements is verified objectively.

Goal 3   Affected groups and individuals are informed of software quality assurance activities and results.

Goal 4   Non-compliance issues that cannot be resolved within the software project are addressed by senior management.

Software configuration management

Goal 1   Software configuration management activities are planned.

Goal 2   Selected software work products are identified, controlled, and available.

Goal 3   Changes to identified software work products are controlled.

Goal 4   Affected groups and individuals are informed of the status and content of software baselines.

■ **The key process areas for Level 3: Defined**

Organisation process focus

Goal 1   Software process development and improvement activities are coordinated across the organisation.

Goal 2   The strengths and weaknesses of the software processes used are identified relative to a process standard.

Goal 3   Organisation-level process development and improvement activities are planned.

Organisation process definition

Goal 1   A standard software process for the organisation is developed and maintained.

Goal 2   Information related to the use of the organisation's standard software process by the software projects is collected, reviewed, and made available.

Training program

Goal 1   Training activities are planned.

Goal 2   Training for developing the skills and knowledge needed to perform software management and technical roles is provided.

Goal 3   Individuals in the software engineering group and software-related groups receive the training necessary to perform their roles.

Integrated software management

Goal 1   The project's defined software process is a tailored version of the organisation's standard software process.

Goal 2   The project is planned and managed according to the project's defined software process.

Software product engineering

Goal 1   The software engineering tasks are defined, integrated, and consistently performed to produce the software.

Goal 2   Software work products are kept consistent with each other.

Intergroup coordination

Goal 1   The customer's requirements are agreed to by all affected groups.

Goal 2   The commitments between the engineering groups are agreed to by the affected groups.

Goal 3   The engineering groups identify, track, and resolve intergroup issues.

Peer reviews

Goal 1   Peer review activities are planned.

Goal 2   Defects in the software work products are identified and removed.

■ The key process areas for Level 4: Managed

Quantitative process management

Goal 1   The quantitative process management activities are planned.

Goal 2   The process performance of the project's defined software process is controlled quantitatively.

Goal 3   The process capability of the organisation's standard software process is known in quantitative terms.

Software quality management

Goal 1   The project's software quality management activities are planned.

Goal 2   Measurable goals for software product quality and their priorities are defined.

Goal 3   Actual progress towards achieving the quality goals for the software products is quantified and managed.

■ The key process areas for Level 5: Optimising

Defect prevention

Goal 1   Defect prevention activities are planned.

Goal 2   Common causes of defects are sought out and identified.

Goal 3   Common causes of defects are prioritised and systematically eliminated.

Technology change management

Goal 1   Incorporation of technology changes is planned.

Goal 2   New technologies are evaluated to determine their effect on quality and productivity.

Goal 3   Appropriate new technologies are transferred into normal practice across the organisation.

Process change management

Goal 1   Continuous process improvement is planned.

Goal 2   Participation in the organisation's software process improvement activities is organisation-wide.

Goal 3   The organisation's standard software process and the projects' defined software processes are improved continuously.

CMM PRACTICES   5.8

In order to provide a more complete picture, it is appropriate to give one specific example of the explosion of a key process area into more detailed specific practices.

The following details for the key process area *Requirements Management* for Level 2: Repeatable are taken direct from the Software Engineering Institute documentation (1993) with the omission of the interpolated notes and explanations.

■ Requirements management

A key process area for Level 2: Repeatable

The purpose of requirements management is to establish a common understanding between the customer and the software project of the customer's requirements that will be addressed by the software project.

Requirements management involves establishing and maintaining an agreement with the customer on the requirements for the software project. This agreement is referred to as the 'system requirements allocated to the software.' The *customer* may be interpreted as the system engineering group, the marketing group, another internal organisation, or an external customer. The agreement covers both the technical and non-technical (for example, delivery date) requirements. The agreement forms the basis for estimating, planning, performing and tracking the software project's activities throughout the software life cycle.

The allocation of the system requirements to software, hardware, and other system components (for example, humans) may be performed by a group external to the software engineering group (for example, the system engineering group), and the software engineering group may have no direct control over this allocation. Within the constraints of the project, the software engineering group takes appropriate steps to ensure that the system requirements allocated to software, which they are responsible for addressing, are documented and controlled.

To achieve this control, the software engineering group reviews the initial and revised system requirements allocated to software to resolve issues before they are incorporated into the software project. Whenever the system requirements allocated to software are changed, the affected software plans, work products, and activities are adjusted to remain consistent with the updated requirements.

■ Goals

Goal 1   System requirements allocated to software are controlled to establish a baseline for software engineering and management use.

Goal 2   Software plans, products and activities are kept consistent with the system requirements allocated to software.

■ Commitment to perform

Commitment 1   The project follows a written organisational policy for managing the system requirements allocated to software.

■ Ability to perform

Ability 1   For each project, responsibility is established for analysing the system requirements and allocating them to hardware, software and other system components.

Ability 2   The allocated requirements are documented.

Ability 3   Adequate resources and funding are provided for managing the allocated requirements.

Ability 4   Members of the software engineering group and other software-related groups are trained to perform their requirements management activities.

■ Activities performed

Activity 1   The software engineering group reviews the allocated requirements before they are incorporated into the software project.

Activity 2   The software engineering group uses the allocated requirements as the basis for software plans, work products, and activities.

Activity 3   Changes to the allocated requirements are reviewed and incorporated into the software project.

■ Measurement and analysis

Measurement 1   Measurements are made and used to determine the status of the activities for managing the allocated requirements.

■ Verifying implementation

Verification 1   The activities for managing the allocated requirements are reviewed with senior management on a periodic basis.

Verification 2   The activities for managing the allocated requirements are reviewed with the project manager on both a periodic and event-driven basis.

Verification 3   The software quality assurance group reviews and/or audits the activities and work products for managing the allocated requirements and reports the results.

APPLYING THE CMM   5.9

The way the CMM is used is covered in detail in the comprehensive set of documents Capability Maturity Model for Software, Version 1.1 (Software Engineering Institute, 1993). We are concerned here more with the general principles of the CMM than with the details of its consistent and fair application in practice to organisational assessment.

The CMM can be applied in a number of different ways, including the following:

■ Self-assessment

Because the document is both detailed and public, organisations can use it for their own self-assessment. There are both advantages and disadvantages in doing so. The main advantage is cost. Though no thoroughgoing appraisal of an organisation's software capability can ever be done cheaply, it is likely to be a good deal cheaper if done in-house than by visiting experts. The disadvantages are lack of assessment experience on the part of the assessment team, as well as disadvantages commonly associated with in-house evaluations: lack of independence, concern about whether top management will take appropriate notice, and bias arising from many vested, possibly conflicting, interests. Nevertheless, self-assessment, possibly guided by a more experienced consultant, can be a very valuable exercise and is often worth carrying out prior to any more formal assessment.

■ Formal software process assessment

This is a structured assessment conducted over about 3–5 days by an independent team experienced in the use of the CMM. It is done to determine the current maturity capability status of an organisation, to identify the high priority areas for improvement, and 'to obtain the organisational support for software process improvement.' It is notable that senior management must be involved in the exercise, and their commitment to improvement obtained.

■ Software capability evaluations

This is where the real teeth are in the CMM. Capability evaluations are used 'to identify contractors who are qualified to perform the software work or to monitor the state of the software process used on an existing software effort.' The use of evaluations in this way by the US Department of Defense has naturally caused all their software contractors to take serious notice of the CMM.

Our treatment is concerned primarily with the first of these uses of the CMM, self-assessment, since most readers of this book will also be concerned with this use. The steps in a software process assessment are typically the following:

■ Team selection

A small team of suitably qualified assessors is chosen. Naturally they should be as independent as possible of what is being assessed.

■ Maturity questionnaire

The maturity questionnaire appropriate to the current level of the organisation (which is included in the CMM document) is administered to a suitable sample of departments and projects within the target organisation. Responses to the questionnaire are analysed to identify areas that need particular investigation or clarification.

■ Site visit

The actual projects are visited, appropriate interviews are conducted, and appropriate documents are reviewed in order first to verify that at all levels the organisation actually does what it says it does and secondly to subject key process areas for improvement to greater scrutiny.

■ Presentation of findings

The findings, which are reviewed with top management, are in two parts, firstly the CMM assessment of the current level of the organisation, and secondly the identification of strengths and weaknesses and a detailed analysis of what needs to be done in the key process areas where improvement is necessary.

It is most important to stress that merely filling in the questionnaires is far from sufficient. Our observation is that the higher the management level at which one asks maturity questions, the better are the answers one obtains. Put another way, management policies for software development are often admirable; developer practices in the same organisations, however, may be execrable. It is one thing to define processes and set standards; it is quite another to ensure that everyone concerned understands them, is adequately trained in using them, and carries them out in the face of schedule and other pressures to cut corners. A thorough review of the development process as it has been and is actually carried out is also essential.

WHAT THE CMM DOES NOT COVER   5.10

It is important not to regard the CMM as the answer to all software maturity and improvement problems. CMM version 1.1 is 'expressed in the normative practices of large, government contracting organisations and these practices must be tailored to the needs of organisations that differ from this template.' In other words, the CMM is targeted at a quite narrow sector of the software development industry. There is an intention to produce tailored versions of the CMM 'for small projects and/or small organisations.'

The authors of the CMM are at pains to point out that it does not address everything that is important for the success of software projects. For example, to date it has ignored human resources issues even though the recruitment and retention of good staff are known to be major factors in successful projects. It also ignores domain dependence and the applicability of specific development methodologies.

CRITICAL APPRAISAL OF THE CMM   5.11

Fundamentals   5.11.1

A number of questions arise about the basic structure, assumptions and provenance of CMM.

The CMM appears to a large extent to be a thorough and logical codification of what is commonly accepted to be good software engineering practice. But is it in fact good practice? Is it the only guaranteed way to produce good software? Should we not perhaps start from the other end by considering good software and asking the questions: How was it produced? and, What made it good?

Is the maturity scale of the CMM really an ordinal one? Are all the key activities of level $n+1$ completely dependent on all the key activities of level n? Clearly many organisations do not think so. Many who are still at Level 1 because they have failed some particular requirement of that level are at some higher level in other respects. There is clearly a logic in the level progression, but is it in reality as much a stage model of natural, observed or likely progression as it is a strict prerequisite structure?

How hard and fast are the level boundaries? The levels are concerned respectively with: Level 2, effective project management, that is, managing whatever it is we are now doing properly; Level 3, software process definition and engineering, that is, making sure that a standard process is defined and appropriate versions of it used in actual projects; Level 4, software process measurement and management in accordance with appropriate quality goals; Level 5, systematic software process improvement. In practice, the issues may not be as separate as the levels would suggest. In particular, can effective project management be separated quite so much from process definition and process measurement? Perhaps an organisation should make steady progress in all three rather than target them one at a time.

Empirical evidence   5.11.2

There is as yet no body of overwhelming empirical evidence that the CMM structure is the right one for software improvement, or that it necessarily results in high quality software. We have all seen examples of individuals and teams who do everything meticulously 'by the book' and produce immaculately documented and impeccably well-structured nonsense. Conversely we have seen individuals and small teams who affect to despise management and seem to follow no defined software process model, who produce software which is manifestly of high quality. Undoubtedly individuals and small teams have many different ways of working which can produce good results. There is perhaps a danger in over-institutionalising and over-constraining software development, which may stifle creativity and ignore the rich diversity of successful ways of doing things. Clearly some discipline and control are necessary, but how much is appropriate for true professionals? Perhaps research is necessary which looks at good software products and asks: 'How was this high quality software produced?' as well as research into the effects of instituting what are currently thought to be good software practices.

Scoring system   5.11.3

A number of objections to the CMM are based on its multi-hurdle scoring system. Such matters, while they are no doubt vital to those being assessed for contracts, are somewhat peripheral to the main concepts and principles of the CMM and will not be further considered, other than under the heading CMM profiles below.

CMM PROFILES   5.12

A CMM profile is a representation, often in diagrammatic form, accompanied by an appropriate report, of the extent to which the goals of the key process areas at the different CMM levels are met. Figure 5.3 is a schematic representation of a CMM profile for a hypothetical organisation. In this particular case, the hypothetical organisation concerned achieves most, but not all of the goals for Level 2, being deficient in three key process areas; achieves the goals for one key process area at Level 3 completely and goes a small way to meeting the goals for two others; and has also made a small amount of progress with one key area at Level 4. The levels are not superimposed one above the other, because they are not related in the way that such a superimposition would suggest. For example, goals for Level 2 are concerned with project management, while goals for Level 3 are concerned with process definition, which is a rather different matter.

FIGURE

5.3

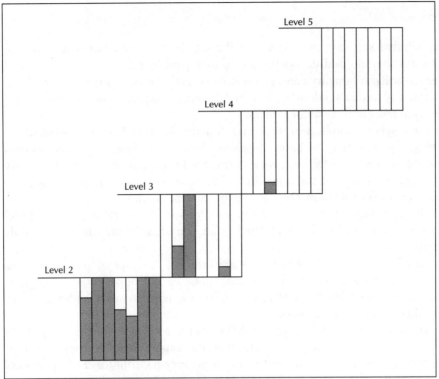

Level 5

Level 4

Level 3

Level 2

Schematic diagram of a CMM profile

Profiles are not only useful for showing the degree to which the organisation has satisfied the requirement of the CMM at its constitutent levels. Some organisations or departments, particularly those in application domains not directly concerned with software contracts for government or defence, may take the view that a particular profile, which spans CMM levels, may be more appropriate to their kind of business than a strict level-by-level progression. In such cases both a target profile showing where the organisation wants to be, and an actual profile showing where the organisation currently is, will be useful.

SPICE   5.13

The CMM has been the main source of inspiration for an ISO initiative called SPICE (Software Process Improvement and Capability dEtermination) (ISO/IEC JTC1/SC7/WG10). Some of the goals of SPICE are that the emerging standard should be independent of development methodology, application domain, cultural differences and organisational size. It is to be hoped that such requirements do not lead to a standard whose lack of specific usefulness is in direct proportion to its generality.

Exercises

5.1 Examine selected software processes in sufficient depth to describe (with reasons) in what ways they do and do not fit the factory paradigm.

5.2 Consider the software quality concepts: reliability, portability, efficiency, user friendliness, testability, understandability and modifiability. Identify possible interactions, dependencies and conflicts among them.

5.3 Choose some specific application type and domain different from US Government contracting, for example, in-house business data processing, or expert system development. Referring to the key process areas for Levels 2–5 of the CMM, identify any that appear to be domain dependent, that is, of greater or lesser importance (perhaps even irrelevant) than they are in the current model.

5.4 Because the vast majority of software organisations in the world are still at Level 1, it has been said that Level 1 is too high. Can you identify and justify a possible level below Level 1?

5.5 Choose an organisation with which you are familiar. Attempt to place it on the CMM scale. Try to find out what is actually done or not done, rather than what is claimed to be done. Identify key process areas for improvement, and attempt to prioritise them for the organisation.

5.6 Given a (hypothetical) organisation at CMM level n with none of the key process areas for level $n+1$ in place, and given that the organisation is constrained to improve incrementally, determine and justify a priority ordering of the key process areas for level $n+1$. This exercise can be done for $n = 1, \ldots, 4$.

References

Basili, V. R. and Rombach, H. D. (1987) Tailoring the software process to project goals and environments, in *Proc. 9th ICSE*, (Monterey, CA, 30 March–2 April, 1987), ACM 345–357.

Basili, V. R. and Rombach, H. D. (1988) The TAME Project: Towards improvement-oriented software environments, *IEEE TSE*, **14** (6) (June 1988) 759–73.

Boehm, B. W. (1978) *Characteristics of Software Quality*, Elsevier North-Holland, New York.

Software Engineering Institute, Carnegie Mellon University, 'Capability maturity model for software, Version 1.1', by Mark C. Paulk, Bill Curtis, Mary Beth Chrissis and Charles V. Weber, Technical Report CMU/SEI-93-TR-24 and 'Key practices of the capability maturity model, Version 1.1,' by Mark C. Paulk, Charles V. Weber, Suzanne M. Garcia, Marybeth Chrissis and Marilyn Bush, Technical Report CMU/SEI-93-TR-25 (Feb. 1993).

Tate, G. Verner, J. M. and Jeffery, D. R. (1992) 'CASE: A Testbed for modeling, measurement and management', *Comm. of the ACM*, Vol. 35 No. 4 (April 1992), pp. 65–72.

CHAPTER 6

Requirements engineering and user participation

Arguably the major reason why requirements are difficult to elicit (and are difficult to understand for systems analysts) is that users, as with all individuals, must express their needs in natural language, which is subject to ambiguity at the best of times, let alone when descriptions of complex interactions between data, functions and organisational dynamics are concerned. This problem is exacerbated several times (often many times!) as the number of users who express their perspective of requirements multiplies.

A further limiting factor is that no individual user is likely to have sufficient global knowledge of the organisation's goals and dynamics to define satisfactorily the requirements of the potential operational system. We maintain that this is true for any non-trivial system, but it is not confined to so-called *large* systems. Our experience with what may be considered small organisations confirms the view that complexity of requirements is such that they defy definition by a single person for all but the most trivial system.

Communication problems between users and analysts   6.1.1

In large part these problems are due to the ambiguity of natural language as discussed above. The user perceives a system requirement, communicates it to the analyst, and believes it to be completely understood within his or her frame of reference. The analyst hears the requirement and interprets it within his or her frame of reference. Unfortunately, the two frames of reference do not always entirely correspond, as illustrated in Figure 6.1. 'But you said . . .', complained the analyst. '. . . and you said you understood', replied the user.

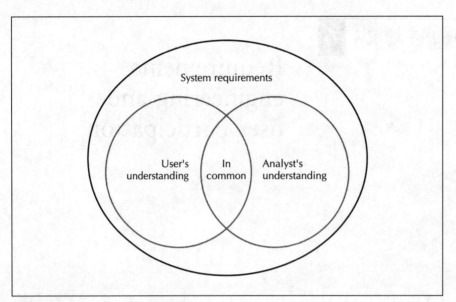

FIGURE

6.1

Problems of understanding between user and analyst

Communication methods and tools   6.1.2

Many attempts at solving the natural language problem have resulted in little progress towards a satisfactory solution. There is little doubt that the most significant advances have been made using not words, but pictures. Structured English (also known as pseudocode), Warnier–Orr diagrams and a host of other techniques have all given insights to the problem and its possible solution, but nothing has made such an impact on this particular problem as data-flow diagrams and entity–relationship diagrams (ERDs); in turn, they model data flow and data structure in such a way that both user and analyst can visualise the interactions of data and functions within the organisational context that will host the eventual system. These tools have more recently become even more popular as communication tools for systems specification with the advent of computer-aided software engineering (CASE). Combined with a system definition approach that incrementally and iteratively develops prototypes as working models of user requirements specifications (see Section 6.4), CASE users report dramatic improvements in user–analyst communication and hence better quality systems. Some of these tools and methods are described later in this book, but some examples are now provided.

Over the past decade the data-oriented specification technique that has emerged as most popular is entity–relationship diagramming (Chen, 1976). (This method is discussed in more detail in Chapter 7). The technique involves identifying entities and classes of entity that exist in relation to the environment being modelled, the attributes associated with those entities, and the kinds of relationships between entities. Symbols are used to represent whether one entity is related exclusively to another entity, whether many occurrences of one entity relate to another entity, and whether or not entities *must* be related for given situations. Figure 6.2 shows for instance, that for any one customer there may be a discount level, but that discounts can only exist for given products. Similarly, all products must have bar codes, but a bar code can only exist if the product exists.

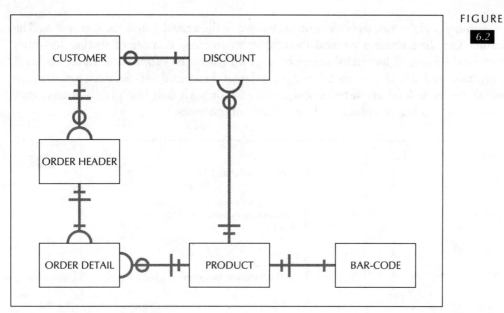

FIGURE

6.2

An entity–relationship diagram

A popular method for describing program structure independent of language implementation is pseudocode. This has been widely promoted (Gane and Sarson, 1979; DeMarco, 1978) as an intermediate program specification technique. It is interesting to note that fourth generation language structures, which are declarative and non-procedural, in many ways closely resemble pseudocode. This is due to the high-level nature of the function declarations. An example of pseudocode is shown in Figure 6.3.

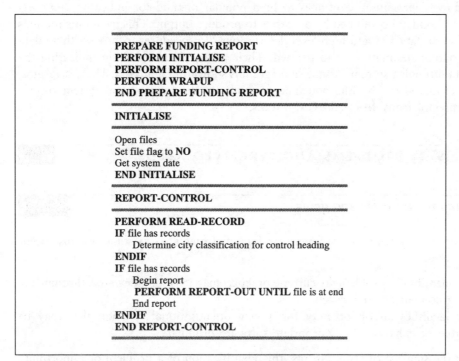

FIGURE

6.3

A segment of pseudocode (adapted from Manning, 1985)

Another widely used specification technique is illustrated below as Figure 6.4. The Warnier–Orr diagramming method treats system structure as a set of smaller (discrete) procedural subsets. A hierarchy structure is set up where the subprocedures are enclosed in brackets and are shown to be part of a larger bracketed set. Subsets perceived to exist at the same level are listed in columnar fashion such that one macro-process may consist of a number of columns of bracketed subprocesses.

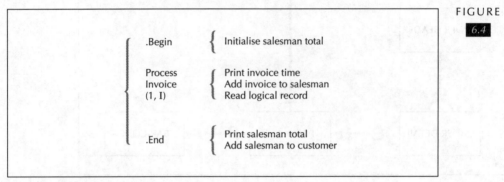

FIGURE
6.4

Part of a Warnier–Orr diagram (adapted from Orr, 1981)

Recently, Petri nets (Petri, 1962), which combine data and process definition, have become popular in systems development specification. Previously applied to engineering applications, including the design of operating systems, Petri nets are diagrams that result from software-generated descriptions of how processes and data are related and in what order system tasks should be enabled and executed. A commonly accepted notation used in Petri net diagrams is illustrated in Figure 6.5.

Data-flow diagramming continues to be a popular method for indicating how sets of data in a system are combined by processes to produce output. This technique requires identification of data sets and high-level descriptions of procedures to process these data sets, with output destinations also defined. Their primary strength is in indicating the flow of data through a system. A sample diagram is shown in Figure 6.6. These diagrams, and those produced by the ER modelling method, are the fundamental system specification features of many front-end CASE tools.

ANALYSIS OF PROBLEMS AND PERCEIVED NEEDS 6.2

Relationship to strategies and goals 6.2.1

Requests for new systems development, or for adjustments to existing systems, occur for two reasons:

1. a user identifies a problem in current practice that may be alleviated through the use of a computer-based system;
2. a user identifies an opportunity for a new organisational function that may be supported or enhanced by appropriate software products.

For all but the smallest of requirements, this identification of a problem or opportunity

FIGURE
6.5

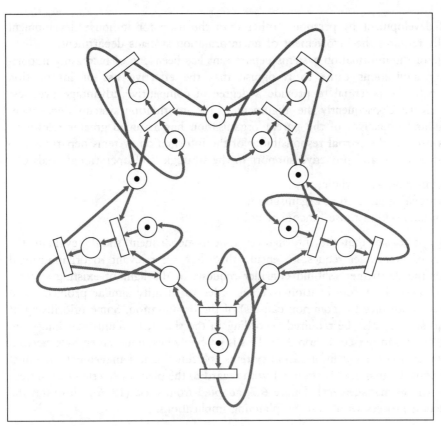

A Petri net representation (adapted from Peterson, 1981)

FIGURE
6.6

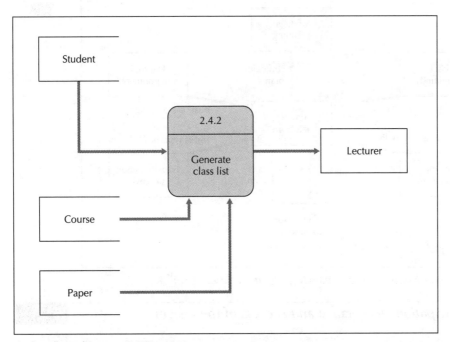

A data-flow diagram (DFD) segment

necessitates development by personnel other than the user; for in-house development this normally requires the involvement of an information systems department.

The role of the information systems department has been one of increasing import-ance since organisations came to recognise that the effective use of information technology held the potential to provide a degree of competitive advantage over less progressive rivals. Consequently the alignment of the information systems department to the goals and objectives of the parent organisation has assumed greater relevance. Thus it has become the partial responsibility of the information systems department to provide both reactive and proactive support to the strategic and operational goals of:

(a) the organisation as a whole;
(b) the functional units of that organisation;
(c) the personnel within those functional units.

This is not to say that the information systems department should evaluate the requirements of every user request to ensure that they are relevant to organisational goals; rather the department should consider requests in the light of existing systems and other requests in a coordination role, in order to identify similar problems and opportunities to advance the common cause(s) of the organisation. Some prioritising of systems requests may also be required according to the short-, medium- and long-term goals of the organisation (see Section 3.5). This is probably best undertaken by a steering committee made up of senior information systems and functional management personnel (see the previous discussion in Section 3.1 with regard to the place of steering committees in system portfolio management). Figure 6.7, adapted from Case (1986), illustrates the project selection process with strategic planning implications.

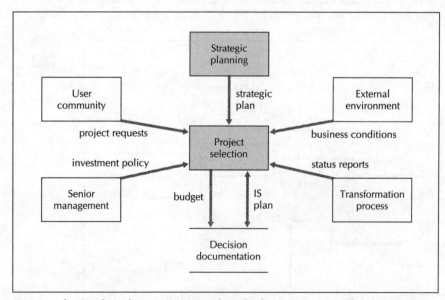

FIGURE
6.7

Project selection based on organisational goals (from Case, 1986)

User participation, acceptance and success of the system　　6.2.2

For many years, system users were the 'poor relation' in the software process, receiving products long after they were due, greatly over budget, and most importantly, functionally incorrect. It soon became evident that to ensure (or at least increase the likelihood of) project success, users had to be considered and actively included in the process. In particular, users now play a vital role in both the early and later stages of the software process:

- in many cases the users provide the impetus for development projects, based on new opportunities or processing problems;
- users must determine, specify and communicate their requirements to the development team;
- active participation in requirements and design reviews;
- users perform and report on system testing;
- the acceptance testing stage is another clear responsibility of the system users;
- delivery of the system incorporates user training, in order to ensure that users are familiar with system operation;
- users also determine requirements for system maintenance.

In some cases, user *management* may have a significant role in the requirements analysis activities, while the actual *users* may have only a minor say in the specification of functional needs. These roles are often reversed, however, in the later tasks specified above. Only the potential system users, not the managers, nor those funding the project, can effectively and critically evaluate the degree to which the system satisfies user needs.

Users are more likely to feel attached to, or have some ownership of, a system they take part in designing. The participative prototyping approach to systems definition has this principle at its heart. Maude and Willis (1991) state that '. . . The key role of prototyping in system development is that it can help to get the critical start-up phases of the project right. . .[this means]. . .

- understanding the problem;
- defining the goals (requirements);
- evaluating possible solutions.'

In other words, prototyping is a way of involving the user right from the beginning of a project, not only in the definition of problems and the 'user's view of the end product', but in the actual construction process. This is illustrated in Figure 6.8; further discussion of the prototyping approach to software development is provided in Section 6.4.

Business process (re-)engineering 6.2.3

One approach to requirements analysis and specification that tends to encourage alignment with organisational focus is *business process (re-)engineering* (BPE/BPR). This approach describes the radical (re)design of business procedures so as to significantly improve costs and/or services. The basic rationale for the emergence of this concept has been the realisation that, in many cases, software systems have been used simply to speed up existing inefficient business activities. The thrust of the BPE/BPR approach is that the fundamental business processes should themselves be examined in detail with a view to developing new, more effective procedures based on the capabilities of information technology. Once this (re)development is complete, new system requirements to support the revamped business processes can be identified.

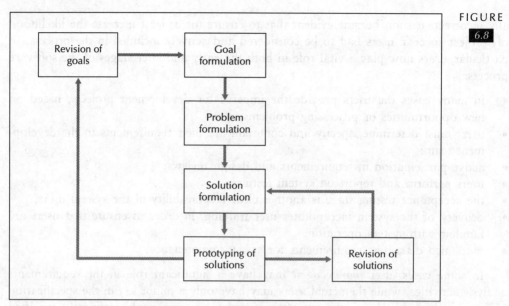

FIGURE

6.8

The use of prototyping for problem solving (adapted from Maude and Willis, 1991)

Reactions of those involved and affected

6 . 2 . 4

Many early software processes were found to be deficient in terms of the relationships that became established between users and developers. Often a significant gulf between the two groups would build up over the life of a project, with minimal interaction being the norm. From the user (normally management) perspective, development personnel were viewed as overly technical, with little grasp of business or organisational reality. Conversely the development team saw the users as naive in terms of their expectations of computers and computer systems. The following process was therefore not uncommon:

1. A few meetings were held between users and developers.
2. The developers drew up what they saw as the user requirements.
3. The users signed off the requirements specification—a document that they did not understand, but that they were told described their needs.
4. After a period of time, often a number of months, the development team returned with a completed system—unfortunately it did not fulfil the users' requirements because (a) their real requirements were not expressed in the specification document (rather, it was what the developers thought the users needed); and (b) their requirements had changed in the interim.

User participation in the requirements analysis process, discussed elsewhere in this chapter, has helped to alleviate this problem. However, the process remains a difficult one, partly because of potentially conflicting objectives. On the one hand the process should result in the development of a document that can be used for effective communication between users and developers—it therefore needs to be relatively simple in terms of the notation and terminology used. The same document, however, must be sufficiently comprehensive, complete and precise, so as to provide a sound basis for the rest of the software development process. If this potential clash were not enough, it is also highly likely that the requirements will change as the organisation evolves.

The following comments are worth bearing in mind when it comes to keeping on the 'right' side of users during the early steps of a project:

(a) Requirements analysis is generally more difficult when there are many users involved. Although the bulk of their requirements may be the same, more often than not, individuals or groups will have their own 'minor' needs. Producing a requirements specification that satisfies all in this situation is clearly unlikely—rational and justified selection of requirements is therefore important at this stage.

(b) If the process is to be successful then the input of users is vital. It is therefore crucial that users are not antagonised by an attitude of superiority or arrogance on the part of developers. (This may be equally applied to the reverse situation.) Meetings should therefore be held on 'neutral ground', perhaps with the independent input of a facilitator. In terms of coordination, initial meetings at least should only include a handful of people—for example, two senior users, one IS manager, one senior project manager, and a facilitator.

(c) Following from the previous point, developers should avoid the temptation to tell users what they need. Certainly some interpretation or clarification of requirements may be needed during the analysis process, but essentially the requirements exist in organisational terms, rather than in the constrained systems structure through which the developers may view them.

(d) It is important that the users themselves be made aware that their requirements will almost certainly change as the project progresses, for reasons discussed previously. Although a signed-off requirements specification provides the basis for subsequent development, the opportunity for changes does not disappear with its production. Users therefore need to be informed of this, together with instructions about the procedure for change requests, so that they do not become increasingly dissatisfied with the perceived inflexibility of the process.

(e) Processes that encourage user ownership of projects also emphasise the concept of shared responsibility. This may be seen simply as an escape mechanism for the developers, in that the 'blame' for problems can be distributed among several individuals or groups. More importantly, however, it tends to create a stronger level of commitment in the users, and their willingness to be involved in the project is generally much greater.

(f) Developers should be willing to acknowledge the limitations of the requirements analysis process, including the probable imprecision of schedule and effort estimates. 'Guarantees' of functionality and cost restrictions are foolhardy at such an early stage of the development process.

FORMALISATION OF REQUIREMENTS   6.3

Can requirements be both formal and understandable to the user?   6.3.1

There is a difference between highly formal systems definitions, such as those defined by specification languages such as Z and the Vienna development method (VDM), and those less formal definitions produced using the conceptual data-flow and data structure models mentioned previously. The latter are most definitely intended as communication tools between analyst and user, whereas the former are primarily intended as formal specification languages, enabling the development of 'provably correct' system descriptions. A much more detailed knowledge of the syntax and vocabulary of Z and VDM is required for understanding than is needed for interpreting an entity–relationship diagram. Doubtless the diagrammatic nature of entity–relationship models makes them immediately less difficult to interpret. A trap for both analyst and user with ERDs is that they allow agreement on the content of the ERD to be an adequate definition of requirements, whereas ERDs do not usually encompass sufficient details of functions and processes to be really adequate definitions of requirements; they are intended purely as data-structure definitions.

We are not in any way dismissing the use (or future use) of formal methods, but for now we believe that the enormous improvement in formality brought about by data structuring techniques like entity–relationship modelling provides a proved and reliable approach to ordering data and organisational elements for the design of implementable information systems. According to McDermaid '. . . The primary strength of formal methods is that they can be readily manipulated by computer programs for various purposes (for example, to check for internal consistency)' (McDermaid, 1989). He goes on to say that, 'It is also reasonable to believe that formal methods will provide the mathematical underpinning to system development. In other words, they potentially provide the mathematical basis for the discipline of software engineering, in the same sense that continuous mathematics underlies more traditional branches of engineering.' Although some work in this area has been undertaken—for example, through the combination of data-flow diagrams and formal methods (Fraser et al., 1991), or with the increasing use of Petri nets in mainstream software development (Tse and Pong, 1989)—this seems a rather large leap from the initial modest claims for specification clarity. There is no doubt that the more precise specifications become, the less ambiguous they will be and therefore, the more correct they will be. Whether they are what the user really wanted when first specified, or during the usual iterations of design, is another matter.

Formal (in the mathematical sense) or not, the concept of refinement is, in our view, essential to the pursuit of correctness in any system specification. McDermaid's concept of refinement is a set of guidelines on how to proceed from a high-level to a low-level specification, with rules for verifying (checking) that this has been done in a consistent manner. He also points out that refinement rules apply to both data and procedures. The difficulty from our perspective is the abstract nature of this process. Data normalisation techniques for database implementation, and indeed entity–relationship modelling itself, are a form of refinement. The difference is that the latter approach uses actual data values for definitive purposes and seldom reduces to abstract or representational symbols for method description. We therefore support the view of Gehani that formal specifications cannot (and should not) replace informal representations (Gehani, 1986). Given that they are complementary, it may be that a combination of the two approaches will prove to be the most effective specification development technique.

Requirements QA
6.3.2

Obtaining user satisfaction for a delivered system, even one that is apparently useful, can never be guaranteed. The prospect of success is clearly more likely, however, if the requirements of the user are fulfilled by the system. Given this condition, one might imagine that successful development would be assured if a delivered system fulfilled the requirements as stated in a given specification. This assumes, however, that: (a) the specification was complete; (b) the specification was correct; and (c) the specification was clear. Unfortunately the reality of the requirements analysis process is such that the achievement of even one of these objectives (for all but the smallest of projects) is unlikely, let alone the achievement of all three. For reasons discussed elsewhere in this chapter and in Chapter 3, it is highly probable that some requirements were specified erroneously, or that inconsistencies were introduced. In order to keep the incidence of such problems to a minimum it is crucial that the process of requirements analysis, as well as the artefacts produced by that process, be subject to previously determined quality control and quality assurance procedures.

The quality process is described by Macro and Buxton (1987) in terms of three components: quality control (QC), quality inspection (QI) and quality assurance (QA). Quality control is the term used to describe the long-established process of internal product review. In terms of the requirements analysis process, this would entail a review of the artefacts produced, carried out by the development team themselves in order to ensure that the user requirements had been specified as clearly, concisely and correctly as possible. This may involve a review of the notes taken at meetings with the user, as well as an examination of any prototype changes requested.

Quality inspection is concerned with the software process, rather than with the resultant products. QI should be undertaken by people other than those involved in the development to ensure that the activities undertaken, in this case during the requirements analysis phase, were appropriate and effective.

Finally, quality assurance is the independent evaluation of process and product quality specific to an individual project, based on predetermined and agreed quality criteria. In general terms this is an independent QC assessment in conjunction with a quality inspection of the process model as it was used in the project at hand. A sample QA checklist that might be used to evaluate the quality of the products of the requirements analysis process is shown in Table 6.1. However, even the most rigorous and comprehensive checklist is unlikely to ensure full compliance with user requirements, owing to the ambiguity of natural language and the likelihood of changing requirements.

Requirements traceability
6.3.3

Previous sections in this chapter have highlighted the importance of a complete and consistent requirements specification. Systems implemented on the basis of incomplete specifications are doomed to failure, at least from the user's perspective. Thus the cost of omitting functionality has been stressed. In a similar vein, the incorporation of *unnecessary* functionality can also have expensive consequences—the development of superfluous functions clearly requires the effort of development personnel and involves the use of costly resources. Furthermore, it may cause the introduction of errors in other functions (due to inconsistencies) and may subsequently result in extensive, but unnec-

Requirements analysis product QA (Adapted from Macro and Buxton, 1987)			TABLE *6.1*
Reference	*Issue*	*Result*	
	1. Does the requirements specification contain: • redundancy? • omission? • error? • ambiguity? 2. Are the objectives of the project stated: • clearly? • concisely? 3. Can this document be used for communication with the users? 4. Have user constraints and conditions been included? 5. Have aspects of solution design been included?		

essary, testing. This leads us to the concept of ensuring requirements traceability. Essentially this is the process by which every system function, as described in the functional specification, can be associated with a stated requirement of the user. In the same manner, each requirement should be linked to a stated need or opportunity. In general, finding erroneously included functions is more difficult than finding those that have been left out of a specification, mainly because users tend to notice what is missing rather than what is included. This task is further complicated by the fact that it can be difficult to break system functions down to the extent that they may be mapped directly to stated user requirements. While these problems are not insignificant, the costs of *not* attempting some form of traceability analysis will almost certainly outweigh them.

PROTOTYPING   *6.4*

The concept of prototyping has been discussed previously in reference to process definition but requires a more detailed treatment. In essence, prototyping is a technique borrowed from engineering which enables a system specification to be developed to the stage of a working model. Some impressions of prototyping are that it is a partial implementation of a design. This may be true in certain circumstances, but essentially it is a full implementation of the design specifications in the form of a working model. This enables very fast examples of what the eventual systems may look like being developed for critical appraisal by users and developers. For instance, sample data-entry and report-format screens can be generated exactly as they would appear in the finished system, without writing all the software that would be required to build their actual content.

Using prototypes, information system users and developers can examine and assess the relative merits of the prototype system and make changes without major rewrites of the original software. This has reduced a level of frustration in the systems development world and has improved system quality and productivity because it has increased system acceptability. It has also helped evolve the concept of real user participation in the system development process.

High-level declarative programming languages, conventionally termed 'fourth generation languages' can facilitate the prototyping process by incorporating screen, menu and report generators using default formats, rather than requiring purpose-built software for each new application. Lantz (1986) in his book dedicated to the prototyping process provides a comprehensive review of the elements of this technique and a deliberate rationale for choosing such an approach for systems development. He also addresses the issues and relative advantages of developing partial (or mock-up) prototypes, compared with 'full' prototypes that include some conventional processing.

Case (1986) makes the useful point that prototyping as a technique is language-independent. He regards prototypes as being functional and semi-functional models of information systems that are built during the development process. The term 'during' is imperative from our perspective. Prototypes are not ends in themselves. They may be further developed as fully functional information systems but should only be regarded as part of the overall development process if they are to retain their 'working model' character. If we start out with the intention of merely extending the functionality of the prototype into a full system, there is a danger of losing the essential 'modelling' nature of what is really an integral part of the system design. Prototypes are in effect system specifications in action.

The impact of prototyping on requirements specification within the software process is well documented by Davis (1993). He maintains that for non-trivial applications, there is an ever-growing and ever-changing set of user needs and expectations. For this reason, if for no other, it is essential to determine at the outset whether the prototype is intended as a 'throwaway' model or as one that is part of the evolutionary development of the system in process. We maintain the position that prototypes should be developed as quickly and efficiently as possible in order to provide an operational version of the system specifications, such that users and developers can participate in the **design phase** of the process, not merely in implementation. From this point of view we would come down on the 'throwaway' side of this issue. There are occasions, however, where some of the prototype software (menu screens, report formats, data-entry verification/validation code) may be reusable in the full system implementation. Where this is obvious, a selective evolutionary process would be appropriate. A direct quote from Davis is perhaps a salutory way to conclude this section and express our view on prototyping. He says, 'It is impossible to retrofit quality, maintainability and reliability.' These attributes must be intrinsic to the final system. One of the costs of system design iteration is to discard what is not absolutely necessary or of the highest quality. When attempting to increase productivity, it should not be at the cost of reducing quality. Prototyping is a technique intended to increase productivity *and* improve quality. If that means discarding the working model in order to incorporate the desired functionality into the final system, then so be it.

Exercises

6.1 List some of the objectives of those stakeholders involved in requirements analysis.

6.2 Compare a selection of user-analyst communication tools. Consider how their effectiveness might change in different application domains.

6.3 Describe how and why the role of the user has changed during the short history of software development.

6.4 Is the allocation of resources for IS projects generally an objective analysis by a steering committee or merely the result of corporate politics?

6.5 How does business process (re-)engineering differ from structured systems analysis?

6.6 Can you think of a method for assessing the reactions of those involved and affected by requirements analysis? How could this be used to impact positively on the effectiveness of the IS portfolio?

References

Case, A. F. Jr (1986) *Information Systems Development*. Prentice-Hall, Englewood Cliffs, NJ.

Chen, P. P. (1976) 'The entity–relationship model: Towards a unified view of data', *ACM Transactions on Database Systems,* 1 (1), March 1976, pp. 9–36.

Davis, A. M. (1993) *Software Requirements: Objects, Functions and States*. PTR Prentice-Hall, Englewood Cliffs, NJ.

DeMarco, T. (1978) *Structured Analysis and System Specification*. Prentice-Hall, Englewood Cliffs, NJ.

Fraser, M. D., Kumar, K. and Vaishnavi, V. K. (1991) 'Informal and formal requirements specification languages: Bridging the gap', *IEEE Transactions on Software Engineering* 17 (5), May 1991, pp. 454–66.

Gane, C. and Sarson, T. (1979) *Structured Systems Analysis: Tools and Techniques*. Prentice-Hall, Englewood Cliffs, NJ.

Gehani, N. (1986) 'Specifications: formal and informal—A case study', in Gehani, N. and McGettrick, A.D. (Eds) *Software Specification techniques*. Addison-Wesley, Wokingham, pp. 173–85.

Lantz, K. E. (1986) *The Prototyping Methodology*, Prentice-Hall, Englewood Cliffs, NJ.

Macro, A. and Buxton, J. (1987) *The Craft of Software Engineering*. Addison-Wesley, Wokingham.

Manning, G. (1985) *Advanced COBOL: A Structured Approach*, Random House, New York.

Maude, T., and Willis, G. (1991) *Rapid Prototyping: The Management of Software Risk*. Pitman, London.

McDermaid, J. A. (Ed.) (1989) *The Theory and Practice of Refinement: Approaches to the Formal Development of Large-scale Software Systems*. Butterworths.

Orr, K. T. (1981) *Structured Requirements Definition*. Ken Orr and Assoc., Topeka, KS.

Peterson, J. L. (1981) *Petri Net Theory and the Modelling of Systems*. Prentice-Hall, Englewood Cliffs, NJ.

Petri, C. A. (1981) *Communication with Automata*, Supplement 1 to RADC-TR-65-377 Vol. 1, Griffiss Air Force Base, New York,—Originally published in German 'Kommunikation mit Automaten', University of Bonn, cited in Peterson (1981).

Tse, T. H. and Pong, L. (1989) 'Towards a formal foundation for DeMarco data-flow diagrams', *The Computer Journal,* 32 (1), pp. 1–11.

CHAPTER 7

Analysis, design and development paradigms

A computer-based information system may be defined simply as the interaction between programs and data: **system = programs + data**. More correctly, programs encapsulate the processes required to operate on the data, such that the functions of the organisations, in terms of their corporate objectives, can be met. For this reason, information systems are more often depicted as **system = processes * data**. The use of an asterisk to illustrate this interaction is probably more appropriate than the + used above in terms of actual system activity. When we talk about process in this chapter, we mean operations internal to a system rather than controls and activities related to the creation of systems, which is the topic of discussion elsewhere in this book.

This elemental model for systems means that other integral components are not represented. The most obvious of these is the users of the system and, in another dimension, the user interface with the system. When we also consider the flow of data through a system and the production of information, we need to depict input and output, internally generated, compared with externally entered data, and the types of data and kinds of transactions within the system.

The issue of user interfaces for systems has recently become a significant area of research known as human–computer interaction (HCI). Work in this area is concerned with designing visual display and printed output information (including user manuals, screen-based error messages, and system help facilities) in forms which are of optimum effectiveness for the users. Recommendations relating to this objective are illustrated in Figure 7.1. Given that the interface is clearly the most visible manifestation of a system for a user, it is crucial that his or her needs be incorporated into the design of the interface if user acceptance is to be obtained. Interface development within a prototyping process has proved to be an excellent approach to facilitate user input. A common problem, no matter what the process, however, is that systems are more often developed for a number of users, each of whom will have individual work patterns, as well as varying levels of ability and system understanding.

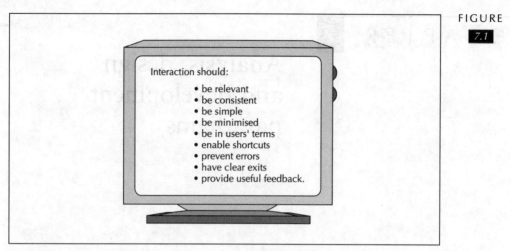

FIGURE
7.1

Interaction should:
- be relevant
- be consistent
- be simple
- be minimised
- be in users' terms
- enable shortcuts
- prevent errors
- have clear exits
- provide useful feedback.

Issues to be considered in information display design (adapted from Nielson, 1993)

A dimension not often depicted in conceptual models of information systems is the size of the system, and the volume of data, transactions or messages being processed by the system. Indications of size can be useful in determining development schedules and plans for resource allocation (see Section 3.3, Section 3.6 and much of Chapter 10) as well as in the prediction of data and code storage requirements.

Non-functional system desirables and constraints   7.1.1

In adopting Gilb's (1988) hierarchy of project requirements in Chapter 4, the notion of 'quality goals' was considered. In contrast to functional requirements, which may be specified in unequivocal and unambiguous terms, quality goals are more often oriented towards non-functional (or non-behavioural) system characteristics. One comprehensive categorisation of these attributes is Boehm's (1978) classification of quality characteristics, shown in Figure 7.2.

Davis (1993) provides extensive discussion on each of the seven characteristics included at the third level of the hierarchy—a brief definition of each is provided as follows:

- *Portability*—How easily can the system be transferred from one environment or platform to another?
- *Reliability*—To what degree does the system perform the required functions correctly and consistently?
- *Efficiency*—To what extent does the system operate in a timely manner with satisfactory use of resources?
- *Human engineering*—How easily can the system be learnt and operated by users?
- *Testability*—How easily can the system be tested so as to ensure correct functionality?
- *Understandability*—To what extent can the system be understood by maintenance personnel?
- *Modifiability*—How easily can the system be adapted, enhanced or repaired?

Many of the characteristics are *non-functional*, since they are not directly related

FIGURE
7.2

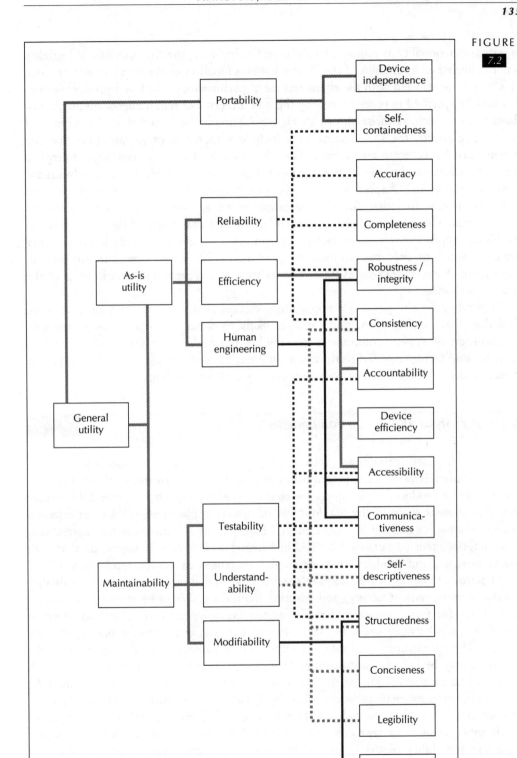

Software quality characteristics (Boehm, 1978)

to system functionality as required by the user. For instance, the characteristic of legibility is not delivered as a function of the system but is a function of the development process. This may be contrasted with the characteristic of performance which is a product feature that may be specified in precise terms by the user. In terms of requirements specifications, characteristics such as those shown in Figure 7.2 might be included at the request of users; for example, the specification may include a requirement to the effect that the system must be accurate and robust. The obvious dilemma with such requirements is that they are immeasurable in this form—just what is a suitable level of robustness? Thus, as stated in Chapter 6, it is imperative that the analysis process produce requirements that are either directly measurable or are at least measurable in commonly agreed terms. This problem is compounded by the fact that some of the characteristics are highly dependent on individuals. For example, if one user finds a system very straightforward to use, but another has extensive difficulties, how can the human engineering characteristics be evaluated so as to give a representative indication of the actual situation?

Depending on the particular application, certain characteristics may also be more 'desirable' than others. Thus, trade-offs are likely to occur: if efficiency is paramount, the inclusion of system components to simplify portability is unlikely. Conversely, a focus on one factor may indirectly boost another; an obvious example of this type of interdependence exists between understandability and modifiability.

Reuse of analysis and design components   7.1.2

We have maintained throughout previous chapters that software process control, management and improvement are prerequisites of high quality software. Given that quality systems *can* be produced, it is imperative that the positive aspects of successful software processes be used again in the development of similar applications—this is an essential part of process engineering as discussed in Chapter 2, and is an important component of the improvement paradigms described in Chapter 5. It is equally important that high quality products and product components also be reused in similar applications.

In terms of the software analysis, specification and design processes, high quality reusable objects, data structures and function definitions should be stored in a component library for future access and retrieval. For example, the hierarchical structure of the relationship between order headers and order details is a common one in business systems. The specification and design components associated with this structure, once validated, may be held for use in other applications, perhaps a system concerned with the recording of information on the constituent tasks of contract jobs (see Figure 7.3).

'Specification by analogy' is described by Maiden and Sutcliffe (1992) as one reuse strategy made more feasible with CASE technology. They cite a number of examples in which applications from very different domains share similar features that immediately encourage reusability. Similarly, one of the most widely cited advantages of object-oriented analysis and design methods is the strong support for component reuse—this is discussed in greater detail in Section 7.6.

It is worth noting that the mere *existence* of a reusable component that is similar to that required in an application does not necessarily mean that it should be used—a careful decision must be made as to the extent of modification required. If the component

FIGURE

7.3

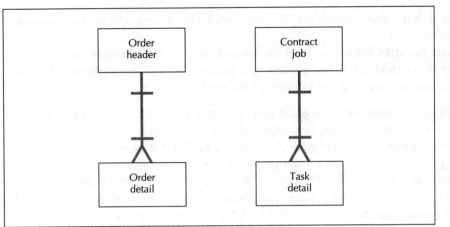

Similarities between data structures

needed is relatively simple, and the degree of correspondence is not overly high, then it may well be more cost effective to develop from scratch.

Finally, a non-trivial issue related to component reuse is its effective management, that is, the efficient storage and browse/retrieval control of the components. It is one thing to save the components for reuse, but this will be of little benefit if the components are inaccessible through poor management. The enforcement of standards is also important in this respect so that the nature and form of all components are consistent.

QA and inspections

Ensuring the quality of the analysis and design processes is generally performed through review and inspection sessions involving all software stakeholders, as well as through in-house self-assessment and external review. If we consider again the requirements of the SEI Capability Maturity Model (CMM) (Software Engineering Institute, 1993), even at Level 2 (of 5), there exists a requirement that quality assurance activities be planned, and that adherence of both products and tasks to quality standards is objectively verified. At Level 3, the quality of all products is required: quantitative measures of requirements defects, design defects and defect density are recommended. Quality assurance in the early stages of the process should help to ensure that standards are achieved before any product is used as a basis for further development. This assessment may take the form of the review described in Section 6.3. Inspection and peer review is equally important, as self-assessment alone may not be comprehensive or thorough enough to highlight areas of deficiency or error.

The requirements review involves contributions from analysts, designers and users/customers. The main objective of the review is to ensure the accuracy of the requirements specification. Pfleeger (1991) suggests the following steps:

- review the project's goals and objectives;
- ensure the traceability of all requirements (see Section 6.3);
- determine and describe the operating environment, to ensure that all system interfaces are correct and consistent;

- ensure that the requirements are compliant with user wishes, and are both consistent and achievable;
- evaluate the risks associated with the project, and discuss alternatives;
- determine methods of future process and product traceability, including the verification and validation of requirements fulfilment.

If a project is sufficiently large, it may be necessary to hold a number of phased reviews before quality tests can be completed to a satisfactory degree.

Quality assurance of design products follows a similar but more extensive approach. Users are generally involved to a lesser degree than in the requirements review, but their input is still needed to validate the claim that the design meets their requirements. Any inaccuracies and inconsistencies discovered should be passed on to those responsible for configuration management (see Section 4.3). Often of more importance at this point, at least in terms of system implementation, is the testing of the design in terms of verifiable characteristics such as modularity, coupling and cohesion. The rationale behind this procedure is an expectation that design components should be as independent and self-contained as possible so as to reduce the structural 'complexity' of the design. Implementation and maintenance of designs that have followed such guidelines are generally simpler than for designs that incorporate many complicated interactions. These attributes may be measured quantitatively by considering the number of control and data links between low-level design components (see also Section 10.8). A more comprehensive examination of design characteristics might include the consideration of portability, modifiability and so on, as described by Boehm (1978) and discussed previously.

Even in these early stages, quality assurance is a vital activity. Software stakeholders—customers, users, developers and project managers—all have different expectations of product and process quality. Reviews, walk-throughs and inspections held during the analysis and design phases should help to ensure that a common understanding of quality requirements is reached between all parties. Having a quality assurance procedure which has been agreed to by all involved is no longer an added option in this process. For high quality to be achieved in software development it is *necessary* to identify the goals and each incremental aspect of the process working towards those goals at the outset of the project. The ISO9000 series of quality assurance standards, as described in Chapter 5, is a framework within which such an agreed procedure can be developed by the collective stakeholders.

A TAXONOMY OF INFORMATION SYSTEMS   7.2

System classification is essentially an arbitrary process, but a categorisation of systems is a useful basis on which to discuss various development approaches. Our taxonomy of systems is shown in Figure 7.4.

Given a classification of this nature, it is inevitable that the software process adopted for the development of the various systems will vary according to system type. For example, the requirements for quality in life-critical process control systems will inevitably place greater demands on testing than say, a transaction processing system controlling stock level updates. Similarly, a decision support system with uncertain functional requirements may be better served by a prototyping-based process than by a more formalised analysis and design approach.

FIGURE

7.4

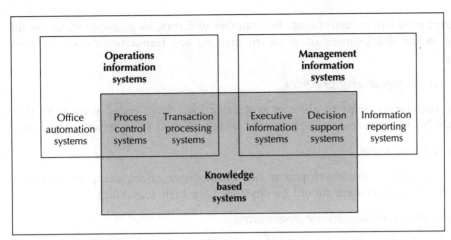

A taxonomy of system types

PARADIGMS AND APPROACHES

7.3

The issues that relate to perceived problems in the software process outlined in Chapter 1 emerge again as a consideration. When deciding upon a specific problem–solution approach it is necessary to understand all the factors that are likely to impact on the success of that system. This would include the applications backlog for a particular organisation, human resource issues, technology impact issues and so on. Brooks (1987) says there is no silver bullet to eradicate these problems as there is fabled to be in the vanquishing of a werewolf. Counter to this, both Yourdon (1989) and Harel (1992) have composed checklists and recommendations in an attempt to create a more positive outlook concerning software engineering and the software process. Among the generic process strategies suggested by Harel (1992) are a number relating to high-level modelling:

- use formalised abstractions to model both static and behavioural system components;
- enable dynamic refinement, compression and expansion of system models;
- enable direct model execution;
- utilise automated generation facilities to produce quality code;
- verify consistency between conceptual and code levels.

Yourdon has provided a more comprehensive and prescriptive list of twelve 'silver bullets':

(a) *Manage human resources more effectively*

High calibre personnel have a greater influence over the success of a project, in terms of achieving standards of product quality and process productivity, than any technology-based tool or technique.

(b) *Use software metrics*

Quantitative, objective assessments of process and product attributes should be used (and refined) to monitor, control and improve both product and process.

(c) *Adopt the best programming languages*

Use those languages that, given their suitability to the application domain, result in the highest productivity and the smallest number of errors, for example 4GLs should be used in the development of small- to medium-size transaction-driven business systems.

(d) Apply reverse engineering practices

Reverse engineering helps to abstract processing logic from coded systems so that they may be re-engineered, reimplemented or redeveloped using newer technology.

(e) Employ software reuse

In order to reduce both development and maintenance effort, components across the entire software process should be developed for high reusability.

(f) Apply the principles of software engineering

This is the adoption of policies, methods and tools that assist in the rigorous pursuit and achievement of quality software development according to time and cost constraints.

(g) Use object-oriented design techniques

Yourdon suggests that these methods are directly relevant to the development of the interactive, graphics-based applications that now dominate commercial software.

(h) Manage the maintenance process

Keeping existing systems functionally up to date is a significant effort component for most development sites—achieving any gains in *new* development productivity and quality can therefore only occur if the maintenance process is carefully monitored and controlled.

(i) Use prototyping

This is among the most effective techniques for determining user requirements, particularly for highly interactive applications.

(j) Adopt CASE technology

Given the right (that is, appropriate) tools, CASE technology can produce real gains in both process productivity and product/process quality.

(k) Manage end-user development

Computer-literate users should be encouraged to develop and maintain their own small (but useful) applications in a controlled and standardised environment, thus reducing the demand for systems placed on the development team.

(l) Undertake quality assurance

Establish and enforce standards and procedures to ensure quality processes and quality products as far as possible.

The central message to be conveyed is that no single development tool, technique, approach or paradigm fits all situations. It may be, in fact, that a combination of aspects and techniques adopted from several paradigms is the most appropriate approach for the development of a particular application. This does not mean, however, that a significant effort should not be made to choose the most appropriate approach. Systems centred around the manipulation and reporting of stock inventory values, for example, may be well suited to a data-centred process. Conversely, the development of a real-time system to control the temperature and humidity of cool stores would probably be better served with a function-oriented approach.

Four contemporary approaches to systems analysis and design are outlined. This book is concerned with the management and improvement of the software process and, therefore, these descriptions are not as extensive as may be found in textbooks that aim to describe each method in detail. Such textbooks are readily available and should be consulted for an advanced understanding of any of the methods mentioned.

THE DATA-CENTRED APPROACH   7.4

Fundamental concepts   7.4.1

We have already seen in Chapter 1 the concept of information engineering (IE) and its fundamental focus on data rather than function. We have also seen in Chapter 6 the entity–relationship modelling technique and its corresponding focus on data rather than function. Both the wider conceptual framework of information engineering and the more specific method of entity–relationship modelling are most obviously illustrative of the data-centred approach to systems development. A number of other techniques have been developed within this paradigm, including Jackson System Development (JSD) (Jackson, 1983) and the data flow models of Gane and Sarson (1979) and DeMarco (1978) as referred to in Chapter 6. As our intention is to illustrate the *paradigm* rather than specific techniques, we have chosen to concentrate on the entity–relationship modelling approach as our example of a data-centred development paradigm. The interested reader is directed to the original references for detailed descriptions of the other techniques mentioned.

Adoption of the assumption that data should be the focal point of information systems resulted in a significant departure from the traditional concentration on the definition of system functions when analysing and designing information systems. In the past, both analyst and user viewed data as the input to functions that were described using flowcharts, structured English, pseudocode, or indeed directly transformed from written descriptions to computer programs. Data of course *is* the input to these functions, but the interaction dynamics of data elements and the 'formal' definition of their interrelationships has come to be regarded (in this paradigm at least) as of paramount importance *prior* to embarking on any functional specification, hence the popularity of methods such as the entity–relationship approach (described below) for data-structure definition.

We believe that data-structure modelling and data-flow modelling cannot occur in a strictly sequential fashion. Both tasks occur simultaneously, but emphasis and time allocation during the specification process will favour one or the other task according to need. If no other concept has been universally adopted by all participants in the analysis and design of information systems, that of iterative development has unquestionable support. The strictly sequential process model of the 'waterfall' systems development life cycle (SDLC) was first discussed in Chapter 2 (Figure 2.2). Simply drawing feedback lines as in Figure 2.1 (page 10) is one way of doing this; attempting to put the entire process into a data-centred approach model as in Figure 7.5 is more ambitious. This latter approach illustrates the simultaneous nature of data-structure and data-flow modelling, which we believe more clearly represents common practice.

FIGURE
7.5

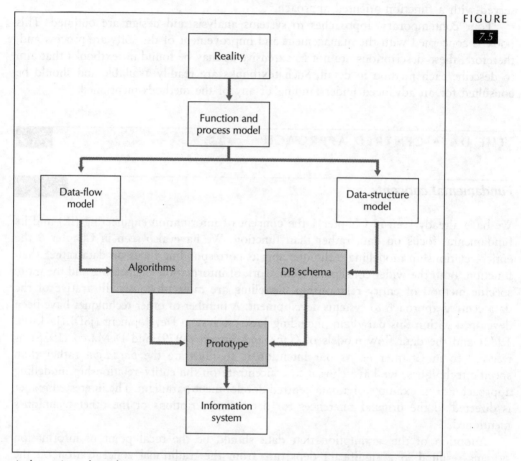

A data-oriented product view of the software process (from Benwell et al., 1991)

From Figure 7.5 it can be seen that, at least conceptually, both data-structure and data-flow modelling methods can (and should) be used to produce a composite data-centred system model as the basis for subsequent development tasks. This approach is well supported, in that it has been suggested that a system developed using a single modelling method is more likely to be inadequate (Mantha, 1987).

The entity–relationship modelling method

7.4.2

Entity–relationship (ER) modelling was initially proposed by Chen (1976) as a method that would enable developers and users of information systems to attain a unified and common view of data. Many extensions to the original model have been subsequently proposed (for example, see March, 1988) but the principal theory remains intact. The ER model (ERM) has two main functions:

(a) it should provide a rigorous basis for database development;

(b) it should serve as an accurate and understandable communication tool for analysts and users (Benwell et al., 1991).

■ Entity–relationship modelling terminology

An ERM depicts the resources and activities of an organisation and the ways in which they are related to each other. It is used to develop a database structure consistent with the needs and operations of the organisation. An ERM consists of the following components:

- *Entity:* A distinct object or activity about which the organisation wishes to store information. Customers, orders and products are all examples of entities. Each entity should have a unique identifier, or *primary key.*
- *Attribute:* Every entity in an ERM is defined by its list of attributes. An attribute describes some aspect of the entity to which it belongs. For example, a customer entity might have attributes like customer number, name, address, phone, credit limit, and so on.
- *Relationship:* A meaningful association between two entities. A relationship has three properties: *cardinality* or *degree, optionality* and *dependency* (all are defined below). Relationships are generally implemented at the database management system (DBMS) level using *foreign keys.*
- *Cardinality or degree:* In a typical orders database, a customer might have multiple orders on file (that is, a customer can be associated with one or more orders) but any particular order can be linked to only one customer (that is, each order can be associated with only one customer). This relationship is a *one-to-many* relationship (customers may be associated with many orders, but each order is associated with only one customer). Relationships may be one-to-one (1:1), one-to-many (1:*n*), many-to-one (*n*:1) or many-to-many (*n*:*m*).
- *Optionality:* Using the same example as above, a customer record might be stored in the database, but have no orders currently on file (that is, a customer can be associated with zero or more orders). An order, however, must *always* be associated with a particular customer (that is, an order is associated with one and only one customer). Thus, in this relationship, the customer entity is said to be *mandatory* (orders cannot exist without an associated customer) and the orders entity is *optional* (customers may exist without associated orders).
- *Dependency:* Although an order is logically a single entity, at the implementation level orders are usually split into two entities: order headers and order lines. This is done to prevent data redundancy and ensure database integrity. Since order headers and lines are logically a single entity, when we delete an order header we must *always* delete the associated order lines, because an order line cannot exist without an associated order header. This is a stronger constraint than just making an entity mandatory to a relationship. In this case, the order line entity is said to be *dependent* on the order header entity, and the order header is known as the *parent* entity.

■ ERM notation

In *Pronto* notation, entities are represented by named boxes (*Pronto* is an ER modelling

CASE tool developed at the University of Otago in New Zealand (Pronto User Manual, 1994)). Relationships between entities are represented by lines between the entities. Figure 7.6 shows a typical ERM drawn using *Pronto* notation.

FIGURE

7.6

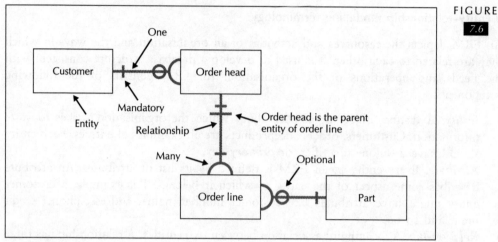

A sample ER model

Cardinality is represented by the semicircles in Figure 7.6. A straight line represents 'one,' whereas a semicircle represents 'many.' Thus, the relationship between customer and order header in Figure 7.6 is one-to-many. Optionality is represented by the small circles and bars on the relationships. The bar represents 'mandatory,' while the circle represents 'optional.' A customer may have many orders on file, but they may also have none, so the order header entity is optional in this relationship. On the other hand, every order must have an associated customer, so the customer entity is mandatory. Dependency is represented by drawing a longer bar just behind the optionality symbol of the parent entity, as can be seen on the relationship between order head and order line in Figure 7.6.

The principal characteristic of entity–relationship models (ERMs) is that they are developed independently of the physical structure in which the data will be stored. This means that the modeller is primarily concerned with developing an appropriate representation of reality from the point of view of the user(s) of the data. Assumptions as to what is an appropriate representation of reality can be built into the model and the data modeller can then verify the assumptions or modify the model as necessary. The model should therefore, at any point in time, represent the modeller's current understanding of reality. This characteristic, combined with the fact that an ERM may be implemented in any one of the major physical database models, has gained the ERM extremely wide acceptance as an analytical tool.

Representing the cardinality and participation of relationships facilitates the development of *normalised* ERMs from which sets of relations conforming to the relational database integrity rules (Date, 1990) can be derived. However, there are various semantic characteristics of data relationships which can also be modelled, thereby enriching the model both as a database design technique and as a means for representing reality. A data model should also include the specification of relevant attributes of entities. Obviously this is essential if the database structure is to support information requirements effectively. For the data modeller, there is a very pragmatic reason for defining attributes early in the modelling process: analysis of attributes provides insight to the semantics of data relationships. Part of the process of attribute analysis is the designation of primary key attributes for each entity, which in turn enables relationships between entities to be represented in a database by foreign keys. Given advances in development automation over recent years, as evidenced by the discussion of the *Pronto* tool above, direct generation of database schema based on rigorously developed ER models is now very much a reality (also see Section 8.3). This should lead to reductions in both development effort and schema errors.

In more general terms, data-oriented development approaches are obviously well suited to the wealth of applications that are centred around the processing and reporting of data element values. In terms of the taxonomy described in Section 7.2, transaction processing and information reporting systems are typical of this class of application. They are used in banks, government departments, retail and manufacturing organisations—in fact, in any enterprise concerned with current transaction-driven data values. In these situations the data objects or elements tend to remain relatively stable, while processes and functions change over time. Thus maintenance is generally simpler if the systems have been developed from a data-centred perspective (rather than from a singular focus on system function).

Davis (1993) has suggested that ER modelling, as a specific instance of the data-centred approach, has too strong a focus on data, in that developers tend to view *database* development as *system* development. Thus the concentration on data tends to dominate the development process to the extent that functional requirements may be glossed over. As stated previously, however, it may be that a combination of data-centred and functionally-oriented analysis and design approaches will produce the most appropriate analysis or design representation. Alternatively, it may be worthwhile considering the techniques of entity-life modelling (Sanden, 1989) and logical access mapping (McFadden and Hoffer, 1988) as methods that incorporate data manipulation and reporting requirements from a functional perspective.

Data analysis representations are generally non-executable, so the behaviour of a system can only be ascertained after it has been interpreted into an executable form. This process of translation creates an opportunity for introduction of inaccuracies and inconsistencies to the system. The ER model does however have a mathematical basis, so the *structure* of a given model can be rigorously assessed. Unfortunately the semantics (or expressiveness) of the ER model is not sufficiently 'rich' to represent the full meaning of some data-centred applications. This shortcoming has, in part, led to the development of semantic, or hyper-semantic, data-modelling methods. These methods extend the capabilities of models like the entity–relationship model to incorporate consistent formalisms of other relationships such as aggregation, grouping, classification and membership (Potter and Trueblood, 1988).

THE FUNCTION-ORIENTED APPROACH 7.5

Fundamental concepts 7.5.1

The main emphasis in any function-oriented approach is on what systems *do*, that is, the functions or operations they perform. Depending on the environment and its terminology, activities, actions, transactions, processes, transformations, procedures or tasks are the things of major interest.

The primary emphasis on function does not necessarily mean that other essential components of systems, such as data, are ignored. It merely means that they 'take a back seat', or are regarded as being of less importance from the point of view of understanding, describing and structuring a system.

The main analysis technique used with the function-oriented approach is **functional decomposition**. This is simply the splitting up of the overall function to be performed into a set of smaller component functions which together achieve the overall function. These smaller functions are then broken down into their component subfunctions, and so on until the lowest level component functions are in some sense self-explanatory, primitive, or decomposed to a sufficient level of detail for the purpose in hand. The term **successive refinement** is also used in some contexts, particularly that of structured programming, as an alternative to functional decomposition. Other terminology commonly used in connection with functional decomposition is the word **explosion**, to denote the refinement of a function into its components, and general terms, such as **hierarchy** or **hierarchical, root, branches, leaves** or **leaf processes**, etc. referring to the basic tree structure.

Functional decomposition is a general process that can be applied to any activities, whether they are software related or not. It is generally considered to be a **top-down** process. The presentation of the results of functional decomposition is certainly top down, but whether the process itself is strictly so in practice is doubtful. As in most human intellectual activities, iteration, adjustment and more complex analysis processes are often at work within the top-down structure.

In its simplest form, functional decomposition is tree structured as shown in the example in Figure 7.7. In this form, a functional decomposition is also called a work breakdown structure (WBS).

Functional decomposition as depicted in a WBS does not show how the components of a subtree at any level fit together to achieve the functional effect of the parent function of which they are a refinement, for example referring to Figure 7.7, how 'divide into modules', 'define module interfaces' and 'design modules' actually work together to achieve their parent function 'design'. For this reason, richer graphical or text-based

FIGURE

7.7

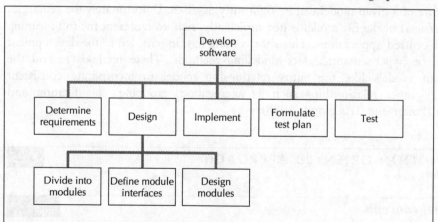

A functional decomposition, or WBS example

notations than simple tree diagrams are often used to support functional decomposition, including structure charts or diagrams, program (or process) design language (PDL) and data-flow diagrams.

Structure diagrams are used mainly to support program design and use the standard structured programming primitive constructs of sequence, selection (or choice) and iteration. Notations vary. In this section we use a largely self-explanatory notation; the square boxes are processes, the angled boxes selections, and the ovals iterations. A subtree of elements (apart from a selection) represents a left-to-right sequence of steps. Such a sequence below an iteration control oval is repeated in accordance with the condition in the oval.

A similar structured-programming-like effect can also be achieved using a process design language. An example in an Ada-like PDL for the same software design process as that shown in Figure 7.8 is given in Figure 7.9.

A functional decomposition approach can also be used with some other common

FIGURE
7.8

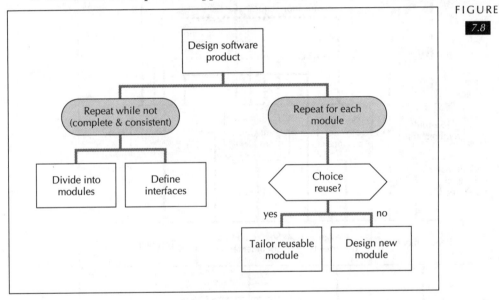

A process structure diagram example

FIGURE
7.9

```
procedure design_software_product is
begin
    while not (complete and consistent)
    loop
    divide_into_modules;
    define_module_interfaces;
    end loop;
    for i in 1 .. number_of_modules
    loop
        if reusable_module_available then
            tailor_reusable_module;
        else
            design_new_module;
        end if;
    end loop;
end design_software_product;
```

An Ada-like PDL example

system description notations, such as data-flow diagrams (DFDs). Here, however, as the word 'data' in data-flow diagram implies, we depart further from a pure functional decomposition approach to include some representation of the data involved, and perhaps other things of interest also, such as external agents. Nevertheless, the main emphasis can still be on the functions and their breakdown into simpler functional components. An advantage of the DFD notation over the structure diagram is that some representation of parallelism is possible. For example, according to the example DFD of Figure 7.10, once a requirements statement is available, one can both 'design software product' and 'formulate test plan'. A disadvantage of DFDs, compared with structure diagrams, is that a single DFD only represents one level of a functional decomposition.

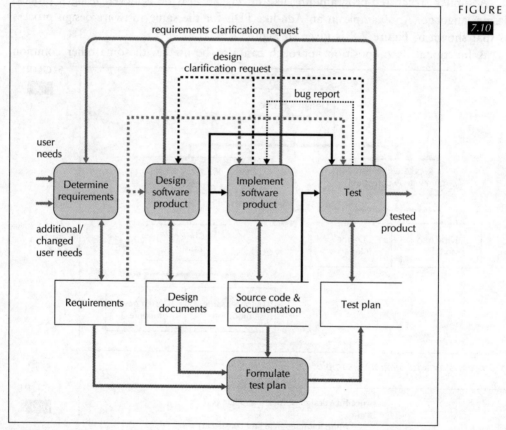

FIGURE
7.10

A DFD example

DFDs can be, and frequently are, used for functional decomposition by concentration on the functions and exploding them into their component functions, and so on. This is not the true nature of data flow, however, which is illustrated in Figure 7.11, showing the derivation of the roots of a quadratic equation, x1 and x2, from its coefficients a, b and c. From this example it can be seen quite clearly that data flow is concerned with the precise dependencies of output data flows on input data flows. True DFDs answer the question: 'What input data flows are necessary and sufficient to produce the required output data flow?'

From Figure 7.11 it can be seen that, at a detailed level, the roles of data and

FIGURE

7.11

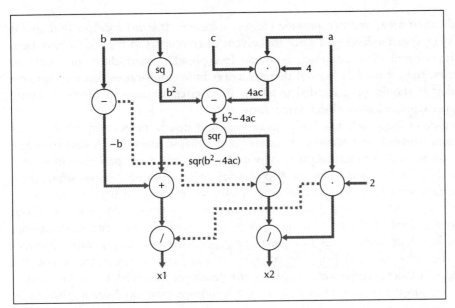

A data flow example

function in data flow are quite intimately related and there is no question of being able to focus on function in any sense at the expense of data. In other words, at a detailed level, DFDs are not really functional decomposition tools. They are much more than this. At a general level, however, DFDs can be, and often are used in a much looser and more permissive way, concentrating on the functions and representing the data flows more vaguely, more generally, or more selectively. This illustrates a general feature of functional decomposition, or successive refinement; that as it becomes more detailed it must also become more precise and, in order to do so, it is also necessary to take the data into account.

The main advantage of the function-oriented approach is its naturalness, not only for developers, but also for customers and users of systems. People in general find it easy to understand and identify with the functions of a system. At the more detailed levels of program design and programming, procedural languages have a long history of successful use. Procedural abstraction (the use of procedures and functions) is still the most commonly used abstraction mechanism, even if it is used with increasing frequency within other more comprehensive abstraction structures, such as abstract data types and packages. There are, however, a number of disadvantages, both of the function-oriented approach generally and also of top-down functional decomposition.

The appropriateness of the function-oriented approach relates to the nature of the system being developed and the types of models which best characterise the system, or the aspects of the system which are of interest. In some systems, for example, *states*, *events* and *state transitions*, together with *actions*, provide more complete, more understandable and much more appropriate models than primarily function-oriented models. As noted in Section 7.4, many systems are naturally data centred and focusing attention on their functions is simply looking at them from a narrow and blinkered point of view which ignores their more fundamental nature and structure. Having said that, however, there are many systems, for example in scientific and engineering computing, where a functional approach is entirely appropriate, fits the natural thinking of the application area, and can provide elegant solutions. It is no accident that by far the majority of systems developed since the advent of computers in the 1950s have been functionally oriented. The approach is much less popular, particularly in computer science circles, than it used to be, but there is as yet little empirical evidence to support the view that it should be discarded in all or most circumstances in favour of more modern approaches, such as object orientation.

The top-down approach has both advantages and disadvantages. An advantage is that it is goal oriented and focuses attention on the major functions. A disadvantage, from an analysis and structuring point of view, is that top-down decomposition into component functions is supposed to happen before the analyst knows what these component functions really involve. In other words, hierarchical structuring decisions, if they are truly made in a top-down manner, are made when one knows least about the later implications of those decisions. This is, in a sense, the opposite of functional abstraction in which lower level functions are generalised into larger, more abstract functions. The risk is that, being in a state of comparative ignorance about the implications of top-level structuring decisions, the developer may well not make the best decisions. One answer to this dilemma is to use top-down functional decomposition to structure a solution which has already been obtained, at least in principle, rather than to obtain the solution in the first place.

THE OBJECT-ORIENTED APPROACH   7.6

Fundamental concepts   7.6.1

Object-oriented techniques, concerned in the first instance with programming languages (notably SIMULA and Smalltalk), have existed for more than two decades. With the advent of the data-centred approach to systems analysis and design, accompanied by the enabling technologies of CASE and relational database schema generators, these techniques have evolved such that an object-oriented methodological paradigm now exists. There is some disagreement as to whether the emergence of object orientation in the software process has been an evolutionary occurrence, or whether this in fact represents a revolutionary departure from the 'traditional information flow' view of software development. We tend to support the former viewpoint. Although a software process centred around objects seems totally natural, and some have expressed dismay that the software industry has been so slow to realise the potential of this paradigm (Coad and Yourdon, 1990), it is unlikely that we would have reached this point had it not been for the use of these traditional methods (that is, those based on data and functional modelling). The acknowledgment of inadequacies associated with these approaches has therefore brought the software industry to the current position of support for the object-oriented paradigm. In this section we outline some of the characteristics of this paradigm as they relate to the software process.

There is a set of five basic ideas fundamental to the object-oriented paradigm:

- objects and classes
- methods
- encapsulation

- inheritance
- requests or messages.

Objects may be observable things, such as invoices, vehicles or customers, but may also be abstract concepts such as airline travel, goods delivery, or customer service. Booch (1994) suggests that an object must have state or form, behaviour and distinct identity. In effect, an object is any thing, which may be physical and observable or abstract, in which we store both data about the object and those operations, or **methods**, needed to process or manipulate that data. The methods associated with an object are essentially algorithmic procedures encoded and awaiting execution. This dual incorporation of data and process in a single object is referred to as **encapsulation**. Sets of objects that have characteristics (attributes and operations) in common are known as **object classes**. In the decomposition of classes into objects, objects at a lower level in the hierarchy by definition **inherit** the operations and attributes of their parent(s). (They are also able to incorporate data and/or operations specific to themselves.) This is illustrated in Figure 7.12.

FIGURE

7.12

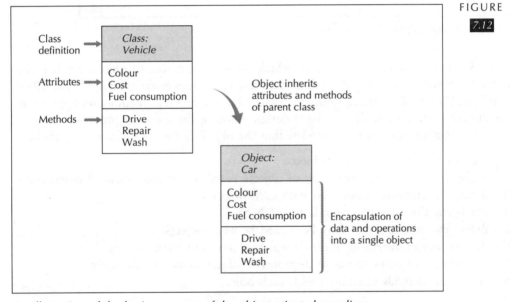

An illustration of the basic concepts of the object-oriented paradigm

In a definitional sense at this level the only difference between an object in this paradigm and an entity in the data-centred approach is that we do not store operations as part of entities in the latter paradigm. Furthermore, some object-oriented notations do not include details of operations in their graphical representation (for example, the notation used by Shlaer and Mellor (1988). Thus the distinction between ER modelling and object-oriented information modelling is in some cases minimal.

Requests are messages that are sent between objects to enable their activation. These requests are in the form of parameters issued from within application software (Figure 7.13).

Just as there are relationships between entities in the ER model of the data-centred paradigm, so there are connections between objects and object classes in the object-oriented approach. These connections indicate the existence of class decomposition

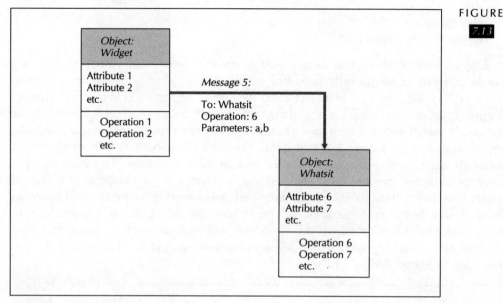

FIGURE

7.13

Object communication via messages

instantiation into objects. Cardinality, which shows the number of objects participating in the relationships, can be shown using the same techniques as are used in ER modelling. Similarly, PDL module descriptions, as discussed in the previous section, are appropriate object representations at the low-level design phase of the software process.

The following steps are common within the object-oriented development paradigm:

1. identify and define the core objects;
2. begin to construct the hierarchy of objects based on attribute/method inheritance;
3. define the attributes associated with each object;
4. determine the relevant methods for each object;
5. define the messages that may be passed between objects;
6. develop object interfaces, through which objects can communicate;
7. determine and refine the most appropriate object model for the system;
8. refine the methods associated with each object.

A number of related benefits can be attained if object-oriented techniques are used appropriately in the software process:

- *Modularity*—objects are inherently modular, owing to their incorporation of method and data. When performed correctly and to an appropriate level of abstraction, object-oriented design results in system representations that can be implemented through direct transformation in a chosen language. This overcomes, to some degree, one of the criticisms directed towards the data-centred development approach, that the emphasis is so much on data that process and function are 'forgotten' in the data-oriented paradigm.
- *Abstraction*—decomposition based on objects and object classes provides a natural mechanism for component abstraction, until self-contained and distinct class instances can be specified, modelled and implemented.
- *Information hiding*—data and operations specific to an object are hidden from other

objects, reducing the likelihood of inappropriate interaction among operations and data elements. Information hiding is generally an objective of the software design process, resulting in a less complex system model for use in subsequent development activities.

- *Reusability*—of all the benefits of object-oriented development, the promotion of component reusability is one of the strongest. With the inherent modularity of objects, and the encapsulation of data and process, object reuse is a clear goal associated with this paradigm. (As discussed previously, however, software reuse must be a managed function.)

Compared to both the data-centred and function-oriented development approaches, the object-oriented paradigm is relatively immature, and standards for both notation and use are still being formulated. This does not detract, however, from the potential that is already being realised under the object-oriented approach.

THE KNOWLEDGE-BASED APPROACH   7.7

Fundamental concepts   7.7.1

Computers are logical machines, performing arithmetic and logical manipulations according to rules. This process clearly assumes that the specification of what is to be performed, and how it is to be performed, can be expressed in these precise terms, and that the data required for this process is accurate, timely and complete. Given these circumstances, systems can be adequately defined, modelled, designed and implemented using the paradigms discussed in the sections above. However, when the situation does *not* match that just described—perhaps where data is unstructured or of questionable reliability, or where levels of uncertainty are involved in processing decisions—other techniques that are said to incorporate the application of knowledge may better serve application requirements. Whereas these approaches are likely to be excessively complicated for the development of traditional transaction processing and management information systems, they are especially applicable for what are normally termed decision support systems (DSS) and executive information systems (EIS).

This section is therefore concerned with techniques that often fall in the category of 'artificial intelligence'. However, since this term is poorly defined and widely misunderstood (Luger and Stubblefield, 1989), we have preferred to use the label 'knowledge-based'. This carries the implication that more than data and logic can be manipulated within software, but that this may not (yet) reach the bounds of intelligence. Although artificial intelligence as an entire discipline has received only scant praise for its endeavours in mimicking human behaviour, a number of subsets of the discipline have been shown to be very successful. We now consider some of them.

▪ Expert systems

Within specified domains, rule-based expert systems have proved their worth in assisting the non-expert user to make sometimes complex, multidimensional decisions that would otherwise have been impossible. Expert knowledge is a function of two components: an understanding of the concepts that make up the domain of interest, and a set of algorithms to solve problems within that domain. Thus a system can be said to be an expert system, according to Black (1986), either if it performs at or near the level of human experts, or if it may be applied effectively to complex problem areas that are normally the domain of human experts. In general, knowledge elicited from human experts in a given area is transcribed into production rules in a form something like the sample shown in Figure 7.14. Processing outcomes generated through rule-based inference are returned to the user normally as recommendations for a course of action. Some expert systems incorporate a degree of certainty or confidence that can be attached to the recommendations produced.

FIGURE

Opening text:
This knowledge base will recommend a hardware configuration likely to meet a user's application expectations, based on a set of criteria supplied by the user. If the criteria supplied are unrealistic (for example, you have under $500 to spend and you require a 486-based PC with a laser printer) then the system will not suggest a choice of systems—it will instead recommend that you rethink your requirements.

Closing text:
The following is a list of the configurations found to best suit your stated requirements. The prices shown are approximations only—special deals may be available.

Sample rule:

Rule Number: 88

IF:
       Cost is $2000–$2500
and   Preferred secondary storage is 160 Mb hard drive with one floppy drive
and   Required RAM is 4 Mb
THEN:
       We suggest a Widget 486, cost is $2200 approx., with 4 Mb RAM and a
       200 Mb hard drive. Probability = 7/10
and   We suggest a Whatsit 386SX, cost is $2000 approx., with 4 Mb RAM and
      a 170 Mb hard drive. Probability = 8/10

A sample set of expert system text and rules

Expert systems have been employed in a diverse range of application areas in which specific detailed knowledge is required. Among the more famous expert systems was MYCIN, developed as part of a Stanford University project during the 1970s. Its task was to advise on the diagnosis and treatment of infectious blood diseases based on data related to a patient's condition. Another was DENDRAL, a system designed to derive molecular structure from information on chemical bonds.

Although clearly useful, expert systems do have a downside. A number of deficiencies have been described by Luger and Stubblefield (1989).

1. The systems contain no 'deep' knowledge of the problem area—for example, the DENDRAL system has no real *understanding* of chemical compounds or structure.
2. Expert systems are generally unable to cope with novel circumstances.
3. They cannot effectively describe the rationale for a given recommendation because of the absence of deep knowledge.
4. It is difficult to prove that expert systems will operate as expected under all circumstances (this is, of course, an attribute of many systems).
5. The performance of expert systems does not improve as a function of time and/or use—'learning' does not occur.

6. Expert systems are often extremely sensitive to small variations in input data values or conditions.

The final two points are particularly important, as they are at least partially responsible for the development of more sophisticated knowledge-based approaches—neural networks and fuzzy systems.

■ Neural networks

Neural network systems, as their name suggests, are an adaptation of brain-like computation devices in massively parallel architectures. They are particularly useful in circumstances where the relationship(s) between input and output values are complex and multidimensional, or are simply unknown. In essence, neural networks are made up of four fundamental components—input units, weighted connections, (layers of) hidden units and output units. The relationship between these components is illustrated in Figure 7.15.

FIGURE

7.15

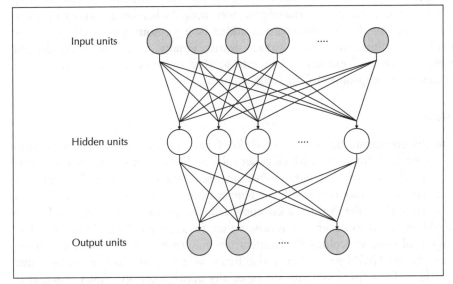

A three-layer neural network showing unit connections

The network receives input data/signals via the input units, causing connections to be 'fired' or activated according to the input values and the weightings associated with the connections. When threshold values are exceeded in the layers of computational or hidden units, further connections are activated until output values are produced at the output layer. This approach differs from that of traditional serial symbolic processing in that all the connections and their various weights contribute to each output value generated.

A network is generally only effective after it has been trained. A set of valid and correct input–output pairs are fed into the network for analysis. Based on the differences, or errors, generated between the expected outputs and the actual outputs, the network adjusts itself, in terms of the threshold values and the connection weights, until the extent of the error is minimised after an optimum amount of training. This process of adjustment is performed in many nets through back-propagation, that is, through feedback from the output units to the computational units. Once the network has been trained to an effective degree it should then be able to generalise the learnt relationship to produce reasonably accurate outputs for new inputs.

Neural networks have been successfully applied to perform complex pattern matching and non-linear prediction in a diverse range of domains, including image recognition, wine analysis and classification, medical diagnosis, and the analysis and prediction of software development effort. Others have also been used in the analysis of time-series data.

However, neural networks are not without their drawbacks. The networks are still sensitive to small adjustments in input parameters (Schoneburg, 1990), and obviously depend on the availability of precise data values for input to the model (compared to fuzzy systems, discussed in the next subsection). There is also a risk that a network may be overtrained so that the error is slowly decreased, but at the same time the generalisability of the model is consequently reduced. Neural networks still provide no degree of explanation for their processing—even if the connection weightings can be accessed, interpretation of this information is generally very difficult. Networks may also suffer from some amount of 'catastrophic forgetting', whereby a trained network cannot subsequently have further information added to it without greatly disrupting or even eliminating everything that it has already learnt. Finally, neural networks depend entirely on the existence of extensive data sets so that the models can be trained, a requirement that may be prohibitive in some domains.

■ Fuzzy systems

In relation to the comments on neural networks, fuzzy systems may be used to good effect within application domains in which exact rules and/or thresholds are not available or are not applicable, but where commonsense heuristics are appropriate. A simple but illustrative example of a fuzzy rule is: 'IF the temperature of the room is COLD, THEN heat output is HIGH'. Under a rule-based approach, the progression from 'COLD' to 'WARM' would be coded to occur at a precise value, for example 6°C. However, 6.1°C does not remove all sense of 'coldness'. Temperature may therefore be treated as a fuzzy variable. Similarly, the HIGH parameter is also fuzzy, as it may not have a precise value or range of values. Thus fuzzy systems are especially appropriate for 'noisy' data, that is, data that cannot be specified totally or precisely. Yet the systems are able to generalise under these conditions of uncertainty.

Fuzzy variables are, by their very nature, specified by membership functions rather than by specific data values. This is illustrated in Figure 7.16 for the concept of temperature. Under this approach you can have degrees of 'coldness' in a bell-like function, rather than as a set of discrete values within a precisely delineated range.

As an example, consider a program that automatically controls the washing time of an automatic washing machine based on two input variables—the 'dirtiness' of the clothes and the extent to which the clothes are greasy. There are no set rules for this task, but there are rules of thumb that may be implemented in a fuzzy system. Thus we need to specify the variables in terms of fuzzy membership functions and we need to specify some fuzzy rules. This then enables us to perform fuzzy inference to determine the washing duration. Dirtiness might therefore be specified as having the values of low, medium and high on a scale of 1 to 100. Similarly, washing time might be very short, short, medium, long, or very long on a scale of 1 to 60 minutes. One of our fuzzy rules

FIGURE

7.16

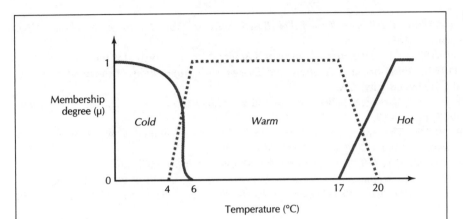

The membership function for the fuzzy variable, temperature

could then be 'IF dirtiness IS medium AND type IS very greasy THEN washtime IS very long'. Based on our membership function for wash time, an appropriate value for the degree of 'very long' can then be determined, and the washing cycle can proceed.

'Fuzzy logic' is currently a popular buzzword—it can even be seen and heard in advertisements for cars (in the control of gears). Other application areas include the control of air conditioning, automatic camera focusing, and also financial domains such as in the assessment of insurance risk.

Exercises

7.1 Why is the concept of software component reuse such an important consideration in terms of analysis and design productivity?

7.2 In terms of software quality assurance, discuss the strengths and weaknesses of the SEI CMM and ISO9000 approaches.

7.3 What are the similarities and distinguishing characteristics of the data- and function-oriented development paradigms?

7.4 Construct a normalised entity–relationship model illustrating the relationships between students, the courses they are taking, and the lecturers on each of those courses.

7.5 Discuss the characteristics and differences between the types of knowledge-based development approaches.

7.6 Comment on the potential of neural networks and fuzzy systems to overcome some traditionally intractable application problems. What obstacles exist to impair their widespread use?

References

Benwell, G. L., Firns, P. G. and Sallis, P. J. (1991) 'Deriving semantic data models from structured descriptions of reality', *Journal of Information Technology* **6**, pp. 15–25.

Black, W. J. (1986) *Intelligent Knowledge Based Systems.* Van Nostrand Reinhold (UK), Wokingham.

Boehm, B. W. (1978) *Characteristics of Software Quality.* Elsevier North-Holland, New York.

Booch, G. (1994) *Object-oriented Analysis and Design with Applications.* Benjamin/Cummings (2nd ed.), Redwood City, CA.

Brooks, F. P. Jr (1987) 'No silver bullet: Essence and accidents of software engineering', *Computer,* April 1987, pp. 10–19.

Chen, P. P. (1976) 'The entity–relationship model: Towards a unified view of data', *ACM Transactions on Database Systems,* **1** (1), March 1976, pp. 9–36.

Coad, P. and Yourdon, E. (1990) *Object-oriented Analysis.* Prentice-Hall, Englewood Cliffs, NJ.

Date, C. J. (1990) *An Introduction to Database Systems* (5th ed.). Addison-Wesley, Reading, MA.

Davis, A. M. (1993) *Software Requirements: Objects, Functions and States.* PTR Prentice-Hall, Englewood Cliffs, NJ.

DeMarco, T. (1978) *Structured Analysis and System Specification.* Prentice-Hall, Englewood Cliffs, NJ.

Gane, C. and Sarson, T. (1979) *Structured Systems Analysis: Tools and Techniques.* Prentice-Hall, Englewood Cliffs, NJ.

Gilb, T. (1988) *Principles of Software Engineering Management.* Addison-Wesley, Wokingham.

Harel, D. (1992) 'Biting the silver bullet. Toward a brighter future for system development', *Computer,* Jan. 1992, pp. 8–20.

Jackson, M. A. (1983) *System Development.* Prentice-Hall International, Englewood Cliffs, NJ.

Luger, G. F. and Stubblefield, W. A. (1989) *Artificial Intelligence and the Design of Expert Systems.* Benjamin/Cummings, Redwood City, CA.

Maiden, N. A. and Sutcliffe, A. G. (1992) 'Exploiting reusable specifications through analogy'. *Communications of the ACM,* **35** (4), April 1992, pp. 55–64.

Mantha, R. W. (1987) 'Data flow and data structure modeling for database requirements determination: A comparative study'. *MIS Quarterly,* December 1987, pp. 531–45.

March, S. T. (Ed.) (1988) *Entity–relationship Approach.* IEEE Computer Society Press, Washington.

McFadden, F. R. and Hoffer, J. A. (1988) *Database Management* (2nd ed.). Benjamin/Cummings, Menlo Park, CA.

Nielson, J. (1993) *Usability Engineering.* AP Professional, Boston, MA.

Pfleeger, S. L. (1991) *Software Engineering: The Production of Quality Software.* Macmillan, New York.

Potter, W. D. and Trueblood, R. P. (1988) 'Traditional, semantic and hyper-semantic approaches to data modelling'. *Computer,* June 1988, pp. 53–63.

Pronto User Manual, (1994) Department of Information Science, University of Otago, Dunedin, NZ.

Sanden, B. (1989) 'Entity–life modeling and structured analysis in real-time software design—a comparison'. *Communications of the ACM* **32** (12), December 1989, pp. 1458–66.

Schoneburg, E. (1990) 'Stock prediction using neural networks: A project report' *Neurocomputing* **2** (1), pp. 17–27.

Shlaer, S. and Mellor, S. J. (1988) *Object-oriented Systems Analysis: Modeling the World in Data.* Prentice-Hall, Englewood Cliffs, NJ.

Software Engineering Institute, Carnegie-Mellon University, 'Capability maturity model for software, Version 1.1' by Mark C. Paulk, Bill Curtis, Mary Beth Chrissis and Charles V. Weber, Technical Report CMU/SEI-93-TR-24 and 'Key practices of the capability maturity model, Version 1.1' by Mark C. Paulk, Charles V. Weber, Suzanne M. Garcia, Mary Beth Chrissis and Marilyn Bush, Technical Report CMU/SEI-93-TR-25 (Feb. 1993).

Yourdon, E. (1989) '12 silver bullets'. *American Programmer* **2** (1), January 1989, pp. 14–16.

CHAPTER 8

Implementation

THE TRADITIONAL ROLE OF SOURCE CODE AS THE ONLY DEFINITIVE SYSTEM DOCUMENTATION

Because of the voluminous nature of difficult-to-change (pre-word-processor) system design documents, the operational computer programs as represented by their source code became *de facto* the only reliable and up-to-date system description. The quality of those descriptions was therefore a direct reflection of the quality of programming style and structure, particularly the use of consistent data names and variable names. Other 'internal documentation', such as comment lines and procedure names that related to system processes and subprocesses, were of critical importance to the quality of 'understandability' that each program reflected.

None of the need for high quality program documentation has diminished, but reliance on programs as the only definitive documentation source has been replaced to a large extent by advances in technology. The word processor, and consequently the ease of amendment of documents, is one reason for this, but a much more significant impact in so far as high quality documentation is concerned, is obtainable through the use of computer-aided software engineering (CASE) tools. These tools, described in some detail in Chapter 9, enable changes to system specifications to occur in the documentation *before* the programs are written. At any time, therefore, the documentation, in terms of data structure and data flow, or the occurrence of data names or other process-related labels, should be up to date and reflect the system as it then exists.

MAINTAINING CONSISTENCY BETWEEN PROCESS PHASES AND PRODUCTS

The use of CASE tools does not, of course, entirely remove the difficulties of keeping programming code in step with the design. Owing to the iterative nature of software development and the reality that some tasks occur simultaneously, it is inevitable that some programming will be undertaken while design that may affect it is evolving at a different rate elsewhere in the development process. Frequent reviews of programs and design phases (monitoring of the development process) is, we believe, the only satisfactory method of avoiding disaster caused by this inherent out-of-step characteristic of the software process. It may not be possible to eliminate this phenomenon, but at least we can attempt to control and manage it (also see Section 4.3 for a discussion on software configuration management (SCM)).

System size is a major factor in the complexity issues associated with keeping code in step with design. The larger the program, the more complex it becomes. The difficulties of program design and construction for large-scale systems are so well realised that the term 'programming in the large' has emerged as a meaningful label in systems development.

An increasingly popular method of monitoring the relationship between program code, design specifications and actual requirements is known as 'forward and backward traceability'. An early successful method for this kind of monitoring was Yourdon's 'structured walk-through' approach (Yourdon et al., 1979). Errors and inconsistencies were detected but not necessarily corrected at the time of discovery. This approach was based on the understanding that if corrections were made 'on the fly' the programs were even more likely to get out of step with the products already developed. Errors were rectified in a controlled fashion as part of a software configuration control process. Design consistency and, in turn, requirements consistency, is maintained by having all participants in the building and use of the system present when the programmer or programming team walk-through their source code. Fagan's Inspection Method (Fagan, 1976), mentioned in Chapter 4, is another approach to the walk-through philosophy. Fagan's approach is directed towards those products developed late in the process; in terms of the 'waterfall' software process, Pfleeger (1991) provides the graphical representation of component traceability shown in Figure 8.1.

Traceability in action requires that a measure be employed to determine the difference between what was stated in the original requirements specification and what is produced in the software. Such a measure with worked examples appears in the appendix entitled 'Measures for Reliable Software' in the IEEE publication *Software Engineering Standards* (Std 982.2-1988) (IEEE, 1988). This paper states that the measure proposed aids in identifying requirements that are either missing from, or in addition to, the original requirements. Each requirement met by the software architecture is counted (R1), as is each original requirement (R2). To compute the traceability measure (TM), the following formula is used:

$$TM = \frac{R1}{R2} \times 100\%$$

If all the original requirements are met in the software, the traceability measure is 100%. Anything less means that some requirements are not present in the software. It may be that the resulting software contains more functionality than the original requirements specified. Indeed, new requirements may have been added after the original specification. Such cases obviously require further investigation. The reader is urged to refer to the IEEE publication for examples of this measure in action and accordingly to follow up the citations there to its application for specifying complex systems.

FIGURE

8.1

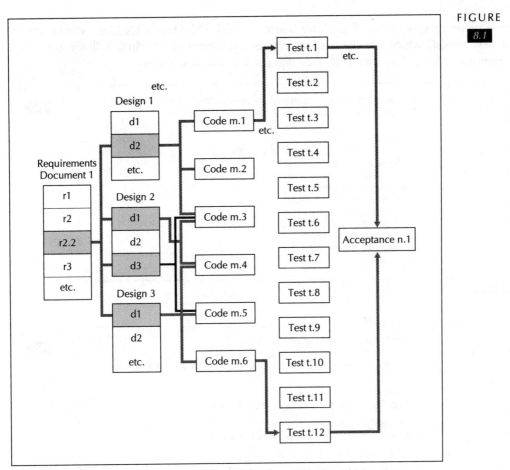

Component traceability through the software process (Pfleeger, 1991)

CODE GENERATORS—THEIR FUNCTIONS AND LIMITATIONS

The automatic generation of programs, and of application systems as a whole, has been considered for a number of years to be the most promising solution to the software crisis. With the advent of fourth generation languages came claims of development without the need for programmers—systems would simply be the final product of a high-level product description. To a small degree, this vision has eventuated. Certainly, within the business application domain, 4GL tools have reduced the need for volumes of high-level language code. Moreover the effective use of tools such as screen and report painters has significantly reduced coding demands, at least in terms of a system's user interface. But what of the data and processing that are the key to a system's operation?

A significant amount of progress has been made in recent years in automatic database schema generation. A large number of CASE tools incorporating this feature are now widely available. For example, *Pronto* is a Macintosh application that assists with the analysis phase of the software process by providing tools for creating and editing ERMs and their associated data dictionaries. It also assists with the implementation phase by generating PDL (Powerhouse) or SQL (ANSI or VAX SQL) schemas from a data model, which can be used to create a database using PhD, Rdb or any other relational DBMS that uses SQL (see Figures 8.2 and 8.3 below).

```
! Schema definition generated by Pronto. Ver. 1.0b4
! SQL definition adheres to ANSI standard SQL
        ⋮
! Developer: SMac
! Generated: 15 June 1994 at 2:21:59 pm
! Create Schema Statement
Create Schema Filename SmythesBuildingBlocks;
Create table Customer
    (AddressLine1 CHAR(20),
    AddressLine2 CHAR(20),
    CustomerNumber CHAR(4) NOT NULL,
    FirstName CHAR(20),
    Surname CHAR(20),
        etc.
```

FIGURE
8.2

ANSI standard SQL code generated by the Pronto CASE tool

```
; PDL—Powerhouse Definition Language.
; Schema Generated by Pronto. Ver. 1.0b4
; PDL/Powerhouse registered trademarks of COGNOS Corp.
        ⋮
; Developer: SMac
; Generated : 15 June 1994 at 2:22:43 pm

; Create the dictionary
Create Dictionary SmythesBuildingBlocks

; Specify elements before files
Element AddressLine1 character Size 20
Element AddressLine2 character Size 20
        ⋮
; Files in the database can now be defined
File Customer &
    Organization Indexed &
    Create

Record Customer
    Item AddressLine1
    Item AddressLine2
    Item AddressLine3
    Item CustomerNumber
    Item FirstName
    Item Phone
    Item Surname
    Item Town

    Index CustomerNumber unique ascending
    Segment CustomerNumber
```

FIGURE
8.3

Powerhouse data dictionary definitions as generated by Pronto

Processing code is normally generated direct from functional descriptions of one form or another, usually some form of pseudocode or structured representation of the interactions between system functions and the data elements that are to be processed. Given that these process descriptions are rigorously developed, we can be confident that the generated code will always be *syntactically* correct. We still need to ensure, however, that it is *functionally* adequate. One example of a functional representation that forms the basis for code generation is the *action diagram*. This is essentially a graphical depiction of detailed program logic—an example is shown in Figure 8.4.

FIGURE

8.4

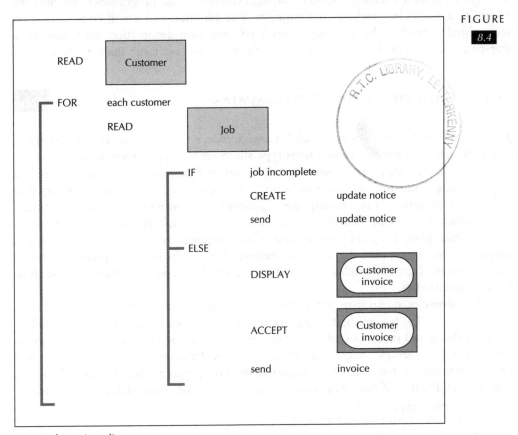

A sample action diagram

Thus the action diagram incorporates graphical and pseudocode-like constructs to describe system functionality. This type of representation can then be directly translated into source code with screen maps and database access calls.

Code generation, like many single tools and techniques, is no panacea. Tools currently available perform a valuable function in the development of relatively small and simple applications, for example, a customer/order database for a small retail outlet, with well-defined data entry, enquiry and reporting functions. For large and/or complex systems, however, the capabilities of code generators remain limited. Furthermore there is still some question as to whether code generation, based on highly detailed process descriptions, provides any significant savings in effort over manual coding from higher-level design representations.

Post-implementation maintenance requirements, as well as requirements for processing efficiency, must also be considered when assessing the worth of code generation. If maintenance is to be carried out on the code itself, one must be sure that the automatically generated programs attain standards of modifiability. If this is not the case, then any savings in effort achieved through the use of the generation tool may be lost in the maintenance phase. In relation to the issue of efficiency, it may be that the priority of a particular system (apart from its functional adequacy) is minimum resource usage. Programs generated by a tool are unlikely to be optimised to the same degree as might be achieved through manual coding, especially if the programmer can tune the system to a particular machine configuration. The adoption and use of code generation tools should therefore be carefully considered—program automation may only be a stop-gap solution which in the long run could prove to cost more than it saves.

THE GOALS OF GOOD PROGRAMMING   8.4

Jerry Smith (1990) in his book *Reusability and Software Construction: C and* C++ states that although software engineering texts typically cover non-programming aspects of the software process ('life cycles', systems analysis and design, process management and so on), software construction was now worthy of inclusion. He makes the point that software construction is not merely 'good programming' in terms of taking advantage of a particular computer's architecture. He refers to 'trick programming' as passé, arguing that 'good programming' is that which produces *readable, maintainable* and *reusable* code. We support this view and believe that for the software process to attain the objectives of greater productivity and higher quality, code must have at least these three characteristics.

The advent of declarative programming languages (often called fourth generation languages or 4GLs) has brought about improvements in each of the areas of readability, maintainability and reusability of code. The very program statements themselves promote readability. For example, ACCESS EMPLOYEES is a valid Powerhouse 4GL[1] file access and open statement. In fact, an entire report-generating program that makes full use of system defaults, one of the more advantageous features of some 4GLs, might read:

```
ACCESS EMPLOYEES
REPORT NAME, DATE-OF-BIRTH, GENDER
GO
```

Through the addition of sort and select statements, this program can take on the appearance of a complex process definition, but one that concentrates on 'what to compute' rather than 'how to compute' the results. For example:

```
ACCESS EMPLOYEES
SORT ON GENDER
SELECT IF GENDER = "F" &
DATE-OF-BIRTH  > "01-01-40"
REPORT NAME
GO
```

could be a program to determine the names of those women in a particular organisation who are entitled by reason of age to an increase in pension allowance, annual leave entitlement, or perhaps the offer of early retirement.

Whatever the example, programs of this form are infinitely more readable than

---

1   Powerhouse is a registered trademark of Cognos International.

many of their 3GL contemporaries. The readability is supplemented in most declarative languages by brevity, adding clarity to the completed code and thereby enabling it to be more effectively maintained. Furthermore, this brevity and clarity brings a simplicity to complex process definitions that generates the potential for reusing the code in future applications. An added advantage, and perhaps the one of most significance, is that the de-emphasis on programming effort is reflected in a greater emphasis on the problem analysis and system design processes.

IMPLEMENTATION VERIFICATION   *8.5*

Verifying, or *proving*, the behaviour of programs has always been the pursuit of programmers. This was mainly an 'informal' activity until the late 1960s and early 1970s, when a flurry of 'formal' methods were proposed and many 'proven programs' were published (for example, see Foly and Hoare, 1971), but much earlier, programmers were aware of the need to verify software in terms of its correctness. In part, this correctness relates to core published algorithms that emanate from computational theory and are mathematically provable; these algorithms are independent of specific problem solutions. An example of such a proof is cited in Berg et al. (1982) and concerns an additive program for realising the product of two numbers. The procedure MULTIPLY below is defined as having three parameters; A and B are inputs and represent the values to be multiplied, whereas R is the output parameter.

```
MULTIPLY (A,B,R)
    begin
        R:= 0; X:=B;
        while X NEQ 0 do
        begin
            R:=R+A;
            X:=X-1;
        end
    end MULTIPLY
```

This procedure written in the ALGOL language can be formally specified as:

$$\{B>0\}R:=0;X:=B\{X=B \text{ and } R=0 \text{ and } B>0\}^+$$

Although we do not go further with this proof, it can be seen that to reduce large programs manually to their verifiable 'proof syntax' could in many cases take a significantly large amount of time. Automatic proofing has therefore greatly enhanced the feasibility and potential of this activity and a great deal of work in developing programs that verify other programs is evidenced in the computer science literature. The reader is encouraged to follow citations from the text quoted above and other more recently published work if this area is of interest.

THE CLEANROOM APPROACH   *8.6*

Developed at IBM in the early 1980s, the Cleanroom approach to software development has at its heart the issue of certifiable reliability: 'The Cleanroom software development approach is intended to produce highly reliable software by integrating formal methods for specification and design, non-execution-based program development, and statistically based independent testing' (Selby et al., 1987). This process is described graphically by Linger (1994) in the diagram shown in Figure 8.5.

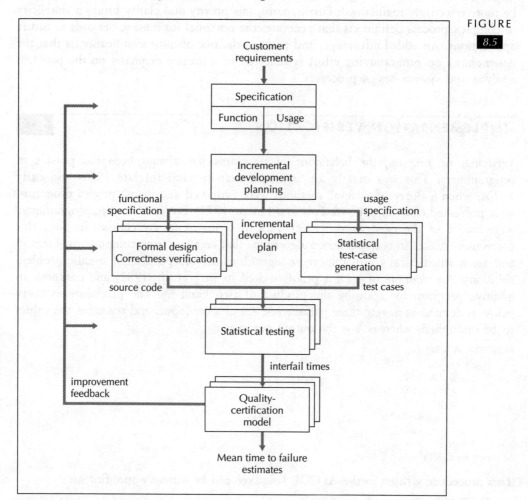

FIGURE

8.5

The Cleanroom software process (Linger, © 1994 IEEE)

The term *Cleanroom* relates to the goal of allowing no errors to enter the software product, with the primary objective of producing zero-defect systems. Furthermore, proponents of the Cleanroom approach suggest that, apart from attaining significant improvements in quality, real gains in productivity can also be achieved. The major components of Linger's Cleanroom process (Linger, 1994) are as follows:

(a) Specification

This is a collaboration between a development team and a certification team, resulting in the production of both functional and usage specifications. The functional specification is a definition of system behaviour under all circumstances, and is the basis for the subsequent incremental development of the system. The usage specification defines all possible usage states, again under both normal and unanticipated circumstances. This 'model' forms the baseline for determining test case adequacy under the requirements for statistical quality assurance.

(b) Incremental development planning

Again in collaboration, the two teams determine an appropriate plan for the phased development of the system.

(c) Design and verification

A repeated process of design-correctness verification is then performed by the development team for each product increment. At the same time, the certification team develops appropriate usage-oriented test cases for each progressive component.

(d) Quality certification

This is an ongoing procedure within the Cleanroom software process. Initially, high-level components are passed to the certification team for verification. This helps to ensure that development effort (and rework) associated with lower-level product blocks is minimised, in that inaccuracies in the high-level product can be identified before significant time has been invested in the development of its subcomponents. The test cases are run against the system, with quality indicators, for example, the elapsed time between failures, collected throughout.

(e) Feedback

Any errors encountered during verification are passed back to the development team for repair. This procedure, like the entire Cleanroom process, is iterative, continuing until the required standards of quality are achieved.

The result of this process is said to be systems of significantly higher quality, at least when first delivered (Hevner et al., 1992). Whereas software typically results in around 30 errors per thousand lines of code (KLOC) at unit test time, the results of seventeen Cleanroom developments produced an average of 2.3 errors/KLOC. The process itself may take longer, but savings in maintenance requirements make the Cleanroom approach an attractive option for large-system development with stringent reliability constraints.

CODE REUSE   8.7

In Section 8.4 on good programming, Smith's (1990) proposals concerning software construction are outlined. He focuses on code reusability in the construction process and takes some care to discuss the attributes of declarative languages in this respect. With 4GLs he points out that procedural details are left to the language translator, thus freeing system developers for more extensive problem analysis and other organisational tasks. Reviewing the object-oriented programming (OOP) paradigm, he points out that proponents see reusability in this domain as being due to its emphasis on abstraction and derivation. He says, 'A fundamental notion of OOP is that of factoring an application in terms of its critical data structures, or objects, and then bundling these objects with the mechanisms or methods that are required for their manipulation.' This is how the OOP approach takes advantage of the declarative paradigm.

The C language, and more especially C++, takes advantage of the declarative paradigm by reducing surface-level complexity through data-hiding techniques—reusing existing code modules and data structures, with their inherent complexity, and merely calling them as objects from the top level. In this sense we would not see OOP as a new paradigm. Indeed, binding external code modules into main programs has been a conventional technique for constructing well-organised programs for more than two decades. The declarative paradigm adds the dimension of readability (and we would say, hence maintainability) thus providing a realistic environment for code reusability.

> 'Software reuse is the application of a variety of kinds of knowledge about one system to another similar system in order to reduce the effort of development and maintenance of that other system. This realised knowledge includes artifacts such as domain knowledge, development experience, design decisions, architectural structures, requirements, designs, code, documentation, and so forth.' (Biggerstaff and Perlis, 1989).

Biggerstaff and Perlis (1989) talk of the concept of code reusability as being full of great promise that has largely been unfulfilled to date. They do say, and we agree, that the reuse of programming code has had some success, whereas the reuse of design specifications has not (see Section 7.1). This could be due to business-oriented matters, such as industrial secrecy and competitive advantage, but is as likely to be due to the poor construction of written specifications, as to any other factor. Ambiguity of language, incompleteness, and a lack of timeliness are, we believe, among the principal causes of analysis and design specifications not being reusable. To some extent, perhaps eventually a large extent, the use of CASE tools that incorporate more formal systems specifications may change this situation. If reusability is widely considered to be a key to improving productivity and quality in the software process, as Biggerstaff and Perlis propose, components of *all* the products in a system (not just code) will need to be potentially reusable. Freed from having to write all the components (or 'symbols') from scratch, the developer should be able to spend more effort on organising those components to suit the solution to a variety of problems. If this occurs, perhaps the so-called 'templates method' of Volpano and Kieburtz in Biggerstaff and Perlis (1989) as depicted in Figure 8.6 will allow the meshing of code fragments to provide cohesive systems that are readable, maintainable, and reusable within a process that encourages and enables high productivity.

Exercises

8.1 Discuss why it is important to keep code in step with design, with particular reference to techniques for assuring code quality.

8.2 What impact have code generators made on software product quality and process productivity and what implementation characteristics have emerged from their use?

8.3 To what extent have fourth-generation languages promoted the goals of good programming?

8.4 The cleanroom approach to software development requires measurable indicators of reliability to be identified. Discuss some of the difficulties associated with the establishment of such indicators.

FIGURE

8.6

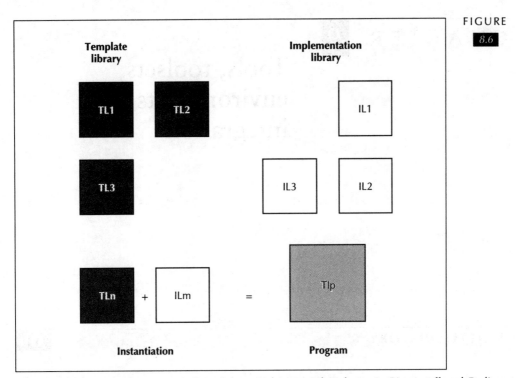

The templates method concept (adapted from Volpano and Kieburtz in Biggerstaff and Perlis, 1989)

References

Berg, H. K. Boebert, W. E., Franta, W. R. and Mohrer, T. G. (1982) *Formal Methods of Program Verification and Specification.* Prentice-Hall, Englewood Cliffs, NJ.

Biggerstaff, T. J. and Perlis, A. J. (1989) *Software Reusability: Vol. 1, Concepts and Models.* ACM Press, New York, NY.

Fagan, M. (1976) 'Design and code inspections to reduce errors in program development', *IBM Systems Journal,* **15** (3).

Foly, M. and Hoare, C. (1971) 'Proof of a recursive program—Quicksort' *Computer,* **14** (4).

Hevner, A. R., Becker, S. A. and Pedowitz, L. B. (1992) 'Integrated CASE for cleanroom development', *IEEE Software,* March 1992, pp. 69–76.

IEEE (1988) 'Measures for reliable software', in *IEEE Software Engineering Standards* (Std 982.2-1988). IEEE Press.

Linger, R. C. (1994) 'Cleanroom process model', *IEEE Software,* March 1994, pp. 50–8.

Pfleeger, S. L. (1991) *Software Engineering: The Production of Quality Software,* Macmillan, New York.

Selby, R. W., Basili, V. R. and Baker, F. T. (1987) 'Cleanroom software development: An empirical evaluation', *IEEE Transactions on Software Engineering,* **13** (9), September 1987, pp. 1027–37.

Smith, J. D. (1990) *Reusability and Software Construction: C and C++.* Wiley, New York, NY.

Yourdon, E., Gane, C., Sarson, T. and Lister, T. L. (1979) *Learning to Program in Structured COBOL.* Prentice-Hall, Inc., Englewood Cliffs. NJ.

CHAPTER 9

Tools, toolsets, environments and integration

Our concern in this chapter is with computer assistance for software development. By analogy with other trades, a piece of software which is used to aid the development or crafting of other software is called a **software tool**. Software tools have a long history, extending at least from the 1950s when **basic assembler** programs were produced to assist the computer program coding process. Basic assemblers allowed programmers to write in a simple symbolic language rather than directly in machine language, using symbolic **operation codes**, such as SUB instead of 010010 (or whatever the machine code for subtract was on the machine to be used) and symbolic **operands**, such as DISCNT, to refer to locations where relevant data items (such as a discount amount) were stored, instead of having to specify the binary **machine address** or location number of that data. An assembler program, or tool, was then used to translate the symbolic program written by (and understandable by) the programmer into machine code understandable by the machine. Another tool, called a **loader**, actually placed the program in the machine, replacing the loader itself, and handed over control to the loaded program for execution.

Soon after the invention of basic assembler languages, more sophisticated **macro assembler** languages and the first **high-level languages**, such as FORTRAN (originally FORmula TRANslation), **COBOL** (COmmon Business Oriented Language) and **Algol** (ALGOrithmic Language) were developed with their **compilers, linkers** and loaders. Macro-assemblers allowed some degree of procedural abstraction through the construction of macros which, in a similar way to subroutines, grouped a number of basic instructions into a higher level, or more abstract instruction. FORTRAN and COBOL were commonly used high-level (or **third generation**) languages, still very much in evidence today, though much expanded and altered from their initial forms. Assemblers have sometimes been called **second generation** languages to distinguish them from **first generation,** or machine languages, and third generation languages. Algol was important as the first language whose syntax was formally defined. Though it is now seldom if ever used, it is the precursor from which the commonly used languages **Pascal** and **Modula 2** have been developed. Linkers are used to combine several separately compiled program units (subroutines, procedures, functions, modules and the like) with unresolved references to other separately compiled program units into a single executable program. It is worth noting that the first libraries of reusable modules (typically called subroutine libraries in those days) date from the early 1960s, if not earlier.

Since those early days the number of tools built to aid software development processes has been legion. We will not review them, which is a massive job, even at the summary level. We merely note several types of tools of interest to the current state of software tool use and research.

OPERATING SYSTEMS—THE UNIX ENVIRONMENT 9.2

As computers grew beyond single-program control and began to handle multiple complex input/output functions, through devices such as punched card and paper tape readers and punches, printers, magnetic tape drives and disk storage, **input–output control systems** and **operating systems** were developed (again around or soon after 1960) for computer resource management. These operating system tools were the distant precursors of **DOS**, **Windows**, **Windows NT**, **UNIX**, and so on. Inevitably, a number of utilities, or software tools, accumulated around operating systems, extending their usefulness by providing a number of additional generic functions, such as text editing.

UNIX was the first operating system to attract a sufficient number of such utilities to form a respectable and easily extensible tool set, and to earn the name of 'the UNIX environment'. Other than in this section, however, we will use the term environment in a different and wider sense. Some features of the UNIX environment warrant inclusion here. In describing them, we view UNIX from the software engineer's point of view, that is, as a framework for the construction and use of tools for software engineering purposes. We do not view it from an operating systems perspective. What, then, does UNIX have to offer the software engineer?

A useful box of existing tools 9.2.1

Apart from a comprehensive set of status, or 'what's going on' utilities, and file management utilities, both of which are tools to support general computer use rather than specific software engineering tasks, perhaps the most commonly used UNIX utilities are text-file utilities. These include editors and simple tools for printing, sorting, rearranging, encrypting and comparing text files. There is also a character, word and line counting utility, one for pattern matching which uses **regular expression** patterns, one for checking spelling, and a group of sophisticated text formatting tools used in text preparation for typesetting or printing.

Of considerable importance to software engineers working within a UNIX frame-work are several general **configuration management** tools, such as *make* and *sccs* (source code control system). Programs, particularly large programs, are typically composed of a number of modules. During development or maintenance, programmers may work on specific separate modules that need attention. These amended modules must then be reintegrated into the large programs or subsystems that use them for system testing and operation. The problem of 'putting all the pieces together again' so that the resulting large program is consistent and complete can be solved using *make*. A *make* file essentially contains a recipe for putting all the pieces together again in the right order into the correct overall structure, but saving time and effort by recompiling only those modules that have been altered since the last time the large program was reconstructed. Without a tool such as *make*, the software engineer would have to go through long, error-prone sessions at the workbench, actually putting the pieces together him/herself instead of specifying once and for all how to make or assemble the large program out of its components. The tool *make* is not only of use for program construction, it can also be used to construct any complex file structure, such as a large report, out of its constituent items. *sccs* is a tool for version control which effectively provides an audit trail of changes and revisions of a file. It also keeps track of who is working on (or allowed to work on) specific revisions of the file. As with *make*, *sccs* was designed with program development in mind, but is also applicable to reports, documentation and specifications.

As one might expect, there is also a number of more specific programming aids for those programming in C. What we have mentioned, however, is only a small selection of the existing tools available to software engineers on a typical UNIX system.

A simple tool composition mechanism 9 . 2 . 2

UNIX has a simple, but very convenient and heavily used mechanism for tool composition, or applying a sequence of tools to a data file. For example, one might wish to apply the following sequence of tools to a program file:

a: a program formatter which arranges each statement (appropriately indented) on a separate line;
b: remove all comments;
c: select all lines containing 'goto';
d: count the lines in the resulting file.

The result would be a count of the number of 'goto' statements in the program.

This can be easily done in UNIX using a 'piped' sequence of commands looking something like:

a progfile I b I grep goto I wc – *l*

where program a formats progfile, program b takes the formatted program file as input and removes comments from it, program grep (c) selects all the goto statements from the formatted non-comment file and program wc (d), using the – *l* or linecount option, counts the lines in the resulting selected goto statement file.

The UNIX metaphor for this type of tool composition is the pipe. Programs a, b, c and d are thought of as filters in a pipeline. Process a, however, is scarcely a filter, except perhaps in the sense that it 'cleans up' progfile. Tool composition is possible in UNIX because, if not otherwise specified, tools have a standard input and a standard output. The standard output of any tool can become the standard input of any other tool, thus giving tool composition. There is also provision for redirection so that instead of taking its input from the standard input, a tool can take it from a specified file, and instead of placing its output on the standard output, a tool can write it to a specified file.

The pipe concept allows compositions of simple generic tools to be used (with suitable options and parameters) to achieve some quite complex processing in a surprisingly simple manner.

Flexible nested tool use 9.2.3

UNIX has a uniform framework for the creation, execution, stacking and termination of processes. A UNIX **shell** is a convenient user interface (among other things) to the UNIX operating system. From the point of view of a software developer or maintainer, all programs, including UNIX shells, utilities, tools and application programs are processes. Where appropriate, UNIX tools have an 'escape to shell' facility. This allows the user to leave the current tool temporarily, use the shell to invoke other tools, and so on, to a nesting depth sufficient for most users. On exit from each current process the suspended process (which was the one left in order to execute the current process) is taken up at the point where it was left. From the point of view of a user of software tools, this means that a software engineer in a UNIX environment can conveniently switch back and forth between tools as required.

Tool use programming 9.2.4

For repetitive use of tools or tool combinations in more complex ways than are permitted by the simple mechanism of pipes, UNIX provides convenient shell programming facilities using one or more of the common UNIX shells, such as the C shell or the Bourne shell. Shell programs allow users to construct new and more powerful shell commands at will. For software engineers, this means that tools can readily be combined, or constrained as the case may be, in predetermined ways using whatever logic is appropriate to the software process being supported by those tools. In this role, shell programs are candidates for software process programming.

TOOLS, TOOLSETS AND ENVIRONMENTS 9.3

It is now appropriate for us to define the concepts that are the subject of this chapter. A multiple-level tool model is defined by Schefström and van den Broek (1993). We will define concepts from the lowest level up.

A **service** is the smallest thing of interest to a developer. It is some piece of software that does something of use to the software engineer.

A **tool** is a strongly related and clearly delimited set of services that a developer regards as supporting a particular job. Examples include diagram editors, such as a data-flow diagram editor, a data model editor or a Booch diagram editor. The relevant definition in Schefström and van den Broek (1993) is: 'A tool is a set of services that show strong internal cohesion and low external coupling.'

Similarly, a **toolset** is a set of tools that show strong internal cohesion and low external coupling. A toolset is typically a group of tools that work together to cover part of the development process, for example, a compiler and its associated syntax-directed editor and debugger, or a group consisting of a data-model editor, a data-flow diagram editor, a structure-diagram editor and a dictionary.

Continuing with the same theme, an **environment** is a group of toolsets that shows strong internal cohesion and low external coupling.

As the scope of the support entity widens from a single tool to a large environment, the degree of cohesion among its components will inevitably decrease. At the same time their coupling may also decrease, or at least not increase. The primary reason for this is that, as the support scope widens, the range of support activities diversifies. Software development planning, for example, will use a very different toolset from software construction (programming, integration and testing).

Schefström and van den Broek also distinguish a **framework** as 'a set of software modules that is expected to be of interest to several tools and is therefore especially well-documented and supported.' The framework can be regarded as a base set of common reusable software services. In this sense, the so-called UNIX environment is more of a framework than an environment.

Figure 9.1 (based on Schefström and van den Broek, 1993) illustrates these concepts.

FIGURE

9.1

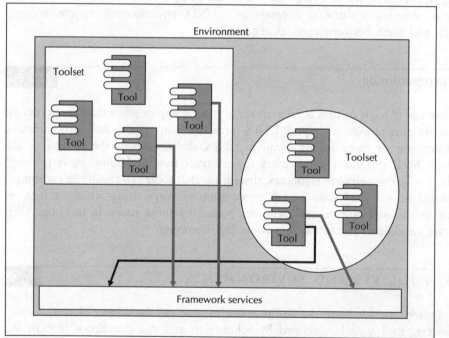

A hierarchy of software support entities

SOME TYPICAL TOOLS 9.4

Diagram editors 9.4.1

In the interests of visualisation, and hence better understanding of software processes, diagrams are used extensively to support all stages of development, but particularly the design stage. Examples include: for structured design, data-flow diagrams, data models and structure charts; for JSD/JSP, entity structure or life history diagrams, system specification diagrams and JSP structure diagrams; for object-oriented approaches, Booch diagrams (Booch, 1994), HOOD diagrams (HOOD User Group, 1992), Buhr diagrams (Buhr, 1984); and so on. Rather than using a general graphics or diagramming tool, it is more user friendly and efficient to use a specific editor for each type of diagram. A diagram-specific editor 'understands' the structure of the diagram type that it supports, and hence it can offer to the user at each stage just those facilities needed. It can also impose integrity constraints, assist with diagram layout, and generally minimise the time and effort a user takes to construct or change a well-presented and syntactically correct diagram of that type. The 'things' depicted in diagrams drawn with diagram editors usually have wider system significance, so their names, structural details and diagram relationships are not restricted to the diagram editor, but are entered into a more widely accessible dictionary as well.

Dictionary/repository   9.4.2

Development support dictionaries were first called data dictionaries because they recorded details of all the items of data created or referred to while using diagram editors or other tools. However, the contents of such dictionaries have been expanded to include information about other development items, such as entities, relationships, objects, processes, operations, external agents, and many others. The dictionary typically contains all the essential information abstracted from the diagram editors, that is, the names, attributes and logical relationships. In some cases the dictionary, or repository, is a central, unifying or integrating tool, used by all other tools. In other cases it is in some sense distributed. We consider the more general problem of sharing essential development data between different development tools in Section 9.5 under the subject of data integration.

Construction/code generation   9.4.3

The diagram editors and dictionary tools contain much information, such as data models/views; structure diagrams; screen, window and form layouts; and data definitions, which can be used directly to generate code for executable system components (also see Section 8.3). Database schemas and subschemas can be generated from data models, views and dictionary entries; program structures from structure diagrams; large parts of screen, window and report programs from the corresponding layouts, and dictionary entries. Detailed, application-specific procedural coding still has to be fitted into these program structures, as well as any database optimisation that may be required. However, if the process specifications which accompany structure diagrams are formal, then code can be generated from them also. Thus, much of the coding and, more importantly, most of the essential structural code, can be generated from design information, thus ensuring consistency of code and design and substantially reducing both coding effort and errors (assuming the design is good). This is true whether we use structured analysis and design, object-oriented methods (with or without real time extensions in both cases), or data-centred methods such as information engineering (Finkelstein, 1989).

DIMENSIONS OF INTEGRATION 9.5

Tool integration within software engineering is different in one important respect from the provision of a general set of inter-operable services such as in a client-server situation. In software engineering we usually have a single product of interest which itself exhibits a high degree of integration. This is not always the case. We may, for example, be developing a set of related but independent services for a client-server system. Even then, however, each service will normally be highly cohesive and integrated. Developers will frequently want to view or browse the structure of the developing system as a whole from various perspectives, for example, data structures, process structures, presentation objects, and to 'drill down' in order to view components of interest in more detail. They will also want to work independently on a specific component, applying a number of related and possibly overlapping tools to the development or rework of that component. Even in this case, however, they will be interested in at least the export provisions of all other components that the development component uses. This need for partial or total views of the developing product implies some strong integration mechanism which can efficiently produce such information from wherever it is held. This does not necessarily mean that there must be a central physical repository, but it means that there must be some integrating service that can effectively assemble the equivalent of repository selections or views as required.

The dimensions of integration that we will consider are the two that are identified in most environments and tool integration situations, that is, data (concerned with the sharing of data between different tools) and control (concerned with interworking of tools and services).

A general issue of importance in integration is **granularity**. In general a greater degree of independence is appropriate to objects with large granularity, whereas it is usually both more convenient and more efficient for there to be less independence between small-grain objects within the same tool or service. *More* and *less* in this context are comparative. The principles of minimising coupling between different components is a rather general one, applicable at many different levels of granularity.

Data 9.5.1

As noted above, any environment needs an **environment database** or set of databases which records the state, or a set of current and past states of each development taking place within that environment. The environment database is often called a dictionary or repository, particularly when it is in some sense centralised. Individual tools need to be aware of that part of the development state that affects them and that they affect. Individual tools, however, will frequently have local data, for example, preferred graphics options for a particular tool, which relate to the development but should not form part of the environment database for that development.

Requirements that environment databases should ideally meet include (Schefström and van den Broek, 1993):

- Normal distributed data management and database facilities.
- Large or long transactions resulting in substantial change, such as might occur in

an extended development session using a particular tool, or perhaps a small set of related tools.

- Effective management of change, and consistency control. Software development is change, so database volatility and the need to propagate changes to all affected components, tools and developers is normal.
- Multiple views. For example, project managers, quality assurance people, data administrators, people concerned with integration or acceptance testing, and programmers will take quite different views of the same development project data.
- Configuration management and support for cooperative and team work.

Control 9.5.2

There are at least three control integration problems:

- The use by some tools of other tools or services.
- The need for tools to inform other tools about what they have done to items or objects of common concern to several tools.
- The sequencing or programming of tool use to fit some defined software process model.

The most efficient and most commonly used means of combining separate modules in a system is through calls to the modules' procedural interfaces. There is, however, some module dependency, in that calling modules must address called modules directly and specifically. Independent tools, however, are not necessarily conceived as modules within a larger system, but more as complete and separate packages. Within such packages, procedure calls are appropriate, but not necessarily between them.

There is a strong desire in some quarters for independence of tools. There are some clear advantages in this objective. Conceptually, at least, it allows a user to extend an existing toolset by introducing useful additional tools as and when necessary or to 'mix and match' independent tools to meet particular requirements. Independent tools must either work very closely with a standard development dictionary or repository, or maintain a dictionary slice, or view, of their own. In the latter case there is a consistency problem if there is any overlap between tools, such that more than one tool can create, delete or alter items which are of common concern.

There are at present a number of control integration mechanisms for independent tools, including the **software bus** and **broadcast messages** (Schefström and van den Broek, 1993). None of them are yet completely satisfactory.

Granularity is an issue in control integration. Within tools, standard calls may be appropriate, whereas between tools, a mechanism which is perceived to be less dependent may be desirable.

PROCESS ADAPTATION AND INTEGRATION 9.6

It is not uncommon for some suppliers of CASE tools, 4GLs and other development support packages to claim that their products can be used with any structured methodology, several object-oriented methodologies, or a range of data-centred approaches, as the case may be. The 'package for all seasons' suppliers provide diagram editors for all diagram types commonly used within any variant of the general family of methodologies which is their target market. Other suppliers target a much more specific market using a particular methodology, or a narrow range of similar methodologies. The extent to which, and the ease with which a particular toolset or environment can successfully support a range of methodologies, or to be more precise, the enaction of a range of process models is a difficult question to answer without conducting appropriate development experiments. Several approaches to the problem are now examined.

Customisation   9 . 6 . 1

Customisation is the tailoring of a set of general facilities provided by a toolset to better fit the user's needs. In practice most customisation is cosmetic: a choice between this form of a diagram or that; a choice between rectangular boxes, boxes with rounded corners or circles; or a choice between different data modelling notations, such as Bachman or Chen. A set of available alternatives is included in the toolset and provision is made for the user to choose those desired. Sometimes this is a choice between alternative tools or services; sometimes it is a choice of parameters for a tool or service. In some cases, for example reporting, greater flexibility is provided. Reports, of course, can only use available information, for example from a repository. However, report specification and generation facilities can provide great flexibility in report content and format at the cost of learning how to use an often quite detailed report specification language.

MetaCASE   9 . 6 . 2

MetaCASE is a computer-aided technology for building CASE technology, that is, computer-aided specification and development or generation of CASE tools. It is more a concept than a full reality, although a small number of metaCASE systems are in commercial use. The goals of metaCASE are: tailoring existing CASE technology, creating new CASE tools, and integrating different existing CASE tools. Some success has been achieved in the first two but not the third. As one might expect, metaCASE is a complex technology, more suitable for use by CASE tool builders or software process engineers than by end-users. 'The future of metaCASE seems constrained by a market that wants "solutions" and not a technology for building solutions' (CASE'92 Workshop Report, 1993). MetaCASE has to a considerable extent been overtaken by software process modelling within experimental software environments and also by various tool integration initiatives.

Software process engineering   9 . 6 . 3

If we take a process view of software development and attempt to use defined software processes, then we need 'the ability to combine and connect tools, methods, data, and people to support the software development process' (CASE'92 Workshop Report, 1993). Software process technology is not yet ready for practical use, but it is a major area of research in which many people are engaged. As such, the role of software process engineering is likely to be clarified fairly quickly. It is clearly important within the overall structure of the software process. It is equally clear that it is a highly complex area which is unlikely to be accessible to most project managers and developers. In this area, as in most areas of software engineering, it is likely that most users will look for ready-made solutions, rather than attempting to develop their own. The suppliers of those ready-made solutions will, however, need software process engineering capabilities if they are to fit solutions to problem areas instead of adopting a one-fits-all approach.

SOME PRACTICAL SOLUTIONS TO TOOL INTEGRATION PROBLEMS 9.7

Provide a single, integrated package 9.7.1

Perhaps the most common current 'solution' to the tool integration problem is to ignore or bypass it by offering a single, integrated package. This is the preferred short-term commercial solution adopted by many suppliers of CASE packages, 4GLs and the like. It is attractive to suppliers because it reduces development effort and tends to lock customers into their product. It is attractive to customers that the product suits and who are comfortable with a single-supplier situation. The downside includes the following:

- A single integrated package will tend to be narrow and inflexible in its applicability. (The vehemence with which supplier salespeople deny this is probably in direct proportion to its truth.)
- A 'closed', rather than an 'open' environment will have limited evolutionary possibilities.
- A single, integrated package is likely to be at risk from a wide range of changes in technology, standards and IT management fashions.
- An integrated package by its very nature, is likely to assume a particular underlying software process, usually undefined, even hidden, because for sales reasons claims are likely to be made that the package depends on no particular methodology or software process, but can support any, or at least many.

Some suppliers attempt to counteract some of the disadvantages by providing options, customisation facilities, import/export facilities and bridges, and so on.

Import/export facilities and bridges 9.7.2

Most single integrated-tool packages provide some kind of (typically non-standard) external interface facilities. For packages providing so-called 'upper CASE' or 'front-end CASE' facilities, planning, analysis and design, general export facilities or bridges to specific 'lower CASE' packages are provided. The export facilities are typically rather basic, being merely a simply-structured output of dictionary contents. A bridge is much more specific, providing the dictionary output in a form appropriate for input to a suitable 4GL or database/SQL package.

Exercises

9.1 List and compare the characteristics of a UNIX toolset as opposed to the package of tools associated with a DOS/Windows environment.

9.2 What software tools are needed as a minimum to facilitate high-quality configuration management?

9.3 How are the following terms defined, as they relate to software engineering configuration management: (a) service; (b) tool; (c) toolset; (d) tool integration; (e) environment; (f) framework?

9.4 What are the primary control integration problems faced by managers of software configuration environments?

References

Booch, G. (1994) *Object-oriented Analysis and Design with Applications*. Benjamin/Cummings (2nd ed.), Redwood City, CA.

Buhr, R. J. A. (1984) *System Design with Ada*, Prentice-Hall, Englewood Cliffs, NJ.

CASE'92 Workshop Report (1993) in *CASE'93, Proceedings of the 6th International Workshop on CASE*, Singapore (July 1993), IEEE Computer Society Press, pp. 380–419.

Finkelstein, C. (1989) *An Introduction to Information Engineering*. Addison-Wesley, Sydney.

HOOD User Group (1992) *HOOD Reference Manual, Issue 3.1.1*, Masson/Prentice-Hall International, Paris.

Schefström, D. and van den Broek, G. (Eds) (1993) *Tool Integration—Environments and Frameworks* John Wiley, Chichester, England.

CHAPTER 10

Software metrics

What are software metrics?

Metrics have to do with measurement. Some definitions, suitably tailored to apply to software, will help us to clarify matters:

- **metric**: a quantitative measure of the extent or degree to which software possesses and exhibits a certain characteristic, quality, property or attribute. The term **measure** is sometimes used (somewhat contentiously) as a synonym for *metric*;
- **unit of measure**: a reference quantity in multiples or fractions in which any quantity of the same kind can be measured;
- **measurement**: a number with an associated unit of measure which describes some aspect of software.

Examples:
(a) Length is a metric; the metre (m) is a unit of measure for length; 3.21 m is a length measurement.
(b) Software size is a metric; the delivered source instruction (DSI) is a unit of software size; 26 154 DSI is a software size measurement.

These examples are instructive. Length is a precise and precisely defined metric. All metres are equal and length measurements take rational values. Software size, by comparison, is not so precisely defined. We need an unambiguous definition of 'delivered source instruction' in order to understand it. Not all delivered source instructions are equal in the obvious sense in which all metres are equal. We might almost say with George Orwell that some source instructions are more equal than others. We can only have an integral number of DSI. Software measurement is not nearly as precise as length measurement.

The need for software metrics

'You can't control what you can't measure.' These are the opening words in Chapter 1 of Tom DeMarco's excellent and readable book *Controlling Software Projects* (DeMarco, 1982). In Chapter 5 we also make clear the need for software metrics in order to assess software maturity and to achieve confirmed software improvement. Without software measurements we have only opinions, and opinions are only as good as the credibility of the person who holds them. Without facts, software managers and developers can only say 'Trust me.' 'Trust me' is not good enough in a multi-billion dollar industry which affects almost every aspect of our lives.

Some of the measurement-related questions that various stakeholders in software development might ask include:

- *General management:* How much are information systems really worth to the organisation? Are we getting value for money from IS?
- *User management:* How much is the proposed system worth? When can we plan to use it in the marketplace? How much user effort do I need to invest in validating requirements? The delivered system? Why do changes to system Q take so long and cost so much? Should we ask for it to be rewritten?
- *IS management:* How do I defend my budget? How do I get good estimates of cost and schedule? How good is our software development process? . . . our software maintenance process? How do I measure the effect of new technologies? How do I know what productivity gains I am getting and where?
- *Purchaser of IS development/maintenance services:* Am I getting value for money? Is the quality satisfactory? How much is improved quality worth?
- *Supplier of development/maintenance services:* How do I bid the right price? How do I ensure adequate quality? What is my productivity, and how do I improve it?
- *Project manager:* How do I know if cost and schedule targets are realistic? How do I measure progress against targets? How do I plan ahead?
- *Software designer:* How do I assess the quality of a design? How do I know design schedules are realistic?
- *Programmer:* I consider myself to be a good programmer, both in productivity and quality, but how do I prove it? How can I argue convincingly for a pay rise?
- *Quality assurance:* How can I assess quality of specification, design, programs, reusable components, systems, activities?

Thus, those concerned with software development all have some interest in software metrics and the effective measurement of many different aspects of software. The questions centre around four main issues:

- *Visibility:* We have noted elsewhere that software is essentially abstract and that visibility into its structure and status is difficult to achieve. Metrics can help to achieve greater visibility and hence more informed and effective management.
- *Planning and control:* In order to plan, we need measurements of previous projects similar to the current project of interest. In order to control, we need measurements of work completed and work in progress, so that we can compare the actual with the planned situation and take appropriate action when *actual* falls behind *plan*.
- *Quality:* This includes reliability, maintainability, usability, and so on. It is widely

believed that improving the quality of all software development products can also improve productivity by reducing subsequent rework.

- *Productivity*: There is a natural concern on the part of management to get better value for money in software, that is, to improve productivity within acceptable quality limits.

The GQM paradigm

Basili's goal, question, metric (GQM) paradigm has been described briefly in Section 5.3. Management sets a goal—possibly concerned with solving a software problem or improving a software process. The goal gives rise to one or more questions concerning how we are going to understand the extent of the problem and to assess the efficacy of the solution. These questions lead us to select or define and use one or more metrics appropriate to the goal. Thus we do not measure software simply because it is there or because the measurements might come in useful some day. We measure software for a very specific purpose.

An example might help both to make the importance of the GQM paradigm more apparent, and to emphasise that the specific choice of metrics can depend on one's point of view. The goals of both producers and consumers in a certain environment are (a) to develop an understanding of software development productivity; and (b) to improve it. There is no shortage of candidate improvement ideas, from introducing CASE to bringing in a facilities management company. The key problem or question is how to establish a development productivity baseline and to measure the effects of whatever changes are made.

We consider the definition of productivity in this context later. Meanwhile, we will take a simple view assuming little variation in software quality. In a general sense productivity is output/input. However, what is output and what is input depends on whether we are producers or consumers of the software being developed. A producer's view might be:

$$\text{Development productivity} = \frac{\text{(all product deliverables + production support products)}}{\text{(all product–related costs + share of overheads)}}$$

However, a consumer may take a different point of view:

$$\text{Development productivity} = \frac{\text{usable functionality of delivered product}}{\text{cost to acquire, maintain and effectively use it}}$$

The producer is concerned with everything needed to produce, whether delivered or not, and whether directly concerned with user functional requirements or essential infrastructure utilities. The consumer is only concerned with functionality directly related to requirements. This may lead to the producer defining productivity more precisely as:

$$\text{Producer productivity} = \frac{\text{(total production SLOC + LOD)}}{\text{(total production costs)}}$$

whereas the consumer might prefer the following definition:

$$\text{Consumer productivity} = \frac{\text{usable functionality in function points}}{\text{acquisition, implementation and maintenance costs}}.$$

The metrics of interest to the producer will then be SLOC (source lines of code), LOD (lines of documentation), all direct and indirect production costs, and the relevant productivity metric. The metrics of interest to the consumer will be function points, relevant costs of acquisition, installation, training, maintenance, etc. and the relevant productivity metric. Both producer and consumer will be interested in changes in productivity as they measure it, as a result of any changes in the production and/or acquisition processes.

SOFTWARE PRODUCT METRICS   10.2

Our treatment of software metrics makes no attempt whatever to be complete. Our concern is with some of the key issues of practical software measurement and management and with some of the most commonly used metrics. **Software product metrics** are measures of the products or deliverables of the software process, including requirements documents, design documents, user and operator documentation, programs, database schemas, and so on. Since software products are almost all available in machine-readable form, it is advantageous for both consistency and economy that product measurements be made automatically using suitable measurement software.

Software product metrics fall into two main classes: **size metrics** and **quality metrics**, though there are some metrics, in particular complexity metrics, which may have both size and quality implications. Size metrics are concerned with the questions 'How much?' or 'How big?' Quality metrics are concerned with questions such as 'How good?' or 'How reliable?' Complexity metrics relate to questions such as 'How complicated?' or 'How difficult?' Size and complexity metrics are clearly related to questions of cost, which are a concern in all software development. The need for software quality, particularly in life- or mission-critical systems, has been stressed in Chapter 5.

SIZE METRICS   10.3

Before we consider specific size metrics, it is appropriate to ask the question: 'What is software size?' The question is not trivial. Software is not just programs. For example, it also includes designs and supporting documentation. As we noted above, in order to be effective, software metrics must relate to clear goals and should therefore be chosen in order to answer specific questions. Different size metrics will be chosen if our concern is:

(a) the total size of all the software products in a project;
(b) the size of the software 'problem to be solved', irrespective of how we choose at a later stage to solve it;
(c) the amount of user or customer functionality that the software delivers;
(d) the amount of code that is written;
(e) the amount of machine code that is finally produced.

If we are interested in the total size of all software products in a project, there is a further problem. There is no obvious common measure for design diagrams, user documentation and programs. They are as different as apples and oranges; in a sense, incommensurate.

In spite of these difficulties, size metrics are essential for cost estimation, productivity studies and as factors in the calculation of quality metrics.

Expanding on Levitin (1986) we can state that a good size measure should have the following properties:

(a) be clearly and unambiguously defined so that it can be calculated automatically;
(b) be intuitively attractive; it should always have a positive value and be additive;
(c) be applicable to a wide range of languages and other development products;
(d) have some correspondence to traditional natural language measures, for example, words, lines, sentences and paragraphs.

The size of the abstract solution to the problem 10.3.1

The size of the abstract solution to the problem to be solved by an information system is itself an abstract concept, investigated by Halstead (1977). It can be thought of as the size of the solution algorithm in some suitable representation or formalisation, for example, in mathematical notation. Halstead expressed size as a function of the number of **operators** and **operands** in an algorithm but, using consistent mathematical notation and formatting, the number of non-blank lines in an algorithm might also be a suitable measure. For example, in the statement:

c := a + b;

the operators are := (assignment), + (addition) and ; (statement terminator or separator). The operands are a, b and c. There are 3 operators and 3 operands in the statement. Alternatively, the statement might be considered to occupy one line of an algorithm.

One reason for being interested in the size of the abstract solution is that it solves the problem completely in principle and, in an ideal world, no further work would be necessary. We would be able to execute the algorithm directly. In practice, the algorithm has to be expressed in some suitable computing language, which will often result in a program of much greater size than the original algorithm. A measure of **language level** can be obtained by comparing the size of the program to that of the algorithm. A low-level language program will be much bigger than a high-level language program, which in turn will be bigger than the algorithm. In a sense, this is the minimum possible size—until perhaps, a smaller algorithm is discovered.

FUNCTION METRICS 10.4

Function metrics aim to measure the functionality of a system/program, that is, how much it does, usually from the point of view of the customer or user. Function metrics include **function points** (Albrecht, 1979), **Mark II function points** (Symons, 1988), **feature points** (Jones, 1986), **function weight** (DeMarco, 1982) and some other variations on the same theme (Reifer, 1989). We will illustrate the principles underlying all of these methods using the most common of the function metrics, function points.

All function metrics are based on a points or weighting system. Different functions are assigned a different weight or a different number of points. The total functionality is measured by the total number of points for the whole system. We first briefly introduce function points to illustrate the concepts. We then very briefly describe the main variations on the function metrics theme.

Function point analysis (FPA) (also described in Section 3.3) was invented by Alan Albrecht in the late seventies. In more recent years IFPUG, the International Function Point Users' Group, has become the *de facto* standards body for FPA which is widely used throughout the world, particularly in commercial IS environments.

In FPA, functions are identified as input, output or inquiry functions; filing functions; and the functions of providing an (external) interface to other systems. There are detailed guidelines for identifying what is, and what is not, an individual function of each type. In summary, the function point counting procedure is as follows:

1. Using the function identification guidelines, IDENTIFY EACH FUNCTION under each of the following function categories;

   input (IF)
   output (OF)
   inquiry (QF)
   entity (internal file) (FF)
   external interface file (EF).

2. Using the complexity guidelines for each function type, RATE FUNCTION COMPLEXITY for each of the identified functions as low, average, or high (using appropriate complexity guidelines). Count function points for each function, depending on its complexity, as follows:

	Low	Average	High
input	3	4	6
output	4	5	7
inquiry	3/4	4/5	6/7
entity/file	7	10	15
external interface	5	7	10

Inquiries are separated into an input part and an output part and are given the function points of an input or an output, depending on which of the two parts has the higher rating.

3. ADD THE FUNCTION POINTS of all components to obtain the raw, or unadjusted, function point count.

4. APPLY AN OVERALL ADJUSTMENT for a number of other (mainly environmental) factors that may influence total system function.

Function points example `10.4.1`

A simple transaction processing application has:

   4 input functions; 1 complex, 1 average, 2 simple;
   5 output functions; 1 complex, 2 average, 2 simple;
   2 inquiry functions; 1 input-dominant, simple, 1 output-dominant, simple;
   6 entities; 1 complex, 1 average, 4 simple;
   no external interfaces.

Assuming that there is no overall environment-based adjustment in this case, then according to the above counting guidelines, this application has 101 function points.

Some FPA details

The concept of function points is simple enough. Consistency in application, however, can be quite difficult to achieve without careful training of function point estimators and quality control of function point estimates. Perhaps the single most critical step in counting function points is the first, identifying the functions. To do this consistently can be quite difficult in some cases. A few selected examples of the kinds of guidelines that might be used are the following for input functions (IF), output functions (OF), and filing functions (FF):

Input data screen	1 IF
Multiple screens grouped together into one transaction	1 IF
Multiple function input data screen, *n* functions	*n* IF
Dual purpose data screen used for both input and output	1 IF, 1 OF
Menu or user control input	1 IF
Function key alternative of user control input	0 IF
Automatically generated input transaction from another application	1 IF
Entity in user-oriented ER data model	1 FF
'Logical' data file	1 FF
Index file	0 FF

Within a specific environment with standard procedures for handling interactive applications, difficult cases can be resolved in a consistent way. Greater variation in counting is to be expected in less disciplined or more varied environments.

Example function complexity guidelines for input functions (low, average or high) depend on the number of different data elements involved and the number of entities or file types referenced, as shown in the following table:

		Data elements		
		1–4	5–15	>15
File	0–1	L	L	A
types	2	L	A	H
	>2	A	H	H

There is no guarantee, however, that the 'A' guidelines will in fact represent true averages for any particular application. Nevertheless, counting conventions adopted by some organisations ignore the complexity ratings and merely take the average function point counts (IF 4, OF 5, QF 4, FF 10, EF 7) for all functions.

The choice of the relative function point weights assigned to the different functions is said to reflect their 'relative value to the user . . . determined by debate and trial' (Albrecht and Gaffney, 1983). There is some debate about the general validity of the relative function type weights, and indeed about the function classifications themselves (Verner et al., 1989). In particular, the basis of FPA was established originally in the late 1970s when batch processing was the norm. In today's almost universally interactive information systems world there is considerable questioning and debate about the suitability of the function categories, several of which are very highly correlated. However, the important issues are consistency, the widely recognised relevance and usefulness of function points for business software, and the strong correlation of function points with both development cost and other size measures, such as lines of code.

Overall adjustment factors include allowances for such functions as data communications, distributed function, performance, complex processing, multiple sites, and so on. These may result in an overall adjustment of at most + or − 35% in the raw function count. It is debatable whether some of the adjustment factors (such as 'heavily used configuration') are truly functional, rather than being more like the cost drivers of COCOMO (see Section 3.3). There is little empirical evidence to support their usefulness conclusively.

As noted earlier, there are many variations on the function point theme, including extensions to real time applications (Jones, 1986; Reifer, 1989). FPA, as regulated by IFPUG, also undergoes periodic updating in order to keep it relevant to new technologies, such as client-server.

The great advantage of FPA is that, where it is appropriate, which is particularly the case for data-centred business systems, it enables a good early estimate of size (and hence cost) to be obtained from suitably complete requirements. There are two main disadvantages. The first is the difficulty of avoiding subjectivity. The second is the limited applicability of function points. They apply well only to systems, typically business systems, which are dominated by input–output and filing functions. Because function points largely ignore internal processing complexity, care must be taken in applying FPA to complex applications, even in the business area. Extreme caution must also be taken in comparing productivities expressed as function points/person-month across different organisations and environments. In terms of Levitin's properties (Section 10.3), function points may lack definition clarity, automatability and possibly additivity.

A particularly appropriate use of function points is the estimation of, and planning for, user involvement in software development and implementation. Since function points measure user functionality, they are particularly appropriate for user-related activities, such as requirements validation, prototyping user interfaces, user interface validation and functional acceptance testing.

CODE SIZE METRICS   10.5

Code size metrics are quite pragmatic. They were first used in punched card days when one program statement was punched into one card. The size of a program could then be easily determined by simply counting the cards. Since those early days, matters have become much more complicated as more sophisticated and higher level free-form languages have been devised. We will examine two classes of code size metrics: line, instruction or statement counts, and token counts.

Line, instruction or statement counts   10.5.1

By far the most common code size metric is 'lines of code' or, to be more specific, non-comment source lines of code (SLOC). A closely related measure is delivered source instructions (DSI). For our purposes, the terms *statement* and *instruction* are synonymous. The measures SLOC and DSI are different in that, in many languages, one statement may occupy several lines and several statements may occur on one line. The measures are similar in that, in most languages, most statements occupy one line. The measures are very highly correlated and often they are little different in value. Most frequently the units of measure employed are in thousands, KSLOC and KDSI. SLOC has the advantage of being (somewhat) language-independent, but may be dependent on source code formatting if this is not standardised. DSI is clearly language dependent and depends on the definition of a statement in the language used. Particular care must be taken in counting nested statements. The important requirement is clear definition and consistency. If source code formatting and statement counting are automated, then consistent source code metrics will be freely and cheaply available. Many of the objections to SLOC and DSI relate to definition and coding style differences. These are very easily resolved in any specific environment.

It is clear that all source code lines, or instructions, are not equal. A null statement, for example, is evidently smaller than a large multi-line print format statement. The LOC and DSI measures therefore rely on the 'swings and roundabouts' principle. In most programs there is a mix of many different kinds of statements and these tend to balance out.

One of the main software estimation problems is determining prior to development what the expected size of a proposed system will be. This can be done by analogy with completed systems of a similar scope and functionality. Alternatively, a function point count can be estimated from requirements and this can be 'converted' to KDSI using a suitable **language expansion factor**, that is, a known average relationship between function points and KDSI for the language in question. Some commonly used language expansion ratios are shown in Table 10.1.

TABLE 10.1

Some commonly used language expansion ratios	
Language	*Source statements per FP*
Unspecified machine language	320
Unspecified macro-assembly language	213
FORTRAN 77	105
COBOL 85	91
Pascal	91
Modula 2	80
Ada	71
Prolog	64
Modern Basic	64
Various 4GLs	20–35
Spreadsheets	6–12

Token counts

10.5.2

Tokens are defined, following Levitin (1986), as 'the basic syntactic units from which a program can be constructed. Each token represents a sequence of characters which can be treated as a single logical entity.' Identifiers, strings, numbers, operators and separation symbols, such as commas and semicolons, are all typical tokens of programming languages. During **lexical analysis**, the first stage of compilation, programs are split into tokens, which can readily be counted at this stage.

Token counts can also be used in other development contexts. For example, a description of an ER diagram will contain entity and relationship names, relationship descriptions in terms of entities related, cardinalities, etc. Such a description consists of tokens which can be counted. Tokens can also be identified in 'fill in the forms' specifications which are common in 4GLs and other non-procedural development products, where each individual entry is typically a token.

In a sense, each token represents an elementary choice or decision, concerning a name, a number, an operator, a list element, and so on. As with lines of code, not all tokens are equal but it is arguable that they are more equal to each other than lines of code are, and therefore a better measure.

Tokens, divided into two subclasses, operators and operands, are fundamental elements in Halstead's **software science** theories (Halstead, 1977), which have been partly discredited (Lister, 1982) and have consequently fallen out of favour, but which nevertheless address, even if they do not solve, a number of fundamental software questions.

In spite of their advantages, token counts are not commonly used. However, confidence in other software size measures is increased if they correlate highly with token counts (Verner et al., 1989).

Size of 4GL and other non-procedural 'code'   `10.5.3`

Many 4GLs and database application languages use screen forms which users fill in to specify many requirements and options within generic functions, such as file specifications, data screen inputs, and reports. It is worth noting that, although screen-based specification forms of this type are themselves non-procedural, the specifications entered into them are in fact parameters to generic 4GL procedures which are instantiated for particular functions in particular applications. Thus, although the specifications are non-procedural, the resulting applications are procedural.

Little work has been done on sizing non-procedural code or, as is more common, applications with mixed non-procedural and procedural code. We have noted above that tokens may be used for both procedural and non-procedural code, though the latter tends not to contain the commas and semicolon separators of the former. It has also been shown in one case study that counts of lines on the screen forms can be used (Verner and Tate, 1988).

SIZE METRICS FOR OTHER DEVELOPMENT PRODUCTS   `10.6`

Object counts   `10.6.1`

The term *object* is used here in the general sense, meaning a thing of interest. Things of interest in ER diagrams, for example, include entities and relationships. If we say that an ER diagram has 20 entities and 35 relationships, then that gives a person with some knowledge of ER diagrams a good idea of its size. Similarly, saying that a rule-based expert system has 213 rules may be more meaningful in many contexts than talking about lines of code. In an object-oriented development, the numbers of objects and methods may be relevant.

Object or thing counts, being like 'apples and oranges', only make sense when like is compared with like, for example ER diagrams with other ER diagrams. In appropriate situations, however, they may be more meaningful than other size measures without necessarily being substitutes for them.

Documentation size   10.6.2

Documentation is of many different kinds, such as requirements documents, design documents, user manuals, operations manuals, reports, change requests, and test plans. It takes many different forms, including text, on-line manuals, diagrams, forms, tables, and mixed documents containing several different forms of information. It is commonly measured in lines (LOD) or pages, where A4 page size is usually assumed. Interspersed diagrams, tables, etc. are often counted just by the number of line spaces or pages they occupy.

A common assumption is that, within a particular environment, LOD is proportional to DSI. However, this is only likely to be the case if the documentation standards do not vary in any way from one project to another. If the quantity and quality of documentation are different, then relying solely on DSI as a representative for the total size of a project's deliverables may be rather misleading.

STRUCTURE   10.7

Software is complex. The data it processes has many complex interrelations and the logic that it implements has many loops and branches. It is therefore natural that software engineers should be concerned with the structure of software as well as its size. There are two main reasons for this. One, to measure **complexity**; two, to assess the **well-structuredness** of a design or program. Complexity is of concern because it is related to difficulty of implementation, understanding, maintenance, and enhancement. Well-structuredness is important because it aims to reduce the effects of complexity by dividing a large and complex system into a structure of smaller components which, as far as possible, exhibit high **cohesion** within each component and low **coupling** of components.

COMPLEXITY   10.8

Before considering the details of some common complexity metrics, it is well to return to the GQM paradigm and ask: 'What do we want complexity metrics for?' This question has been partly answered above, to help us to estimate the difficulty, and hence the effort needed, in development, maintenance and enhancement. This being so, we are primarily interested in **cognitive complexity** rather than **structural complexity**, that is, we are concerned with the human difficulties of understanding and working with the software rather than with such measures as the number of independent paths through a program. Of course, cognitive complexity and structural complexity may be more or less strongly related. Empirical work is necessary, however, to confirm such a relation and to indicate which one from a plethora of structural complexity metrics is the most appropriate for any particular type of software activity.

Cognitive complexity   10.8.1

Relatively little work has been done in cognitive complexity as opposed to structural complexity. If we restrict our attention at this stage to programs in text rather than visual form, it appears that, in attempting to understand programs, developers do two basic things, called **chunking** and **tracing**. *Chunking* is the process of mentally dividing a program (the top-down view), or grouping program elements (the bottom-up view), into comprehensible chunks, each of which a developer can grasp mentally as a single building block. *Tracing* is the process of resolving references or connections between chunks. Forward or backward tracing may be necessary to do this. A trace may be simple and short or may involve several steps and large 'distances' within the program or between programs. There are other complications. For example, chunks may be nested within other chunks. Empirical work on cognitive complexity typically involves timed program comprehension or maintenance tests. The times required to answer certain comprehension questions correctly or to perform certain maintenance tasks can then be correlated with various candidate complexity measures in order to choose the most suitable one.

Selected structural complexity metrics   10.8.2

Given the inherent complexity of software it is not surprising that there is a very large number of structural complexity metrics. One study (Munson and Khoshgoftaar, 1989) identified some 35 program complexity metrics, without considering metrics for architectural or design complexity at all and even omitting one or two of the better known program complexity metrics. However, there is a good deal of overlap between these metrics. Factor analyses of five sets of empirical data identified three very clear intuitively meaningful imputed factors, namely 'control', 'size', and 'modularity'. The imputed factor 'control' relates to control flow complexity, that is, the numbers of branches and loops. The imputed factor 'size', or using Halstead's terminology, volume, simply relates to how big a program is, bigger programs being more complex. The imputed factor 'modularity' relates to nesting structures and fanin (see the following subsection). Two other imputed factors, 'action' and 'effort' are not so satisfactory, either intuitively or in the number and nature of complexity metrics that characterise them best. 'Action' relating to the number of statements and operators has considerable overlap with size. 'Effort' relates not to actual effort, but to two of Halstead's so-called effort metrics for which the theoretical and empirical basis is at best tenuous. There is perhaps some basis to support a classification of complexity metrics as control, size and modularity. We might also add information flow complexity to this list since the information-related complexity is arguably as important as the processing logic complexity. Software size metrics have been studied above. We now consider several complexity metrics that belong to the other three classes.

Cyclomatic complexity

One of the simplest and most widely used measures of control complexity for procedural languages is McCabe's cyclomatic complexity (McCabe, 1976). The executable statements of a program are represented as a **strongly connected graph,** that is, a graph in which any node is reachable from any other node. An example will illustrate the metric. Figure 10.1 is a graph for the BinarySearch program which follows. The nodes represent executable statements or sequential groups of executable statements. Splitting nodes, where control flow branches, represent conditional or loop statements, such as **if then else, case** and **do while.** To make the graph strongly connected, an arc from the exit point back to the entry point of the procedure has been added—the dotted arc.

FIGURE

10.1

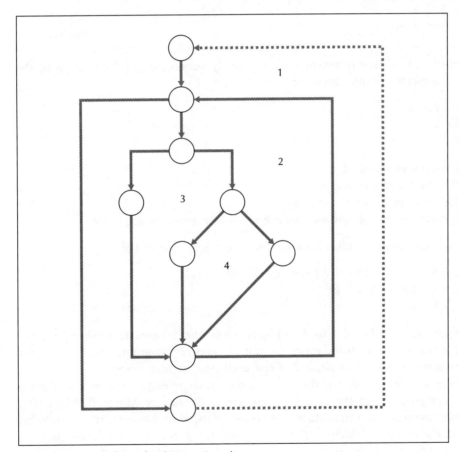

Strongly connected graph of BinarySearch

```
procedure BinarySearch(var L: list;
                       target: keytype;
                       var found: Boolean;
                       var location: integer);
{from Robert L. Kruse (1984) Data Structures and Program Design 2nd ed. Prentice-Hall, p. 165}
var    top,
       bottom,
       mid:integer;
begin
```

```
        top := L.length;        {list structure contains list length field,
                                  together with an array of entries, each
                                  consisting of a key and a value}
        bottom := 1;
        found := false;
        while (not found) and (top >= bottom) do
        begin
                mid := (top + bottom) div 2;
                if target = L.entry[mid].key then
                        found := true
                else if target < L.entry[mid].key then
                        top := mid – 1
                else
                        bottom := mid + 1
        end;
        location := mid
    end;
```

When a program has been represented as a strongly connected graph in this way, the cyclomatic complexity is calculated as:

$$E - N + 1$$
$$\text{or } S + 1,$$
$$\text{or } R$$

where E is the number of edges
N is the number of nodes
S is the number of splitting nodes
R is the number of regions—areas bounded by non–crossing edges,

in the strongly connected graph. Thus for the BinarySearch example:

$$C = E - N + 1 = 12 - 9 + 1 = 4, \text{ or}$$
$$C = S + 1 = 3 + 1 = 4, \text{ or}$$
$$C = R = 4$$

The regions are numbered 1 to 4 in Figure 10.1. The cyclomatic number gives the number of different paths from entry to exit through a program. This is also the minimum number of test cases needed to test each path at least once.

Ten has been recommended as the 'maximum ideal complexity' for a module though 'for a very complex system the cyclomatic number . . . may be larger' (IEEE, 1988). Clearly, large complex programs which *can* be modularised in a natural way should be. However, modularisation which is dictated by arbitrary size or complexity measure limits, and has little functional justification, should be avoided. There is no way to reduce the complexity of an inherently complex system. One can only construct suitable abstraction hierarchies and trade off intra-module and inter-module complexities in order to control the complexity by making the system more comprehensible.

Information flow complexity   10.8.4

Under this heading we consider a number of variations on a theme relating to information and/or control flow into and out of a procedure, module or other program unit. If we consider flows into and out of a module, then **fanin** is the number of inflows and **fanout** the number of outflows. The metric:

(fanin * fanout)^2

is called the information flow complexity and the metric:

size * (fanin * fanout)^2

is called the weighted information flow complexity (Henry and Kafura, 1981).

It is thought that modules with high values of either measure are more error prone than those with low values. High information complexity measures may indicate a lack of cohesion (more than one function) or excessive functional complexity (which is similar) in the module. It may also indicate an area of high information 'traffic'.

The flows may be procedural or informational. **Procedural fanin** is a count of the number of modules that call (or otherwise pass control to) a given module. **Procedural fanout** is a count of the number of modules that a particular module calls (or otherwise passes control to). **Informational fanin** is a measure of the amount of information flowing into a module. It can be defined as procedural fanin plus the number of data structures from which the module receives data either directly or via **in** parameters. **Informational fanout** is a measure of the amount of information flowing out of a module. It can be defined as procedural fanout, plus the number of data structures into which a module stores data either directly by writing, or assignment, or via **out** parameters. These general definitions can be more specifically instantiated for a particular environment and programming language. As with other metrics, it is best if their computation is automated both for cost reasons, and to ensure clarity of definition and consistency of measurement.

One problem with the metrics is that modules with a zero value of either fanin or fanout are assigned zero complexity, which is counter-intuitive. This can be overcome by stipulating a floor of one for fanin and fanout values.

There is nothing sacrosanct about the specific form of information flow metrics. There are few compelling theoretical or empirical reasons why (fanin * fanout) should be squared, nor why information flow complexity should be weighted by size. Indeed, since size tends to be highly correlated with almost all other complexity measures, including information flow complexity, weighting by size may be overkill. For example, cases have been made for the usefulness of informational fanin alone, and informational fanout alone, as useful indications of error proneness (Henry and Kafura, 1981; Kitchenham et al., 1990). The suggestions of Kitchenham et al. with regard to the practical use of control flow metrics are worth noting:

- ensure that modules with large fanout do not perform too many functions;
- ensure that programs with large fanin (commonly used subroutines, for example) are kept small and simple;
- review the design of modules that have both large fanin and large fanout, since this is a likely indication of inadequate decomposition.

RELIABILITY 10.9

More work has been done on software reliability than any other aspect of software quality, so much so that, in some quarters, reliability and quality have been treated as synonymous. There are two good reasons for this. First there is a large body of reliability research concerning other products, much of which is applicable to software. Secondly, reliability is easier to define and measure than other qualities, such as understandability, maintainability, and usability, for example. This does not make it any more important, only easier to investigate. We will consider only one reliability metric. The interested reader who wants to know more is referred to IEEE Std 982.2, *IEEE Guide for the Use of IEEE Standard Dictionary of Measures to Produce Reliable Software*, one of the most readable and educational of standards documents.

Mean time to failure 10.9.1

If t_i is the elapsed time between the $(i-1)$th and the ith failures, then mean time to failure (also called mean time between failures) if n such time intervals have been recorded is:

$(\Sigma t_i)/n$, for $i = 1$ to n.

Careful and accurate recording is necessary, using the computer system clock if appropriate. Normally we only record the time that the system, subsystem, module or other component of interest is actually in use. If appropriate, the metric can be used for faults of different severity levels. One can use a moving average of say the last k time intervals between failures. This should increase as software reliability increases, though sometimes new bugs are introduced when existing ones are fixed.

The observed times between failures can be input to one of several statistical models of software reliability to obtain a failure rate model showing the increase in reliability as a function of test time (Littlewood, 1980).

REQUIREMENTS TRACEABILITY 10.10

It is not only necessary to get the right requirements for a system, but also necessary to ensure that those requirements, and only those requirements, are actually implemented. Requirements traceability links architecture, design or implementation to requirements. It can be regarded either as a product metric or as a process metric depending on one's point of view. (A metric for traceability has been described in Section 8.2; it is reiterated and extended here.) If R is the number of agreed requirements, RI is the number of agreed requirements implemented and RE is the number of implemented requirements not in the agreed set, then:

requirements traceability = (RI / R) * 100%.

One will normally also be interested in the percentage of non-agreed introduced requirements:

(RE / R) * 100%.

One might well ask, where do new unagreed requirements come from? Who would want to introduce them and why? There are several possible answers to these questions. The original agreed requirements might have holes in them, which the implementers decided to fill. If so, the additions should be agreed and the requirements amended appropriately (through software configuration management as described in Section 4.3). The implementers might have thought some additional things were a good idea and added them. Such additions are often in the form of 'gold plating', or the addition of unnecessary embellishments. Why should anyone want to do this? One answer is pride and individuality. An implementer might want to stamp something of her or his personality on what is done, or attempt to impress the project manager or the user by the supposed additional 'quality' of the work. Such independent action is not in the spirit of so-called 'ego-less' programming and is generally to be discouraged.

QUALITY IN GENERAL   10.11

Our concern for software quality is seldom confined simply to reliability. If this is the case (and indeed whether or not it is the case) then the more general recording of defects, faults and failures may be appropriate. It is well to distinguish between these terms. A **defect** is anything that is wrong with a product, whether an omission, imperfection, ambiguity or fault. It is the most general indicator of some actual or potential problem. A **fault**, or **bug** is the cause or potential cause of a failure. A **failure** is either a breakdown of some sort or the production of wrong or otherwise unsatisfactory results. An **error** is a human action or mistake that results in a software fault.

Figure 10.2 represents relationships between failures, faults, defects and errors. The arrows start with the detection of the problems and point towards their causes. Failures can occur in test or in operation. Not all failures are due to software faults. Some will be hardware failures. Some will be due to user error, for example putting the wrong disk into a PC. Other failures will be traceable to software faults. During development, certain development products, such as software designs, may be inspected. Such inspections, particularly if they are formal inspections (Fagan, 1976), will identify defects. Defects in development products may also be detected by developers when they are working with those products. For example someone doing detailed design may find defects in the architectural design document from which they are working. These defects may be also classifiable as faults, particularly if they are in code. In some cases, for example in user documentation or program comments, they may indicate an unsatisfactory state which may not be a direct cause of failure but may adversely influence the usability, understandability or some other important quality of the software.

A much quoted analysis by Boehm (1981) indicated that the cost to remedy a software defect rises exponentially with the number of phases that pass before the defect is finally detected. A requirements error not discovered until coding may take 10 times the effort to fix that it would have taken in the requirements phase where it occurred. If it is not discovered until acceptance testing, the cost might be 50 times, and at operation, up to 200 times the cost to fix at requirements phase. Similarly design errors not discovered until acceptance testing might take 10 times the effort to fix at the design phase.

Defect density, defined as the number of defects above a certain severity level per software product size unit, is a useful measure of quality for any software product, whether it be requirements, design, code or other documentation. Defect densities are frequently expressed in defects per KDSI, but they can be expressed in defects per function point or even defects per 100 function points. For defect densities to be

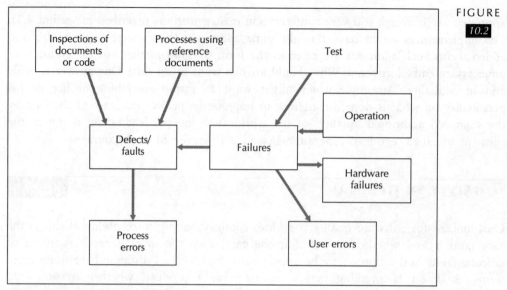

FIGURE
10.2

Failures, faults, defects and errors

comparable, care must be taken in the definition and classification of defects and in ensuring the consistency of inspections.

SOFTWARE PROCESS METRICS   10.12

The process view sees software development as a complex process, itself made up of a number of (sub)processes which produce a variety of products, including designs, test plans and programs. Depending on one's viewpoint, several processes may relate to one product, or one process may affect several products. For example, the processes 'design from specifications', 'incorporate specification change in design', and 'correct design error' may all relate to a single design product. The process 'correct (a specific) system fault' may affect specification, design, program and testing products. The constituent processes may overlap, or occur in parallel, and be subject to choice and iteration, depending on the software process model being enacted. Some measurements, such as effort and elapsed time, apply primarily to processes rather than to products. However, where products can be linked precisely to the processes which contribute to them, such process measures as effort and elapsed time can also, of course, be associated with products.

In a sense, product measures can be regarded as measures of the processes that contribute to the creation of a product, but the situation is often not clear cut. For example, the quality of a program does not depend simply on the programming process. It also depends on the specification and design processes. Only where these have been constrained to be of a certain uniform quality can we associate the quality of a program more directly with the programming process.

Software process metrics are typically concerned with consumption of resources during a process, with process control, or with the association of errors or faults with particular processes. The main reasons for collecting process metrics are to understand, control and improve software processes.

MANAGEMENT CONTROL MEASURES   10.13

Management control measures deal with matters such as identifying how many defects are introduced, and where and how much it costs to remove them or reduce their incidence. Some measures apply to specific processes; for example fault days (the number of days faults spend in software from their introduction to their removal) will normally relate to testing or verification processes. Error distribution by phase, or by activity in a defined software process model, can indicate where attention is necessary to improve the work in particular phases or activities. Error distribution by cause or reason for errors (for example lack of experience, lack of knowledge, inadequate documentation, non-conformance to standards, omissions in requirements) can indicate in a different way where attention is necessary, for example, education to correct lack of knowledge or to reduce the effects of lack of experience. Error distributions which analyse why errors have not been detected earlier (for example omitted or inadequate review, omitted regression testing) can also help managers to focus on where the software process can be tightened up to improve quality and to reduce costs by catching errors early when they are easiest and cheapest to fix.

TEST COVERAGE   10.14

Following the *IEEE Guide for the Use of IEEE Standard Dictionary of Measures to Produce Reliable Software*, test coverage is defined as:

$$\frac{\text{(implemented capabilities)}}{\text{(required capabilities)}} \times \frac{\text{(program primitives tested)}}{\text{(total program primitives)}} \times 100\%.$$

The first factor represents the proportion of requirements actually implemented. Clearly one cannot test conformance to requirements which have not been implemented, so these should be discounted. The second factor represents the proportion of program primitives, be they independent program paths, statements, predicates, or whatever is appropriate to the programming languages and testing tools used, which are actually tested. Test coverage is a measure of the completeness of the testing process from both the developer perspective (the second factor) and the user perspective (both factors). As such it is a process measure for the testing process.

EFFORT   10.15

Effort is person time. It is measured in person hours, days, months or years, with a time granularity appropriate to the context. If days, months or years are used, we need clear definitions of precisely how many hours there are in a standard day, how many days in a standard month, and so on. The time used for effort measurement is working time, not elapsed time (see Section 10.16). Effort measurements are most useful when related to specific development activities and specific individuals or skill groups, for example programmers doing development programming or programmers doing rework. At first sight one might think that effort was one of the easier process attributes to measure. Unfortunately that is far from the case. Developers often switch from one development activity to another. They sometimes think about particular development problems when they are far from the office. They take part in courses and discussions as well as scheduled and *ad hoc* meetings. Sometimes they are pulled off a project temporarily to do urgent fixes to systems with which they are familiar. Sometimes they do a lot of overtime, paid or unpaid. Developers as a race are often impatient of bureaucratic authority and regard time sheets as a chore to be put off as long as possible and completed in the shortest possible time at the last possible minute, even if the result is more fiction than fact.

One crude approach to effort measurement is to take a cost rather than an effort view by booking all the paid normal and overtime hours of all those assigned to a project, to the project. Unpaid overtime can be considerable in some situations and can distort the effort picture significantly. This may not matter if the unpaid overtime practices do not change significantly over time. If they do change, however, due to a change in work practices, bonus schemes or whatever, the whole effort pattern may also change. In such cases the validity of historical effort data for use in effort estimation for new data may be called into question.

With the increasing use of CASE tools, software engineering environments, IPSEs and other automated aids to development, there is the opportunity to record automatically development time spent at the workbench. Even here, however, there can be difficulties. If there is no activity on the workbench for, say, an hour, should this time be counted or not? If the developer was thinking, or discussing the development problem with a colleague, then perhaps it should be counted. If the developer was organising the office end-of-year party, then perhaps it should not be. To capture such information, some kind of time and activity management front end to the workbench development tools would seem to be necessary in which the developer states his or her intentions when logging on, enters details of related off-workbench activities (for example thinking, discussions) since the last session, then engages in planned development work and finally makes any necessary adjustments to the effort records when logging off. In this way the effort record becomes a sufficiently accurate representation of the effort on defined process activities during the session and related off-workbench activities. Effort information, in particular, assignment of effort to development process activities, is likely to be more accurate if we collect it close to when the effort is actually expended.

In the collection of reliable effort data, as with all software metrics, there is no substitute for developer motivation. If it is in the interests of the developer and of the development team to collect reliable effort data, then good results can be expected. If there is any suggestion that the data will be used unfairly or to the disadvantage of developers, then data collected from them is more likely to represent what might be in their best interests than what actually happens. Developers committed to software improvement within an agreed process assessment and improvement framework (which is in everyone's interest) are more likely to provide the necessary measurements conscientiously.

TIME   10.16

Time is measured either in working hours, or days, not counting holidays or other non-productive time (working time), or in calendar days counting all elapsed time whether productive or not. For many development purposes, for example, time-to-market or resource availability planning, elapsed (calendar) time is important. Time actually working is needed in effort measurement. Project management software facilitates the mapping of activities requiring a known or estimated amount of working time onto a calendar which blocks out holidays and the like. In this way working time can be converted into calendar or elapsed time from any specific date at any specific place.

PRODUCTIVITY   10.17

The measurement and improvement of productivity is a matter of concern to most organisations. In concept software productivity is simple enough, being software output or value per unit of input, usually measured in effort and/or $. However, obtaining clear and consistent definitions of software productivity is not a simple matter. Figure 10.3 (adapted from Grady and Caswell, 1987) gives an excellent conceptual view of the components and some of the important influences on software productivity. The downward pointing arrows connect contributing factors to software productivity and its measurement. The upward arrows lead from influence factors. Thus the value of software is influenced by customer and corporate needs and the difficulty of producing it by the complexity of the problem and the tightness or otherwise of the environmental constraints to which the development is subject.

FIGURE

10.3

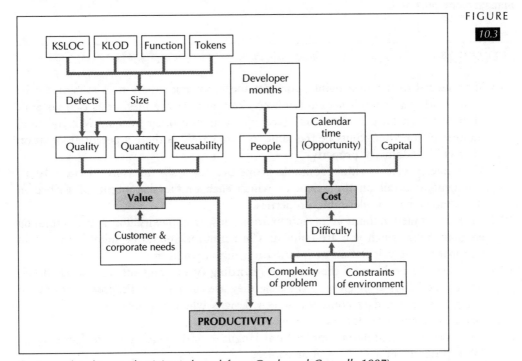

Factors related to productivity (adapted from Grady and Caswell, 1987)

Value is typically measured in quantity terms, mainly as function points or as KSLOC, though quality is becoming much more important. We are concerned not only with quantity, but also with quantity at an acceptable quality level. From a producer's point of view this is no doubt reasonable, because it costs the same amount to produce one quantity unit, regardless of its usefulness or value to the customer. From the consumer's point of view, quantity may be a less useful surrogate for value, however, unless the customer has been very careful about requirements. Size is a contributor to quality measurement in that quality is frequently measured in defects per size unit. Reusability is a recent addition to the value side of the productivity relation. Reusable components represent value in a similar fashion to inventory items in a factory.

On the cost side we have people costs or effort as the main component in most cases. Calendar or elapsed development time can be important where an application has economic importance, contributes to market share, or is for competitive advantage. In such cases early implementation can produce benefits which offset costs, whereas late installation can be very costly. Capital costs are for development hardware, software, and the like.

Software productivity is notoriously difficult to measure with any degree of accuracy, consistency and confidence. Great care has to be taken with the definition of the units of size and effort and similar care has to be taken with their measurement. Attempts to compare productivities, for example in function points per person month, between different organisations, are fraught with many difficulties due to differences in measurement practices and should in general be avoided. Using careful, consistent measurement within a single organisation and environment, significant productivity trends should, however, be detectable and measurable with a satisfactory degree of accuracy for management purposes.

Exercises

10.1 With regard to function points, consider the following situation. A system can be treated either as a single system (with no external interface files) or as two systems, both of which have external interface files with the other system. Will the total number of function points be the same in both cases? Is there a potential violation of Levitin's additivity property?

10.2 With reference to Levitin's desirable properties for a size measure (Section 10.3), comment in detail on the extent to which each of the size metrics described in this chapter has the desirable properties.

10.3 Give a detailed definition of information flow complexity for a programming language with which you are familiar. The definition should be suitable for use in automating the calculation of information flow complexity.

10.4 Consider the problem of the accurate recording of on- and off-workbench development activities at or close to the time they are carried out. Propose methods for doing this, giving data collection screen designs where appropriate.

10.5 Define size measures for the following:
   (a) a program/module in a procedural language with which you are familiar;
   (b) a program in a 4GL of your choice;
   (c) a program in a logic programming language (for example Prolog);
   (d) a program in an object-oriented language (for example Smalltalk, C++);
   (e) a program in a language using some other paradigm, for example a functional language.
   Identify the difficulties in each case.

10.6 Write a program to measure size consistently and automatically for one of the cases in Exercise 10.5. By consistently, we mean that the same program should be the same size, whatever its formatting.

10.7 Define complexity measures for individual modules for the language types in Exercise 10.5 (a) to (e).

10.8 Write a program to collect several different complexity measures automatically for modules in one of the language types referred to in Exercise 10.5.

10.9 The complexity measures of Exercise 10.7 concern module complexities. Define architectural or inter-module complexity measures for systems written in the languages in Exercise 10.5 (a) to (e).

References

Albrecht, A. J. (1979) 'Measuring application development productivity', in *Proc. Joint Share/Guide IBM Application Development Symposium* (October 1979), pp. 83–92; also reprinted in Jones, T. C. (Ed.), *Programming productivity: Issues for the 80s*, IEEE Computer Society Press (1981), pp. 34–43.

Albrecht, A. J. and Gaffney, J. E. (1983) 'Software function, source lines of code, and development effort prediction: a software science validation', *IEEE Trans. Software Engr.* Vol. 9, No. 6, (November 1983), pp. 639–48.

Boehm, B. W. (1981) *Software Engineering Economics*, Prentice-Hall, Englewood Cliffs, NJ.

DeMarco, T. (1982) *Controlling Software Projects*, Yourdon Press, New York, NY.

Fagan, M. (1976) 'Design and code inspections to reduce errors in program development', *IBM Systems Journal*, 15 (3).

Grady, R. B. and Caswell, D. L. (1987) *Software Metrics: Establishing a Company-wide Program.* Prentice-Hall, Englewood Cliffs, NJ.

Halstead, M. H. (1977) *Elements of Software Science*, Elsevier, New York.

Henry, S. and Kafura, D. (1981) 'Software structure metrics based on information flow', *IEEE Transactions on Software Engineering*, 7 (5), pp. 510–18.

IEEE (1988) Std 982.2-1988, *IEEE Guide for the Use of IEEE Standard Dictionary of Measures to Produce Reliable Software*, IEEE.

Jones, T. C. (1986) *Programmer Productivity*, McGraw-Hill Book Co., New York, NY, USA.

Kitchenham, B. A., Pickard, L. M. and Linkman, S. J. (1990) 'An evaluation of some design metrics', *Software Engineering Journal*, 5 (1), pp. 50–58.

Levitin, A.V. (1986) 'How to measure software size, and how not to', *Proceedings COMPSAC '86*, Chicago, IL, pp. 314–18.

Lister, A. M. (1982) 'Software science—The Emperor's New Clothes?' *Australian Computer Journal* Vol. 14, No. 2, (May 1982), pp. 66–70.

Littlewood, B. (1980) 'Theories of software reliability: How good are they and how can they be improved?' *IEEE Trans. on Software Engineering*, Vol. 6, No. 5, pp. 489–500.

McCabe, T. J. (1976) 'A complexity measure', *IEEE Trans. on Software Engineering*, Vol. SE-2, No. 4, (Dec. 1976), pp. 308–20.

Munson, J. C. and Khoshgoftaar, T. M. (1989) 'The dimensionality of program complexity', *Proceedings 11th International Conference on Software Engineering*, Pittsburgh, PA, pp. 245–53.

Reifer, D. (1989) *Asset-R Manual*, Reifer Consultants Inc., 25550 Hawthorne Boulevard, Suite 208/ Torrance, CA, USA.

Symons, C. R. (1988) 'Function point analysis: Difficulties and improvements', *IEEE Trans. on Software Engr.* Vol. 14, No. 1, (January 1988), pp. 2–11.

Verner, J. M. and Tate, G. (1988) 'Estimation of size and effort for a fourth-generation development', *IEEE Software* (July 1988), pp. 15–22.

Verner, J. M., Tate, G., Jackson, B. and Hayward, R. G. (1989) 'Technology dependence in function point analysis: A case study and critical review', *Proceedings 11th International Conference on Software Engineering*, Pittsburgh (May 1989), pp. 375–82.

Index

Page numbers in *italics* indicate figures